D0991226

THE NEW
MULTILATERALISM IN
JAPAN'S FOREIGN POLICY

THE NEW
MULTILATERALISM IN
JAPAN'S FOREIGN POLICY

DENNIS T. YASUTOMO

St. Martin's Press
New York

338.9152
Y29n

THE NEW MULTILATERALISM IN JAPAN'S FOREIGN POLICY
Copyright © 1995 by Dennis T. Yasutomo

All rights reserved. Printed in the United States of America. No part of this book may be used or reproduced in any manner whatsoever without written permission except in the case of brief quotations embodied in critical articles or reviews. For information, address St. Martin's Press, Scholarly and Reference Division, 175 Fifth Avenue, New York, N. Y. 10010

ISBN 0-312-04778-9

Yasutomo, Dennis T.
    The new multilateralism in Japan's foreign policy / Dennis Yasutomo.
        p. cm.
    Includes bibliographical references and index.
    ISBN 0-312-04778-9 (alk. paper)
    1. Economic assistance, Japanese. 2. Japan—Foreign economic relations. I. Title.
    HC60.Y372 1995
    338.9'152—dc20   95-16441
                                                       CIP

Book Design by Acme Art, Inc.

First Edition: September 1995
10 9 8 7 6 5 4 3 2 1

CONTENTS

University Libraries
Carnegie Mellon University
Pittsburgh PA 15213-3890

ACRONYMS

ADB	Asian Development Bank	JECF	Japan-Europe Cooperation Fund (EBRD)
ADF	Asian Development Fund	JSF	Japan Special Fund
AFDB	African Development Bank	LDC	Less developed country
AFDF	African Development Fund	MDB	Multilateral Development Bank
AFIC	Asian Finance and Investment Corporation (ADB)	MIGA	Multilateral Investment Guarantee Agency (IBRD)
AID	Agency for International Development (U.S.)	MITI	Ministry of International Trade and Industry
ASEAN	Association of Southeast Asian Nations	MOF	Ministry of Finance
BHN	Basic human needs	MOFA	Ministry of Foreign Affairs
CAR	Central Asian Republics	NIES	Newly industrializing countries
CIS	Commonwealth of Independent States	OCR	Ordinary Capital Resources
DAC	Development Assistance Committee (OECD)	ODA	Official Development Assistance
DMC	Developing member countries (ADB)	OECD	Organization for Economic Cooperation & Development
EBRD	European Bank for Reconstruction & Development	OOF	Other Official Flows
EC	European Community	OPEC	Organization of Petroleum Exporting Countries
ECAFE	Economic Commission for Asia and the Far East	PHRD	Policy and Human Resource Development Fund (IBRD)
ECU	European Currency Unit	PLO	Palestine Liberation Organization
FSU	Former Soviet Union	SAL	Structural Adjustment Loan
IADB	Inter-American Development Bank	SCI	Special Capital Increase
IBRD	International Bank for Reconstruction and Development	SECAL	Sectoral Adjustment Loan
		SDPJ	Social Democratic Party of Japan
IDA	International Development Association (IBRD)	TASF	Technical Assistance Special Fund (ADB)
IFC	International Finance Corporation (IBRD)	UN	United Nations
IFI	International Financial Institution	UNCTAD	United Nations Conference on Trade and Development
IFMP	Institute of Fiscal and Monetary Policy (MOF)	UNDP	United Nations Development Program
IMF	International Monetary Fund	UNTAC	United Nations Transitional Authority for Cambodia

INTRODUCTION AND ACKNOWLEDGMENTS

The study of Japan's Official Development Assistance (ODA) policy continues to draw the intense attention of academic observers, policymakers, and the private sector. The interest in Tokyo's foreign aid is no longer restricted to technical aspects but extends to diplomatic implications, especially in a post–Cold War international environment that has produced yet more nations in need of massive capital and technology transfers to effect historic transformations of their societies. The popularity of the Japanese ODA as a topic of research and analysis has caught its second wind in the 1990s. However, most of the current studies in both English and Japanese omit any detailed treatment of one of the most significant developments in recent ODA policy—the increased emphasis on multilateral aid, especially assistance channeled through international financial institutions. Aid literature continues to focus almost exclusively on bilateral ODA. Yet it is difficult to understand the dynamics and significance of Japan's overall ODA policy without incorporating the analysis of recent movements on the multilateral side.

Multilateral institutions are especially important for understanding Japanese diplomacy. The study of multilateralism has gained renewed interest among policymakers and academics. These institutions, still proliferating, are considered potential pillars of any new world order in the post–Cold War era, much as they were considered one of the pillars of the old world order created at the end of World War II. The United Nations is receiving renewed attention in Japan as policymakers and the public debate the nation's involvement and role in peacekeeping operations. International financial institutions receive less attention, but it is in these agencies that Japanese diplomatic activism has reared its head and taken root since the late 1980s. Japan has become a visible participant in the operations of these institutions, with its contribution transcending its traditional role as a source of money but not necessarily personnel and policy. Multilateral development banks, in particular, offer instructive case studies of this new activism.

Our question is, how do we analyze and interpret the new multilateral activism in Japanese diplomacy? We begin by assuming that ODA and multilateral development bank (MDB) policies are not isolated cases but rather components of a new activism in Japan's overall foreign policy. Therefore, in order to understand ODA and MDB policy, we may need to develop analytical frameworks that revise or replace the traditional ways of interpreting Japanese foreign policy, especially those that emphasize passivity and reactivity as congenital conditions of the Japanese state. Reactivity remains the more convincing and popular explanation of Japanese diplomacy, but as we enter the next century, Japan's recent activism forces a reassessment of the tenets of this particular way of interpreting Tokyo's diplomacy. The onus to provide alternative explanations is actually on those who harbor doubts about reactivism. This study takes up that challenge and in that process attempts to address not only ODA and MDB policies but also the more ambitious question of how we can explain Japanese diplomatic behavior in the 1990s and beyond.

This study is, therefore, a personal exploration of the behavioral and attitudinal roots of Japan's twenty-first century foreign policy using ODA and international organization policies as case studies. In it I attempt to clarify my long-standing concern about reactivism versus activism. The study is not meant to be definitive but the beginning of a long-term process of hypothesizing and testing in other policy areas.

I owe a deep debt of gratitude to several organizations that assisted in the completion of this project. The Japan–United States Educational (Fulbright) Commission provided, during its fortieth anniversary year (1992-93), a generous grant that allowed me a year-long research stay in Japan. I would especially like to extend my personal appreciation to Caroline Matano Yang, the executive director, and the entire staff of the Fulbright Commission office for their support and assistance in conducting research.

I would like to thank the Social Science Research Council (SSRC) and American Council of Learned Societies (ACLS) for allowing me to utilize its professional grant for write-up purposes upon my return from Tokyo. This book could not have been written so quickly had it not been for SSRC'S understanding and support.

I also appreciate the financial support provided by Smith College's Committee on Faculty Compensation and Development and by the Picker Fellowship, made possible by the generosity of Jean and Harvey Picker. This funding enabled summer visits to Japan that allowed me to gather the information needed to secure the Fulbright and SSRC grants. And I am extremely grateful for the generous leave of absence that gave me the opportunity to use the fall 1993 semester to write up the results of my stay in Japan. Needless to say, I owe my Government Department and East Asian Studies Program colleagues, and my students, a debt of gratitude for supporting my long absence from administrative and teaching duties. The Japanese Ministry of Finance (MOF) deserves special thanks. I appreciate the efforts of the then-vice minister of international affairs, Chino Tadao, for sponsoring my candidacy to the ministry's Institute of Fiscal and Monetary Policy, which appointed me as a visiting scholar for a nine-month period during my year as a Fulbrighter. The institute provided office facilities, and its hard-working staff arranged numerous interviews with MOF officials directly involved with multilateral development bank policy. I offer sincere thanks to Mssrs. Naito, Kitaura, Shintani, Kobayashi, Myoga, and Yamamoto. I cannot leave out the acts of kindness by Ministry of Foreign Affairs officials, especially Deputy Foreign Minister Matsuura Koichiro and director of the multilateral aid division, Sugimoto Nobuyuki.

This book also reflects and embodies the assistance and friendship provided by numerous colleagues over the years. The list of colleagues is long, and it includes many of the individuals on the roster of interviewees at the end of the bibliography. However, there are a few individuals whom I must single out for special thanks. Skipp Orr and Alan Rix deserve special mention as comrades-in-arms in the study of Japanese aid policy. I have enjoyed our periodic exchanges of ideas and opinions over the years and only wish that these meetings could be more frequent. In addition, I treasured the support and encouragement of Nakahira Kosuke, Paul White, Miyamura Satoru, Lisa Twaronite, Okuma Hiroshi, Brian Crowe, Kitamura Takanori, Kinoshita Toshihiko, Kojima Seiji, and Kobayashi Eiji. Each has contributed in some way over the years to the completion of this project.

I must also extend an apology to my family, Maura, Deirdre, and Siobhan. They exercised great patience and tolerance during the research and drafting of this book, enduring everything from frequent absences to uprooting to a foreign country for a year. Their sense of humor, though often at my expense, sustained me throughout this project.

Finally, deep appreciation goes to Simon Winder at St. Martin's Press for his patience, understanding, and generosity with deadline extensions.

Incidentally, all Japanese names follow the Japanese order—surname first—except in footnotes, where the standard format is observed.

I absolve all of the above-mentioned institutions and individuals from any responsibility for the accuracy of my information or for my conclusions. Whatever errors or flaws readers may find in this study, these individuals are not at fault.

This book is dedicated to James William Morley, professor emeritus of Columbia University, who started it all for me as teacher, adviser, mentor, friend. If there are errors and flaws, it's all his fault, of course.

Dennis T. Yasutomo
Northampton, Massachusetts
May 1995

PART I

FOREIGN AID AND FOREIGN POLICY

1

—◆—

THE EVOLUTION OF JAPAN'S AID
DIPLOMACY AND THE NEW AID DEBATE

The price of greatness is responsibility.

—Winston Churchill

Old warriors seldom trade stories around the campfire about their country's great foreign aid campaign of yesteryear. They do not brag about the wounds suffered in the taking of that hill, inch by inch, to measure the effects of acid precipitation on the rain forest; the building of schools in developing nations seldom triggers the intense reaction of trade wars; and foreign aid technicians seldom are assumed to be courting the kind of danger confronted by soldiers sent to foreign lands. Foreign aid, in other words, is deemed as low, rather than high, politics.

This may be different, however, in the case of Japan. Tokyo's rapid rise in stature from defeated enemy nation and aid recipient to economic great power and the world's largest aid donor symbolizes its determination that ODA (Official Development Assistance), not military activities, would be Japan's international contribution in the postwar period. ODA is considered a key to Japan's status and survival as an accepted member of the world community, and it has engendered its own types of "war stories." ODA also has triggered emotional criticisms of foreign aid boondoggles and harm to aid recipients, and it also has produced the first casualties of its foreign aid campaign—aid technicians who died in the field as a result of political upheaval or accidents. For Japan, ODA is high politics in a post–Cold War world where economic competition increasingly defines international relations.

Japan's foreign aid has become an integral component of an overall diplomacy that stretches from Cambodia to the Persian Gulf, from Latin

America to Africa, and from East and Central Europe to almost all international organizations. It is used to fund global tasks that range from Palestinian and African refugee assistance and environmental protection to Asian poverty alleviation and the dismantling of nuclear weapons in former Soviet republics. Aid is no longer a unidimensional arm of foreign economic policy, obsessed with selfish economic gain at the expense of developing nations. It is a means of defending the nation against the threats of the post–Cold War world, of raising a national status tarnished by war, and of avoiding international criticism and isolation by contributing positively to a world community sensitive to trade imbalances. Many observers, therefore, view ODA as Japan's first genuine step toward accepting the kind of international responsibilities required of greatness.

Japan's rise to aid great power status resulted from necessity and accident, pragmatism and idealism, fortuitous timing and opportunism. It was the result of a coalescing of evolutionary and revolutionary changes in the postwar international system and of consciousness-raising and design at home. But if we accept the traditional depiction of Japanese foreign policy as passive and reactive, mired in domestic political turmoil and bureaucratic politics, bereft of principles and values, subservient to the United States, and trapped by the neoisolationist heritage of the past ODA, activism should not have happened. Therefore, the challenge in the analysis of Japanese ODA policy is to explain the new activism, to bring clarity and conciseness to a policy arena that defies both because of its rapid development and its natural and intended ambiguity.

Four developments define the evolution of Japan's ODA policy since its inception in the 1950s: diversification, or the emergence of multiple uses of ODA for broader foreign policy objectives beyond development, plus the globalization of ODA policy beyond the Asian region; politicization, or the use of ODA not only for national economic gain but also for wider political and strategic diplomatic objectives; multilateralization, or the increased utility of coordinating ODA with fellow donors and channeling aid through international institutions rather than relying only on bilateral aid; and philosophizing, or the fashioning of aid principles and strategies that allow Japan to contribute not only money but also "ideas."

The evolution of these themes has been gradual, cumulative, and often overlapping, with diversification and politicization appearing in the 1970s and 1980s, and multilateralization and philosophizing emerging as 1980s and, especially, 1990s themes. These themes are important not only for understanding ODA policy but also for anticipating the themes and behavioral patterns of Japan's overall foreign policy in the twenty-first century. Of these themes, as this study will demonstrate, multilateralism has increasingly become the framework within which diversification and politicization are evolving, while new philosophies attempt to explain the substance of a policy in constant motion.

Subsequent chapters will chart the ascendance of multilateralization in ODA policy and in Japan's overall foreign policy, but the necessary first step is to provide the policy and literature context of the new multilateralism. This chapter surveys both the emergence of activism in Japan's postwar ODA policy from its inception in the 1950s to the mid-1990s and the Japanese aid literature that seeks to explain this phenomenon. It reveals that multilateral financial institutions come into view only in the most recent phase of aid policy's evolution and that multilateral aid has yet to make any notable appearance in the literature on Japanese aid policy. Because of this, we can question the utility of aid literature in providing guidance toward an understanding of recent policy developments. The general conclusion is that we are heading toward relatively uncharted territory in the study of Japanese ODA and foreign policy.

THE EVOLUTION OF AID DIPLOMACY: DIVERSIFICATION AND POLITICIZATION

The Japanese quickly channeled the smoke that rose from the embers of defeat and destruction in World War II into the smokestacks of reconstructed factories. By the end of the 1950s, reconstruction had been completed successfully, and Japan entered the decade of the "economic miracle." The secret of that miracle lay somewhere in the nation's human resources, bolstered by unity of purpose, supported by a good education system, and driven by memories of what could have been. It was forged by astute government economic policies, a dynamic private sector, and an inviting international economic system. The miracle also was helped by foreign aid, provided bilaterally by the Americans during and since the occupation period (1945-1952) and supplemented thereafter by the World Bank, wherein Japan trailed only India as the second-largest borrowing nation.

Japanese ODA was born in this crucible of despair and hope, and its personality in the 1950s and 1960s reflected the nonpolitical temper and economic needs of the times. Japan was simultaneously a developing and a developed nation, and an aid borrowing and aid-giving nation. Japan's first steps toward aid great power status began in 1954, when its multilateral aid started with membership in the Colombo Plan, and in 1958, when Tokyo approved its first bilateral yen loan (to India). Japan's motive for aid-giving to developing countries was identical to its reason for aid-borrowing from the World Bank: economic growth. The commercial interests of the nation reigned supreme, and ODA was a low-key policy tool that found a small niche in the nation's foreign economic policy. At the time, the Japanese used the term "economic cooperation" rather than "ODA" or "foreign aid" to camouflage the sparseness of concessional official flows compared with the massive proportion of private flows.

Political interests were muted and implicit, confined to the main objective of restoring good relations with Asian victims of wartime aggression, the main ODA recipients during the early stage. In a sense, Japan's aid implied strategic interests because of the attention given to Asian members of the Free World camp in a bipolar Cold War world. Politics and economics functioned as two sides of the same coin, for economic relations often depended on political stability in these countries. It is thus possible to argue that ODA did have a political agenda, although Japan focused on the opposite reasoning: that political stability depended on economic success. However, one must concede that political and strategic objectives were secondary, and even avoided and denied officially, in favor of the pursuit of economic interests. Under a policy of "separation of politics from economics," the political dimension of Japan's aid was, in large part, a concession to the American hegemon, while economic objectives constituted Japan's indigenous national interest.

The turning point for aid policy activism came in the 1970s. Two of our four themes—diversification and politicization—emerged on the scene, and by the 1980s, Japanese ODA policy became less one-dimensional and less regionally focused. As a result of the historic events of that period, it became more political, more global, and more independent as well as more generous.

The globalization actually occurred in the midst of a renewed emphasis on aid to Asia in the 1970s. Asia policy received increased attention because of the Vietnam War and America's defeat in 1975, the Sino-American rapprochement of 1971, and the implications for Japan and Asia of the 1969 Nixon Doctrine. For Japan in particular, Prime Minister Tanaka Kakuei's (1972-74) trip to Southeast Asia in January of 1973 proved a critical turning point in the evaluation of ODA's diplomatic utility. Tanaka was greeted in Indonesia and Thailand by street riots, a result of disaffection of opposition forces in these countries with their government's as well as with Japan's commercial "overpresence" there. The riots shocked Japan, coming after the 1960s when it aspired to a leadership role in the region.

The immediate result was that economic assistance to the region received a heightened priority.[1] ODA terms and conditions softened; aid amounts rose; recipients increased; untying progressed; and new aid forms emerged. Tanaka's successor, Prime Minister Miki Takeo (1974-76), announced an "Asian Marshall Plan," designed to incorporate Japanese technical and financial assistance in a rice production doubling program in Asia. Japan eventually carried the plan to the Asian Development Bank (ADB). Miki's successor, Fukuda Takeo (1976-78), announced his "Manila Doctrine" in 1978, which envisioned a Japanese contribution of $1 billion to five Association of Southeast Asian Nations (ASEAN) projects.

The Fukuda Doctrine also illustrated a growing political agenda in Asia. In the 1970s, Japan initiated ODA to Communist countries, beginning with Mongolia and extending to Vietnam after the 1975 fall of Saigon. One of the doctrine's objectives, in addition to improving Japanese relations with ASEAN nations, was the mitigation of tension between ASEAN and Hanoi after the U.S. withdrawal. Tensions rose between the ASEAN states and a unified Socialist Republic of Vietnam. These efforts came to naught with the 1979 Vietnamese invasion of Cambodia, but Japan embarked on another type of political use of ODA: economic sanctions in support of the West's and ASEAN's tough policy toward Vietnam. Japan froze its aid package to Vietnam, though reluctantly, and applied sanctions against other nations, including Afghanistan after the 1979 Soviet invasion.

The 1970s thus witnessed the initial molding of ODA as a consciously used diplomatic tool in Asia. Economic interests were still paramount, but the political-strategic dimension became more visible as a covert component of ODA policy. The diplomatic utility of ODA hit a takeoff point during this decade, but Asia was not the only arena for this kind of experimentation.

The catalyst for this globalization was the 1973-74 OPEC (Organization of Petroleum Exporting Countries) oil shock. Japan showed considerable independence from the American position by supporting the Arab and the Palestine Liberation Organization (PLO) stance on Middle East issues, and followed its policy change with increased economic and technical aid to the region. Japan's objective was to secure sources of energy. The Middle East, hardly among the neediest of Third World regions, thus figured prominently in Japanese ODA flows in the mid-1970s. Japan subsequently dispatched envoys to the region, including high-ranking government officials and ruling Liberal Democratic Party (LDP) members; it endorsed Arab-Palestinian positions in the United Nations; it cooled relations with Israel; and it invited both Egyptian president Anwar Sadat and PLO chairman Yassir Arafat to Japan. Sadat's assassination aborted the trip to Japan, but

Arafat's visit resulted in the opening of a PLO office in Tokyo. [2] In other words, while economic-resource motives triggered Japan's decision to emphasize the Middle East, political-strategic issues quickly gave its ODA flow a political coloring.

Japan's search for alternative sources of energy also led beyond the Middle East to Africa and Latin America. ODA flows to these regions showed a marked increase as Japan attempted to avoid keeping its energy sources in one basket. Throughout the 1960s, Asia received nearly 100 percent of Japan's ODA. By the end of the 1970s, the Middle East, Latin America, and Africa equally shared roughly 30 percent of the ODA budget. The government unofficially attempted to maintain a level of 10 percent of total ODA flows to each of these three regions, with 70 percent earmarked for Asia. The actual division of shares fluctuated wildly over the next decades, but the principle and reality of globalization beyond Asia remained intact. By the end of the 1980s, the percentage to Asia dropped to the 60 percent range; by 1992, Asia's share hovered around 50 percent. The overall effect of the oil shock loosened the fixation of Japan's ODA with Asia and added a previously missing political and strategic dimension.

This reduction in the percentage of total aid to Asia does not reflect a downgrading of its priority for Japan. The earmarking of 50 percent of a nation's aid to one region still represents a strong commitment. The drop in the proportion of aid to Asia represents an attempt at greater balance, for while the percentage decreased, the absolute amount increased greatly. And Asian nations maintained their positions on the top-ten list of aid recipients, dominated usually by South Asian and Southeast Asian nations plus China. Therefore, one can argue that the globalization of Japan's ODA was premised on the continued priority given to Asia, which reflected Japan's official insistence that its international contributions started there.

The culmination of the globalization of ODA in the initial period was the 1977 Bonn Summit pledge by the Fukuda Cabinet to double cumulative ODA in five, later reduced to three, years. This was the first of four aid-doubling plans that would span the next decade and a half. [3] In 1980, Japan's cumulative ODA flow totaled $3.3 billion, and Japanese pledges jumped dramatically thereafter, to $50 billion in 1986 and $70 to $75 billion in 1993. ODA policy now became a principal contribution that Japan could make to the international community, one that would appeal to both the Third World and to fellow First World donor nations as well as to the Japanese people, who favored international nonmilitary contributions.

The greatest test of a globally oriented ODA policy came in the last half of the 1980s. ODA became a pillar of Japan's approach to the Third World's accumulated debt crisis. In the same year that Japan became the world's largest creditor nation, 1985, the developing world's accumulated debt surpassed $1 trillion. The simultaneous rise of Japan as the world's largest creditor, with surpluses approaching $100 billion at the time, and the descent of Third World countries into a debt crisis provided an opportunity for Japan to address both problems at once: recycle the surplus to debtor nations. Between 1986 and 1989 Japan devised three debt relief plans totaling $65 billion; the plans focused heavily on the disbursement function of international financial institutions but also emphasized bilateral channels.[4]

By the 1980s, as Japan attained the status of largest creditor nation and international financial superpower, and as it amassed large surpluses and competed with the United States as the world's largest aid-giver, ODA entered the mainstream of Japan's external policy. Fellow donors, developing nations, and international institutions welcomed Japan as a major alternative to or supplement for American's relative decline as the world's banker.

The political-strategic dimension that appeared in Asian and Middle Eastern aid gained momentum throughout the 1980s. The government began to consider political and strategic objectives more than before. Until the 1990s, it was careful, however, to either deny or camouflage this motive. The government was concerned primarily with retaining the consistently strong support for aid among the Japanese people, who viewed ODA as a humanitarian rather than political gesture. One of the main objectives was burden-sharing, based on a recognition that the United States was weakened by domestic economic difficulties and pressed to become more selective in fulfilling its overseas security commitments. The politicization of ODA also responded to increased pressure from the Jimmy Carter administration (1976-80) for increased Japanese defense spending. Japan viewed ODA as its contribution to the bilateral strategic relationship.

The use of ODA for political purposes experienced rough spots in the 1980s, but the momentum was maintained. In 1979, the Ohira Masayoshi cabinet (1978-80) instituted ODA for "countries bordering conflict," a term used to describe Japanese aid to three "front-line" states important to Western allies: Thailand, Pakistan, and Turkey. Ohira also inaugurated ODA to the strategically important People's Republic of China in 1979-80 as one means of supporting the modernization efforts of a post–Mao Zedong China. However, the Suzuki Zenko cabinet (1980-82) stepped back from explicit political-strategic rationales for ODA, adopting comprehensive national security as national policy and preferring to sugar-coat political aid with the term "ODA" to "areas which are important to the maintenance of peace and stability of the world." On the other hand, Prime Minister Nakasone Yasuhiro (1982-87) pushed through a controversial $4 billion aid package for South Korea, acknowledging Japan's debt to Seoul for its defense efforts on the Korean Peninsula.[5] And the 1987 "Kuranari Doctrine," named after Nakasone's foreign minister, explicitly linked aid to countering increased Soviet presence and influence in the South Pacific.[6] Succeeding cabinets continued to use aid for political support purposes; cases include the transfer of power in the Philippines from Ferdinand Marcos to Corazon Aquino and the suspension of aid to Myanmar after the declaration of martial law. In addition, at Toronto in 1988, Prime Minister Takeshita Noboru (1987-89) expanded the use of economic resources to peacekeeping operations, at that time unaware of the impact Saddam Hussein would have on that pledge in 1990.[7]

As the 1980s came to a close, the world's largest creditor nation also became the world's largest aid donor, surpassing the United States. Japan entered the 1990s as an aid great power. However, as in the 1970s, domestic and especially international developments again rocked the aid establishment in the 1990s. The bursting of the Japanese economic bubble, the Gulf War, Tiananmen Square, Cambodia, and the collapse of East Europe and the Soviet Union laid the foundation for a new stage in the evolution of aid diplomacy.

THE EVOLUTION OF AID DIPLOMACY: MULTILATERALIZATION AND NEW PHILOSOPHIES

Four major developments characterize Japanese ODA policy in the first half of the 1990s: The political and strategic use of ODA became explicit and acknowledged, rather than implicit and camouflaged, and expanded to East Europe and the republics of the former Soviet Union; ODA's Asian policy began to change in character, responding to new economic miracles and adopting new recipients; disparate principles and themes coalesced into Japanese-style ODA philosophies, including an official ODA charter; and multilateral aid received new emphasis and expanded into new areas.

The political-strategic dimension of Japan's ODA policy came out of the closet after 1989. Three specific events triggered the new openness: First, the collapse of East Europe in 1989 and the Soviet Union in 1991 focused attention on the importance of the transformation of these nations' political and economic systems. The "victory" of democracy over communism ended the Cold War and seemed to validate the universal correctness of democratic and free enterprise values and systems. The promotion of democratic and capitalistic principles, including the promotion of private flows to the European theater of the former Second World, became an integral objective of Western governments. This helped legitimize the insertion of political and ideological content into Japan's ODA policy, leading to a weakening of the separation of politics from economics approach. In the 1990s, Japan's ODA especially to East and Central Europe contains requirements for a commitment to democratization, multiparty political systems, the rule of law, human and civil rights, and a transition to free enterprise systems on the part of aid recipients.

ODA also became intimately linked with peacekeeping operations of the United Nations (UN). Prime Minister Takeshita had incorporated peacekeeping efforts as one of the main pillars of his 1988 "international cooperation initiative," and two years after its declaration, Iraq's invasion of Kuwait tested this pledge. After strong American criticism of Japan's initial lukewarm support for the U.S.-led United Nations effort to roll back Baghdad, Tokyo committed $13 billion to the Gulf War effort and to specific Middle Eastern countries affected by the conflict. It also contributed to the Palestinians in support of the Israeli-PLO peace agreement in 1994, and it dispatched a fleet of minesweepers to clear the waters of the Persian Gulf after the end of hostilities. Once again, as in the 1970s, the situation in the Middle East and Persian Gulf served as a catalyst for significant changes in Japan's ODA policy.[8] In the 1990s, Japan had two ODA-related concerns: placating critics of its hesitant support for the multinational effort, and a nagging feeling that its economic cooperation to Baghdad prior to the invasion helped enable Iraq to invade Kuwait.[9]

The Gulf War had the most catalytic effect on the use of financial resource flows in support of peacekeeping activities, but Japan also contributed aid to the UN's humanitarian mission in Somalia, though the mission took on the characteristics of a military operation. In Rwanda, Japan pledged over $40 million in 1994 to the UN High Commissioner for Refugees, the Red Cross, and the World Health Organization for relief efforts in the wake of the Hutu-Tutsi civil war. In 1993, Tokyo participated in United Nations Transitional Authority for Cambodia's (UNTAC) effort to bring peace and free elections to Cambodia. Japanese aid was accompanied, along with civilian election observers, by the historic dispatch of Self-Defense Force troops onto the Asian mainland for the first time since World War II. In this sense, ODA has been linked, however indirectly, under a multilateral banner, with Japan's use of military might abroad. The complementary use of ODA and military forces is a 1990s phenomenon that would have been unthinkable in previous years.[10]

Finally, the Tiananmen Square massacre of students and workers in June 1989 triggered international economic sanctions against China. Japan initially joined the Western powers, but reluctantly. In fact, Japan immediately worked to soften the sanctions at the July Paris Summit and eventually restored aid flows with the tacit consent of the West.[11] Tiananmen Square forced the Japanese to consider seriously the political ramifications of taking diplomatically harsh steps against its neighbor at a time of increasingly close relations and an exploding Chinese economy. But more than this, Tiananmen Square provided the Japanese with a convenient opportunity to voice doubts openly about the appropriateness of sanctions in effecting political change in recipient countries. Japan had followed the lead of Western nations on sanctions against Vietnam, Afghanistan, and other nations in the 1970s and Myanmar in the 1980s, but China was different. Japan viewed continued ODA flows as more effective than sanctions in promoting human rights and greater political liberalization there. Therefore, its hesitation on China reflected not the wish to depoliticize the human rights issue but rather its strong belief that ODA, used politically as a positive rather than negative sanction, could act as an agent of democratization.

This also applied to countries other than China, most notably in the case of Alberto Fujimori's Peru, when Japan hesitated on sanctions and continued financial support. And Japan lifted sanctions on Iran and Vietnam, with aid flows starting again in 1993. In other words, in the 1970s and 1980s, Japan instituted economic sanctions in step with Western partners, but in the 1990s, Japan lifted, avoided, or softened sanctions in line with its conviction that they were either ineffective or counterproductive in the long run. Again, this represented not a Japanese attempt to escape from political uses of ODA but rather a clearer conceptualization of how to utilize aid as an effective political tool, a view that often conflicted with American preferences.

A second development in ODA policy involves the change in the nature of Japan's aid to Asia in the 1990s. Japan maintains its focus on the region, arguing that it is still home to the largest number of the world's poorest people. However, Asia's record as the fastest-growing region of the world economically challenges its need for increased Japanese aid. Many Asian nations have graduated or are on the verge of graduation as aid recipients, with some, such as South Korea, Taiwan, and Singapore, themselves becoming small-scale donor nations. Japan thus needs a new rationale, or new targets, for its ODA.

As a result, Japan is looking beyond the traditional recipients. China, a new recipient in the 1980s, became the largest bilateral recipient throughout most of the decade, instead of the traditional South and Southeast Asian nations (although Indonesia returned to its top position in the 1990s). Japan intends future development of its aid relationship with Beijing, though not at the expense of ASEAN recipients, which retain about one-third of total Japanese aid flows. Japan considers Vietnam to be a possible new frontier; Cambodia is a potential new target; and Tokyo has taken a leadership role in the democratization and liberalization efforts in Mongolia. Japan also is taking the lead in defining the Central Asian Republics of the former Soviet Union—Kazakhstan, Uzbekistan, Turkmenistan, Tajikistan, and Kyrgyzstan—as "Asian" developing nations: Tokyo successfully pushed for their inclusion on the OECD's (Organization for Economic Cooperation and Development) Development Assistance Committee list of developing nations in 1992, thereby making them eligible to receive Japanese ODA, and supports dual membership in both the European Bank for Reconstruction and Development and the Asian Development Bank (ADB). Therefore, Japan is not only fashioning new rationales for Asian aid but also recruiting new regional members.

The third recent development concerns aid philosophy. With the rapid expansion of ODA policy, the Japanese government found itself hard-pressed to provide a coherent explanation that kept up with the transformation of ODA objectives, character, and status. Policymakers came to feel the necessity for some kind of philosophy to placate domestic aid critics who demanded official guidelines and statements of intent; to maintain the support of the Japanese public for ODA, which had always soared around an astounding 80 percent level but had begun to slip as the nation's economic bubble burst; and to explain aid motives and objectives to foreign audiences. The lack of an official "philosophy," and the general and vague principles set forth by Foreign Ministry officials in the 1980s, left ODA vulnerable to the charge that economic objectives constituted Japan's sole reason for aid-giving. Therefore, in the 1990s, Japan unveiled its first official ODA philosophy.

Japan first embarked on an effort to develop an aid philosophy that could explain, clarify, and garner support for its rapidly expanding aid policy in 1981. The Ministry of Foreign Affairs publication *Keizai Kyoryoku no Rinen: Seifu Kaihatsu Enjo wa Naze Okonau no ka*[12] attempted to provide a conceptual framework to explain Japanese aid motivations. It introduced two principles that still stand as Japan's official aid policy rationales: humanitarianism and interdependence. It also linked ODA to "comprehensive national security," the concept unveiled by Prime Minister Ohira's study group, with its inclusion of nonmilitary threats to national security and the need for emphasizing nonmilitary countermeasures such as ODA.[13]

This "philosophy," however, did not openly acknowledge the political and strategic character or objectives of aid, preferring vague, antiseptic umbrella terms to camouflage the political-strategic dimension. Hence, Ohira's "countries bordering conflict" and Suzuki's "areas important to the maintenance of peace and stability of the world" and "comprehensive national security" enjoyed a separate existence from "humanitarianism" and "interdependence." Only the latter two concepts survived the 1980s, although the basic assumptions of comprehensive security remained in force throughout the 1980s and the term "front-line states" reappeared in 1991 to justify aid to Egypt, Jordan, and Turkey.[14]

The 1990s aid policy rationales exhibited some continuity and much change. Political-strategic uses became open and touted as national policy, and the targets and actual content of this aid changed. In the 1990s these previously little-acknowledged objectives were transferred from the periphery to the explicit core of ODA policy in the 1990s. Rationales were now molded to the new political imperatives of the post–Cold War era. Prime Minister Kaifu Toshiki (1989-91) declared the primacy of political objectives of aid to East Europe. After the Gulf War, when Japan was stung by criticism for inaction, Kaifu announced his ODA guidelines: Japan would pay close attention to recipient country military expenditures, their development and production of weapons of mass destruction and missiles, their arms exports, their efforts toward democratization and the introduction of a market economy, and their guarantee of basic human rights and freedoms. Kaifu not only made these a priori political conditions, something the Japanese studiously avoided in their old ODA policy, but he also extended them to all Japanese aid: "Democracy, freedom and a market economy must be the framework for *any country* offered assistance."[15]

The Miyazawa Kiichi cabinet (1991-93) incorporated these principles into the "ODA Charter" of 1992, adding the global environment to military expenditures, weapons of mass destruction, democratization, market economies, and human rights.[16] The collapse of East Europe and the Gulf War resulted in an ODA Charter that announces to the world that Japan's aid, the prime example of the "separation of politics from economics" policy, now gives priority to diplomatic and political objectives. This development gives the startling impression that Japan has, almost overnight, shed its economic animal coloring in favor of standing tall as the champion and protector of democratization, arms control, economic liberalization, and the preservation of the global environment.

The charter has its critics, but it now stands as Japan's official aid philosophy. However, as we will soon see, another candidate challenges the charter as Japan's development philosophy. At this point, it is sufficient to note that the appearance of an official philosophy—and a political one at that—after decades of aid-giving without one is, in itself, significant.

The fourth significant change in Japanese ODA policy in the late 1980s and 1990s is the emphasis on multilateral channels. Three strands in Japan's multilateral diplomacy in the 1990s can be identified.

UNITED NATIONS–RELATED ACTIVITIES. Japan joined the UN in 1956, and the Kishi Nobusuke cabinet (1958-60) designated UN-centered diplomacy as a major pillar of Japan's foreign policy. However, it is fair to say that Japan has not played a major role in that institution until recently. By the 1990s, however, Japan's contributions to and through the UN system serve as one of its primary arguments for inclusion on the Security Council as a permanent member.[17] UN diplomacy currently consists of two major types of activities: peacekeeping-related efforts, as discussed earlier, and global environmental aid, for example, a pledge of $7 to $8 billion over five years at the 1992 Earth Summit in Rio de Janeiro.

MULTILATERAL DEVELOPMENT BANK-RELATED ACTIVITIES. By the end of the 1970s, Japan attained membership in the international financial institutions (with the exception of the European Bank for Reconstruction and Development, which was established in 1991, and the African Development Bank, which did not welcome nonregional members until 1983, although Japan was a member of the African Development Fund from 1973). However, at that time, Japan's presence was hardly felt, except in the Asian Development Bank. In general, Japan was not a significant financial contributor, a political voice, or a presence in the management or staff in these organizations.

Japan's presence came to be felt in the 1980s because of its increased financial weight, but only at the end of the decade did the nation embark on a more active and visible course of action within these institutions. Japan's recent activism initially revolved around financial contributions and commensurate vote shares. By the 1990s, Japan was in the number two spot in most of these institutions. But the opening round of this activism can be dated from the announcement and implementation of Japan's surplus recycling plans of the late 1980s. As we will see in later chapters, Japan earmarked a total of $65 billion for Third World debt relief, with the MDBs, especially the World Bank and the Asian Development Bank, serving as principal conduits for the recycled funds. In addition, and more significantly, Japan also has spoken out more in these institutions, articulating its views and proposing changes in standard operating procedures and assumptions. The new 1990s Japanese theme for MDBs is "ideas, not just money," and these new "ideas" center on the potential applicability of Japan's own development experience to the nations of the Third and former Second worlds.

GROUP OF 7–RELATED ACTIVITIES. The G-7 has been called upon to deal with many of the major issues of the post–Cold War world. Japan has become a presence at the annual summits, and what this study will reveal is that G-7 policies serve as the framework for much of Japan's ODA and MDB policies in the 1990s, ranging from East European to environmental aid.

The four themes introduced in this chapter—diversification, politicization, multilateralization, and philosophizing—all converge in Japan's policies toward the multilateral development banks in the 1990s. Multilateral bank policy provides one concrete handle on the question of how Japan will define and fulfill its appropriate international role. It is in these institutions that Japan is finally accepting an agenda-setting and rule-making role through greater assertiveness and involvement in funding, management, and operational dimensions. It is in these agencies that Japan is making full use of its nonmilitary resources, unfettered by any required commitment of military power (which partially explains the difference between Japan's hesitant multilateral Gulf effort and multilateral bank activism). And it is in these agencies that Japanese independence from the United States seems to have reared its head.

In other words, in the 1990s, international financial institutions seem to represent one of the testing grounds for Japan's twenty-first century diplomacy. Given the international emphasis on economic, financial, technological, and human resources in defining the power of nation-states in the post–Cold War era, Japan seems well suited to contribute actively in the creation of a new world order that must address global problems ranging from East European and Russian transformation to environmental and debt issues. The new multilateralism in international relations appears fortuitous for a Japan that is searching for ways to channel its new activism.

In sum, aid diplomacy evolved from a minor component of Japan's foreign economic policy to a pillar of its future role in the world. Aid diplomacy does not constitute the total of Japan's diplomacy, but at times and in certain circumstances, it has come close. As a result, ODA policy can no longer be understood in one-dimensional terms. It is a diverse, multidimensional policy tool with multiple objectives. The challenge for aid analysts is to provide a convincing explanation of the new activism and to speculate on its implications for future Japanese foreign policy.

THE AID DEBATE

The analysis of the motives, form, substance, and future of Japan's ODA policy leaves much room for debate. Ambiguities abound because of a policy process that lacks transparency and an official policy rationale that lacks clarity and consistency. The Japanese literature on foreign aid, relatively scanty until recent years, has addressed these issues in a serious and concerted manner only in the last few years. In many ways, the literature reflected the consensus that existed in aid analysis in previous decades and the diversification that occurred in aid policy during the 1980s in particular. Japan experienced two major booms in its aid literature. The first explosion occurred in the mid-1970s, especially from 1973 to 1975.[18] It is tempting to credit the OPEC oil shock, and the resulting use of ODA in Japan's resource diplomacy, as the spur to the publishing boom. However, the oil shock occurred during the winter of 1973-74. Thus, many of these studies appeared prior to the oil shock; given the time lag between drafting, submission, and actual publication, the research and writing actually occurred primarily in 1972 and 1973. Other explanations for this aid literature boom include Japan's "economic miracle" and its transformation into a surplus country in 1968, allowing Tokyo to consider a role as a capital exporting nation, and the utility of ODA as an effective means of mitigating the anti-Japanese attitudes revealed during Tanaka's trip to Southeast Asia.

   This literature neither reflected nor triggered an aid debate. Many of the works were merely descriptive, focusing on recent developments in ODA policy. There was also a basic consensus on the major issues, including Japan's motives for giving aid, on the shape of the policymaking process, and on the characteristics and conditions of ODA policy. In short, both government supporters and critics of aid agreed on the primacy of economic and resource motives for aid-giving, on the primacy and problems of the bureaucratically dominated four-agency aid policy structure, on the toughness of aid conditions, and on the regional concentration on Asia.[19]

   The only real debate focused on calls for the government to improve ODA conditions and increase aid amounts, but even these demands found agreement, in principle, within the government. Perhaps the most controversial issue was the American factor, with critics charging the government with subservience to U.S. security policy in making aid decisions (especially the restriction of ODA to non-Communist Asian recipients). But even this view approached consensus if rephrased as an ODA policy determined within the Cold War political, strategic, and economic framework of the U.S.-Japan alliance.

   A serious aid debate ensued only during the second boom in aid literature. This debate reflected the changes in ODA policy and culminated in the publication of a myriad of ODA-related books from the late 1980s and into the 1990s. These works were penned by Japanese academics, journalists, government officials, aid practitioners in the field, think-tank researchers, and foreign observers from both donor and recipient nations whose books were translated into Japanese. Parallel with Japanese analyses of Tokyo's ODA policy, numerous English-language studies of Japan's ODA emerged abroad in academic[20] and official circles[21], with some being incorporated into the debate in Japan.[22] International ODA conferences in Japan also contributed to both foreign and Japanese interest in Japanese ODA.[23]

The debate emerged as a response to numerous interrelated developments since the mid-1970s. These include Japan's emergence as the world's largest creditor nation in 1985; a persistent recession with the bursting of the economic "bubble" of the 1980s, resulting in even greater concern with trade friction and national budget expenditures; the spotlight on ODA policy in Japan's political arena, especially in the Diet; the proliferation of critical articles on aid in the print medium; the concern among "taxpayers" (in whose name everyone speaks) with effective use of their money; the proliferation of non-official, mostly academic, aid analysts who have first-hand opportunities to visit and evaluate ODA projects; the focus on the link between ODA and diplomacy, especially since the Gulf War and Tiananmen Square; and a general aspiration in Japan to find ways to contribute more fully to the world community through nonmilitary means.

In many ways, aid policy analysis fought to keep up with the rapid pace of change in aid policy itself. Rapid change often results in awkward, uneven, and disjointed policies, and ODA literature feasted on the contradictions and ambiguities of a policy that may have changed too fast. In the midst of greater activism, the general consensus found in earlier aid policy analysis broke down, yielding an actual, sometimes bitter, debate with clearly defined differences of opinion.

The debate centers on aid rationales, conditions, politicization, effectiveness, impact on recipient governments and peoples, and the policymaking process. Opinions divide along two dimensions of Japan's ODA policy, with positions determined by a positive or negative answer to the following questions: Is Japan's ODA a negative force that serves only the donor's interest, harms the recipient, and corrupts both donor and recipient, or is ODA a positive, constructive, and even noble force that promotes the public good for both donor and recipient? Does Japan have a coherent ODA philosophy that serves as a moral guideline and national interest compass, or is ODA policy bereft of any guiding principles, moral or otherwise, as a rudderless, reactive rationalization for mercantilism?

These dimensions may over simplify a complex debate, and there is always the danger of building an analytical Procrustean bed, especially when "schools" of thought have just begun to appear. However, a look at the current aid debate through these two dimensions will yield a useful framework for the analysis of Japanese ODA that will transcend the persistent one-dimensional debate among non-Japanese aid analysts (i.e., is Japanese ODA policy mercantilistic or not?). Perhaps it is time to give Japanese analysts center stage to see how they would evaluate ODA policy rather than to rely primarily on foreign interpreters of that policy.

The first dimension basically asks if Japanese ODA is a force for good or evil. From the beginning of Japan's ODA efforts in the 1950s to the current day, the "evil" school of thought has prevailed in Japan. This is the mainstream view, the orthodoxy, of Japanese aid analysis. However much Japanese aid may change, however much aid supporters point to successes or benefits, the "original sin" school of thought concentrates almost exclusively on the evil intentions or effects of Japan's ODA policy. Some may favor ODA in principle, but almost never do they give *Japanese* ODA the benefit of the doubt.

In recent years, the adherents of the "evil" school of thought are centered in academia and the mass media, especially newspapers. Academics are prolific and make a strong case based on personal experience in the aid field, including evaluations of ODA projects. In the 1990s, the most widely cited spokespersons for the ODA-as-evil school are Sumi Kazuo and Murai Yoshinori[24], and ODA supporters often singled out among newspapers the *Mainichi, Asahi,* and *Tokyo Shimbun* for an obsession with ODA scandals and project failures.[25] In addition, aid critics populate certain political parties, primarily the opposition parties of the era of LDP rule (1955-1993), especially the Social Democratic Party of Japan (SDPJ) and Komeito (Clean Government Party). Critics also are scattered throughout nongovernmental organizations, citizen's groups, and the university student population.

While the critics of ODA articulate the mainstream view, oddly enough, opposition parties have supported the passage of the economic cooperation budget each year without incident, and Japanese public opinion in general supports ODA to developing nations, consistently registering a support level of around 80 percent. These forces consider ODA Japan's humanitarian responsibility to developing nations but consistently find fault with the motives and record of their own government's aid. That is, Japan's ODA motives are suspect and its performance congenitally flawed and in need of radical improvement. It may, therefore, be fairer to distinguish between the hard-line critics and "associate critics": As hard-liners, opposition party members tend to be equally caustic and consistently severe toward Japan's aid but more selective (paying attention to ODA scandals rather than success stories) or sporadic (vocal in Diet deliberations but not in the print medium) in their criticism. And public opinion supports humanitarian aid in principle but criticizes wasteful, inefficient, and scandalous uses of their tax dollars.

The Japanese ODA-as-evil school concentrates its fire on several specific negative features and consequences. The main areas of concern follow.

The principal indictment is mercantilism. Critics argue that the ultimate objective of Japanese ODA is self-centered economic gain. ODA is merely a tool—along with trade and overseas investment—of a predatory mercantilistic national policy that colludes with Japanese general trading companies and engineering and consulting firms. The objective is not to assist developing nations but to enrich Japanese private sector interests by utilizing ODA to open, or maintain, overseas markets for manufactured goods, technology, and services, or to secure and maintain sources of raw materials and energy resources.

Through this prism, the striking increase in Japanese ODA is attributable to foreign economic policy. ODA helped stimulate the domestic economy during periods of slowdown, providing overseas opportunities for, as an example, the construction industry during the recession of the early 1980s. Or ODA is a convenient response to criticism of Japan's huge annual surpluses by trade partners; for example, the recycling plans could help reduce that surplus by funneling it to LDCs.

Corruption is another target. Do taxpayers really know where their money is going? The critics' answer has two dimensions: into the pockets of LDC elites and into the coffers of Japanese elites. Aid studies have uncovered numerous cases of inflated costs, aid money laundering, and under-the-table payments that have ended up in the hands of political, bureaucratic, or private sector elites in the recipient nation, with Indonesian and Filipino cases especially prominent in the literature. Aid, in other words, does not reach the masses, where the need is greatest.

On the other hand, ODA flows back to one of its sources—the politicians in the Diet who appropriated the funds in the first place. Observers have criticized Liberal Democratic Party politicians for taking bribes for supporting a specific project or for receiving kickbacks from companies that received a contract. Most critics believe the root of corruption is the collusive relationship between the government and business sectors.

Critics have focused increasingly on quality-of-life issues in the 1990s. They charge that Japanese ODA has a tremendously negative impact on the peoples of recipient nations. Many Japanese projects destroy the natural environment through environmentally unsound dam, bridge, and other infrastructural projects. Whether destroying rain forests in South America or plant and animal life along a river in India, Japan's main impact on Third World environments is negative. The degradation of the natural environment is paralleled by the disruption of the local inhabitants' lifestyle. Not only are quality-of-life issues raised, but recent cases of forced, uncompensated evacuations of local villagers have been uncovered. Critics' charges thus range from destroying and polluting virgin territories to ethnocide in the pursuit of profits. Effectiveness remains a concern for critics. ODA spending basically wastes taxpayer money. Critics cite project after project that seem to reveal some kind of boondoggle, from providing television sets to a village without electricity to projects that never seem to end because of cost overruns and deadline extensions.

Aid types continue to be a traditional target. The problem with Japanese ODA is its concentration on infrastructure projects. More profit can be made by building bridges, roads, dams, airports, or ports than by any social infrastructure projects, thus making Basic Human Needs (BHN) projects less desirable. The health, educational, and other needs of the local inhabitants are thus treated as secondary and not the stuff of development.

Aid critics also insist on the depoliticization of ODA and condemn the Japanese government's perceived political agenda. The charge of politicization entails two primary complaints: First, the Japanese government is accused of utilizing ODA to make friends with despotic, authoritarian governments in the Third World. Japan averts its eyes when it provides ODA to countries with atrocious human rights records. Not only does Japan subsidize greedy elites, but it also props up oppressive elites while ignoring the people who are striving for democracy or even survival. Second, Japanese ODA is viewed as subservient to American influence. Some critics doubt the independence of Tokyo's aid policy, which they consider to be an arm of U.S. political and strategic policy. During the Cold War, Japanese ODA followed the anti-Communist, anti-Soviet, and pro-West dictates of Washington. Japan's principal aid recipients were thus non-Communist nations in the Free World, and even nonaligned recipients were basically pro-West in economic and foreign policies.

From this viewpoint, the official rationales for aid-giving—humanitarianism and interdependence—were plainly a facade for the underlying political and strategic objectives of the United States. To the extent that official aid rationales pertained to Japanese, rather than U.S., national interests, they related to the economic security of the nation. Aid to ASEAN nations, for example, is critical for keeping the Malacca, Lombok, and Sunda straits open to Japanese ships.

Critics also focus intently on policymaking. Japan's aid policymaking structure and process are antiquated and in need of reform. The main problems include the collusive relationship among the government, bureaucracy, and Japanese firms; the lack of transparency in the policy process, where aid policy decisions remain hidden from the public eye; and the decentralization of the aid bureaucracy, which results in jurisdictional squabbles and uncoordinated policies.

Finally, all critics call for reform. All of the preceding problems demand a basic reform of Japanese ODA. A general consensus seems to exist on two fundamental starting points. First, critics argue for the passage of a basic ODA law, modeled on the American Foreign Assistance Act, to spell out Japan's ODA philosophy and objectives and to provide greater opportunities for the Diet to exercise oversight functions over ODA policy. Second, they argue for a restructuring of the aid policymaking apparatus, favoring both greater transparency in decision making and greater centralization through the creation of an economic cooperation ministry or agency of some kind.

In sum, ODA critics argue that Japanese ODA is self-centered, exploitative, wasteful, and destructive and, therefore, requires considerable reform through rethinking aid rationales, Diet oversight, consideration of recipient people's interests, and greater transparency in and centralization of the aid policy apparatus and process. The bottom-line assessment, however, is that Japanese ODA is basically incapable of doing good, and the extreme argument prefers that Japanese ODA be eliminated entirely.

By the early 1990s, a large body of literature began to challenge the orthodox view of Japanese ODA policy. Of course, government ODA white papers always have served as the official retort to aid policy critics,[26] but aid proponents now include government officials and aid practitioners,[27] some conservative politicians,[28] private sector organizations and firms,[29] and a few development economists and academics who have evaluated aid projects.[30] These "revisionists" bring greater balance to the aid debate by responding directly to the critics' arguments and, while acknowledging problems, by pointing out the positive features and impact of Japan's ODA.[31]

The pro-Japanese ODA "school"[32] response to critics ranges from personal to philosophical. The debate has become quite bitter among some participants, with both sides criticizing the other side for bias, faulty research methods, poor understanding of the field, and for pursuing personal, political, and financial agendas.[33] The substance of the pro-aid faction's position focuses on the refutation of the critics' indictment and on emphasizing new aspects of ODA policy.

Revisionists respond to the charge of mercantilism by noting that all donor nations pursue their own economic interests, with West European nations such as Germany and France especially notable. Even the United States makes sure that there is a return on American development assistance, and the new Clinton administration has focused explicitly on linking ODA with business opportunities for American firms.

Contrary to the orthodox view, they insist, Japan's aid is the most liberalized of all the donors. It is now the most untied, with Japanese private sector procurement of aid projects dropping into the 20 percent range. In fact, Japanese companies are upset with the government for favoring non-Japanese procurers from developed and developing nations over Japanese firms. As one example, Japanese executive directors on the board of directors of international financial institutions refrain from lobbying for contracts for Japanese firms, unlike many other executive directors.

Government officials in particular respond that ODA should not, in fact, be considered in isolation, separate and distinct from a nation's trade and investment strategies. ODA can contribute significantly to LDC development, but ODA is not enough. A coordinated strategy is required that encompasses semiofficial and private flows if the problems of development are to be addressed. Therefore, to be effective, a comprehensive approach is necessary, one that incorporates ODA, semiofficial, and private flows. The Japanese thus conceive of a graduated weaning of recipients from concessional public to commercial private flows rather than the abrupt cessation of ODA upon "graduation."

Finally, Japanese aid is no longer one-dimensional. Economic objectives were paramount in ODA's early days, but by the 1990s, Japan has incorporated strategic, diplomatic, political, and philosophical components into its aid policy. This is reflected in the 1992 ODA Charter, which attempts to blend a diversity of objectives, ranging from environmental concerns and women in development, to democratization and attention to military spending.

Corruption is unfortunate, but this is not the fault of ODA or Japanese policy. The problem rests with the greed and general quality of domestic and recipient country elites. Japan plays the hand that is dealt; that is, many less developed countries (LDC) are under the rule of oppressive and corrupt elites. While respecting the international principle of noninterference in the internal affairs of other nations, Japan still must attempt to improve the livelihood of the masses.

In addition, ODA can be an agent of change. Experience has shown that for many LDCs, development gives rise to new internal forces. Citizens, often representing a rising new middle class, begin to demand greater political freedom and economic liberalization as living standards improve. ODA can plant the seeds of democratization and liberalization from within, which is the most effective type of political and economic freedom. What is needed is patience on the part of the donor and self-determination and self-help on the part of the recipients.

Japan also understands the link between development and the quality of life, especially environmental degradation. After all, that was its experience during its economic miracle. Japan is still coping with the after-effects of that period. However, Japan moved decisively to reverse environmental damage and, in that process, learned much that may be of use to less developed countries facing similar prospects. Japan will now take the lead in the field of the environment, and ODA will be a major means of environmental preservation. If there is one area where Japanese ODA policy is attempting a leadership role, it is in the environmental field, with the 1992 Earth Summit commitment of $7 to $8 billion constituting the opening shot.

Revisionists contend that ODA is effective. It is not a waste of taxpayers' money. The government is emphasizing closer monitoring and frequent evaluations of projects. Critics focus only on the failures and those projects that are beset with problems. They ignore evaluation reports revealing that the majority of Japanese ODA projects are relatively successful.[34] Newspapers especially seek out boondoggles because they make the headlines and sell papers, but if they bother to look, they will find numerous projects in every recipient country that actually contribute to the welfare of the people.

The best evidence of ODA's effectiveness is the record of Japan's principal aid recipient—Asia. Its top recipients have effected their own economic miracles as the world's fastest-growing region economically. Some of these countries are now becoming aid donors themselves, creating their own aid agencies, with some modeled on Japan's aid policy and structure. Japanese ODA is not the only reason for their success, but it did contribute its fair share.

On aid types, aid policy defenders insist that Japan does pay attention to social infrastructure, and ODA does reach the masses in the areas of health, education, community development, and agriculture. Japan's recent aid to Sub-Sahara Africa is weighted heavily toward Basic Human Needs and humanitarian aid. However, infrastructure is important and should not be slighted. For example, funding food production is fine, but dams are needed for irrigation, roads and bridges are needed to transport these goods to market, and ports are needed to export these products abroad to earn foreign currency. The Asian experience in particular has especially focused attention on the need for adequate infrastructural development.

On the charge of politicization, aid practitioners argue that Japanese aid is fundamentally nonpolitical in intent. Japan's overall foreign policy has followed the formula of "separating politics from economics," and this principle has carried over to ODA policy. This not a unique Japanese concept but a general approach to international relations and development. The principle is, in fact, codified in the charters of most international financial organizations, which reflect the principles of its founding nations. Japan supports the basic principle of noninterference in domestic affairs. However, it also supports universal principles of human and civil rights, democratization, and free and open economies. ODA has been used as a diplomatic tool to promote these principles, with the Japanese government codifying its commitment to these principles in the ODA Charter.

Neither is Japanese aid the handmaiden of American policy. Japan has supported the United States as a loyal ally throughout the Cold War period, but it has also pursued its own interests when different from the United States. ODA for Arab states following the first oil shock reflected Japanese interests, with its endorsement of Arab and PLO, rather than Israeli and American, positions. Japan also took the lead in reinstating aid to China despite Tiananmen, thawed the freeze on Vietnamese aid ahead of the United States, and decided to start the flow of assistance to Iran despite U.S. and Western difficulties with Teheran. The United States is supported when appropriate, but Japan also expresses its concern with American approaches and takes independent actions when necessary.

As for policymaking and reform, the ODA policy structure and process have their problems, but it all works rather well. Resources are pooled; a functional division of labor is organized according to technical expertise; consultation is extensive; all relevant actors are involved and have their say; and coordination has not been a problem. This decentralized, "bottom-up" approach is more appropriate for a Japanese setting than a centralized "Western-style" system. Reform may be necessary to increase transparency and efficiency, but not the kind advocated by the critics. A foreign assistance law would just make policymaking less effective, creating more red tape and stretching out the time frame of policymaking. Besides, the desire for a law reflects politics, with opposition party supporters looking for yet another way to embarrass the government. That is the real objective of the demand for transparency. And when these opposition parties became ruling parties in the coalition government that toppled the Liberal Democrats in 1993, they were very quiet on the issue of aid legislation and reform.

Centralization of the policy apparatus is unrealistic. Any aid agency, whether attached to the prime minister's office (PMO) or independent, will suffer from the usual Japanese organizational problems. For example, the staff will more than likely come from existing ministries and agencies and from the private sector. And the underlying (unrealistic) assumption for creating a PMO agency is that political leaders possess the expertise about developing nations' cultures, economies, politics, and history necessary to implement ODA policies effectively.

Finally, aid critics refuse to acknowledge a new development in ODA policy—the use of ODA to define Japan's role in the world. Because of suspect motives and the obsession with only the negative impact of ODA, critics cannot argue that foreign aid serves a positive role as Japan's contribution to the international community. However, this belief forms the core of recent aid proponents' literature. These writers grapple with the road Japan will travel into the twenty-first century and conclude that ODA fits perfectly into the emerging Japanese aspiration for an international role that combines globalization and politicization through nonmilitary means. ODA has a role to play as a diplomatic tool that combines Japan's national strengths—finance, technology, knowledge, and human resources.

In sum, aid proponents argue that aid criticism is biased, ill-informed, and out of date. They also open up discussion of a new dimension, namely, ODA as a principal pillar of Japan's future role in the world. In other words, aid supporters are not merely defensive, responding only to criticism, but also discuss ODA as an integral component of a Japanese vision of the future.

Interestingly, it is difficult to categorize studies of Japanese ODA written by non-Japanese observers. Some fall into the mercantilist mainstream category,[35] but most fall into an intermediate category, either those that consider Japanese ODA policy as "basically bad, but not evil" or "basically good, but needs improvement." The bad-but-not-evil perspective focuses on the lack of an aid philosophy, a dysfunctional policymaking process, a susceptibility to reactiveness, and poor aid conditions. These studies share the aid-as-evil school's advocacy of reforms but reject the view of Japanese ODA as predatory, exploitative, and mercantilistic.[36] On the other hand, some foreign observers consider Japanese ODA as basically positive in either intent or direction, the result of an evolutionary process characterized by greater activism, awareness of problems, and sincere efforts to change. The major task is not so much radical reform but greater clarity of purpose, effectiveness in implementation, and fine-tuning of the policy process.[37] Both views share in common the belief that Japan needs to continue aid activism while making changes in the policy process. But they ultimately differ in their confidence in Japan's ability actually to make those changes; the former view is skeptical while the latter view is willing to give the Japanese the benefit of the doubt.

AID PHILOSOPHY

The second dimension of the aid debate focuses on whether Japan has an aid philosophy. While it may seem that this aspect of the debate could produce a simple yes or no answer, there are many dimensions and variations on both sides of the issue. Unlike the question of whether Japanese aid is good or bad, most foreign observers have vocally joined this debate, mostly on the negative side. [38]

The mainstream view holds that Japan does not possess an ODA philosophy. There are five variants of this "school."

The most frequently cited reason for a lack of philosophy is simply that Japan is incapable of formulating an aid philosophy. There are, in turn, three arguments here that can be distilled from the literature. First, Japan lacks a philanthropic tradition. A society traditionally composed of groups with a highly defined sense of us-them, we-they ethic has not developed a philosophy of extending a hand to outsiders. Japanese society reflects this tradition by lacking the various types of nonprofit and philanthropic organizations that dot the American landscape. Second, Japan's bureaucratic policy process makes it impossible to develop a comprehensive aid philosophy. Whatever rationales or philosophies that have appeared to date reflect the attitudes and interests of the specific ministry that produced that philosophy.[39] The ODA Charter, for example, reflects the thinking of the Foreign Ministry, and its principles are not fully supported by other ministries. Third, a Japanese philosophy would contradict the traditional practice of request-based procedures and the principle of self-help. Japan has not placed rigid conditions on its aid to LDC nations. Rather, the assumption is that the recipient nation knows its own needs best, thus leaving the initiative to the recipient. Japan's ODA is designed to supplement and support the recipient's self-help efforts. Any overarching philosophy that Japan might attempt to force on the recipient contradicts the assumption that the recipient knows best.

A second variant is that Japan does not have a philosophy because it does not need one. The reason is simple: Japan's ODA is designed merely to enrich its own companies and national economy. A sophisticated, comprehensive philosophy is, therefore, superfluous and deceptive. Since commercial gain is the real objective, any philosophy or principle, such as humanitarianism or interdependence, would just be a public relations attempt to cloak the real intention of aid.[40]

A third version of this argument insists that Japan does not have a philosophy because it should not have one.[41] Japan should maintain its traditional request-based approach, with its adherence to noninterference in the recipients' domestic affairs, its confidence in their ability to recognize their own needs, and its reliance on LDCs' self-help efforts. Japan should not attempt to impose its own universal philosophy or self-interested conditions on recipients. This lack of a philosophy or conditions makes Japan's ODA unique among donor nations, and recipient nations greatly appreciate Japan for this. The bottom line of ODA should not be beautiful, dazzling philosophies or donor national interests but results. The effective use of ODA is far more important than its political, economic, and public relations rationalizations. Japan is better off without a bothersome philosophy.

The fourth argument believes that Japan has no philosophy because it allows foreign influences to define ODA policy. Japan merely borrows the existing philosophies of others, thereby obviating the need for its own, original philosophy. Since Japan is ignorant of the cultures, politics, and economies of developing nations, it is incapable of formulating its own development strategies for others to emulate. Therefore, Tokyo either borrows American philosophies and aid strategies, [42] such as Basic Human Needs, or aid principles culled from other international sources. For example, Japanese aid rationales in earlier periods borrowed heavily from the Pearson (humanitarianism) and Brandt (interdependence) Commission Reports [43] to formulate the 1981 philosophy.

A final strain of thought in the no philosophy camp decries this lack and calls for the creation of a new philosophy. [44] In recent years, many Japanese acknowledge and condemn the lack of an indigenous philosophy. These advocates range from newspapers and opposition and ruling party politicians to academics, bureaucrats, and private sector representatives; they come from both critics and revisionists. Their reasons for promoting the formulation of a set of ODA guiding principles may differ, but their objectives—clarification and persuasion—and their target audiences—Japanese citizens and foreign countries—are similar.

The government needs a philosophy to explain ODA to the Japanese people and to maintain their support, especially in the face of the media's fixation on aid scandals and in the midst of an economic recession. Aid supporters also feel the need to respond to foreign criticism of Japan's aid policy, especially in the wake of the Gulf War and the Tiananmen Square incident. Lack of information and, therefore, understanding is regarded as the main source of criticism; hence, a philosophy would explain Japan's policy. Aid critics want a clear philosophy that encompasses noble, humanitarian guidelines and rejects commercialism, corruption, and self-interest. Lack of transparency and information is regarded as the main cause of hidden waste and irregularities.

On the other side of the coin, among those who argue that Japan does indeed possess an aid philosophy, there are three strong retorts. First of all, some argue that Japan not only has an aid philosophy, it has had one from the very beginning. What is this philosophy? Three possibilities exist: First, commercialism is not the reason why Japan lacked a philosophy. It was, and is, Japan's ODA philosophy. According to ODA critics, mercantilism itself has constituted the philosophical underpinning of Japanese ODA since the 1950s. ODA began with wartime reparations and economic cooperation agreements designed to rebuild Japan's war-torn economy; ODA helped Japan survive the effects of the oil shock in the 1970s; and ODA helped recycle trade surpluses to LDCs as one means of reducing trade friction. In all these eras, the common philosophy was the promotion or maintenance of Japan's economic growth and standard of living. Self-help actually meant helping Japan, not the developing nations.

Second, Free World political principles, under the rubric of anti-communism, constituted Japan's philosophy. Japan borrowed the American principles of democracy and free enterprise and shaped its aid policy along the lines of Washington's Cold War containment policy. Thus the common bond with aid recipients until the mid-1970s had been the ideology of capitalism and anticommunism. [45] With the end of the Cold War, the "victorious concepts"—democratization, privatization, free markets, human and civil rights—form the basis of Japan's ODA, as codified in the ODA Charter, but these are merely a continuation of Cold War principles. Therefore, new philosophies have not arisen from whole cloth but from looms constructed at the inception of ODA policy.

Third, Japan's philosophy is not a political but rather a development philosophy.[46] Anticommunism, democracy, strategic objectives, diplomatic uses—all of these simply get in the way of the real objective of Japan's ODA: the economic development of developing nations. From the very beginning, Japan's aid philosophy has been clear: a belief in self-reliance and self-help on the part of the recipient; a request-based aid philosophy; separation of politics from economics; emphasis on infrastructure; attention to the social infrastructure and the welfare of the masses. All of these constituted a Japanese development philosophy that has guided ODA all along. It was practical and results-oriented rather than political and ideological, which as a rule are obstacles to genuine and effective development.

The second response to the no philosophy camp acknowledges the lack of a philosophy during the early phases of ODA's existence but insists that things have changed. Tokyo now possesses a newly created aid philosophy.[47] Again, one can view this recent development from different angles.

For example, it is possible to argue that Japan's current aid philosophy is the result of a cumulative process. Japan lacked a philosophy in the 1950s and 1960s. The change began in the late 1970s with the early concepts of Comprehensive National Security and "countries bordering conflict"; it took hold through the 1981 economic cooperation principles of humanitarianism and interdependence; it evolved toward the Kuranari Doctrine and Takeshita's international cooperation initiative; and it culminated in the Kaifu principles and the ODA Charter, which now stands as Japan's official philosophy.[48]

Another view rejects the cumulative interpretation, arguing that the ODA Charter would not have been possible during the early phases. Only the special circumstances surrounding the Gulf War and the end of the Cold War caused Japan to devise such a philosophy, the contents of which are basically foreign to previous concepts. The philosophy, especially its political principles, is thus unprecedented and marks a new phase in Japan's ODA thinking. However, the corollary is that because this philosophy appeared suddenly and reactively, questions can be raised about its genuineness and depth. The suspicion is that the charter is more a public relations exercise hurriedly patched together in order to mitigate foreign criticism. Despite the charter's activist cast, Japan still prefers the request-based, separation of politics from economics intent of its ODA policy.

The third variation propounds a philosophy-under-construction perspective. These proponents argue that the new philosophy is still in its gestation period—on the verge of birth—but that it has little to do with the ODA Charter. Here, the distinction between political-diplomatic and economic-development philosophies rises to the fore.[49] In the early 1990s, widespread discussion occurred, especially among development economists and some policymakers, about what Japan could contribute to development. A popular conclusion is: lessons from Japan's own development experience, which seem similar to the experiences of Asian neighbors. This Japanese or Asian development model, to be discussed in detail later, constitutes Japan's newly emergent ODA philosophy and development strategy, not the ODA Charter with its political-diplomatic roots and agenda. The tenets and dynamics of the Asian model remain somewhat ambiguous, in need of further study and definition. Numerous Japanese are doing just that, seeking a coherent and comprehensive set of principles and guidelines. In the meantime, Japan has increasingly become the principal advocate of the Asian model in multilateral banks and other international fora. In short, a new philosophy is rooted in the common features of the "economic miracles" of the Asia Pacific region.

THE AID DEBATE AND MULTILATERAL ASSISTANCE

One of the main lessons we learn from Japanese aid literature is that multilateral aid can be ignored. It is on the periphery of the aid debate. On the whole, it is hard for observers to isolate and identify Japan's specific contributions to international financial institutions. Project boondoggles are usually not the fault of any one member, and it is difficult to track a specific policy through the maze of a massive international organization in order to assign sole responsibility to a specific country. On the other hand, the pursuit of national interests in these institutions is often tougher than bilateral diplomacy: Policies get watered down by the need to compromise with other members, or restricted by the strictures of these organizations' charters, or criticized for the hubris involved in grabbing sole credit for an international institution's policy success.

Japanese critics do not waste much energy directly attacking MDBs—unlike many studies in the West that lambast the motives, impact, and character of these institutions[50]—and they do not explain clearly Japan's overall MDB policy or policy toward specific MDBs. They tend to focus on specific projects or narrow policy issue areas, latching on to Japan's economic designs.[51] Critics find it difficult to peer into these massive institutions, and besides, Japan's role in them is perceived to be weak and relatively peripheral anyway. It is therefore difficult to accuse Japan of being the driving force behind destructive policies emanating from these banks. To a great extent, these institutions buffer Japan from direct criticism, which forces critics to focus their attacks on the more vulnerable bilateral aid dimension.

On the other hand, although aid supporters are more comfortable with these banks, sometimes they are at a loss to detail the substance of Tokyo's record in these institutions, and they have yet to articulate the exact role these banks play in overall foreign policy beyond the obvious financial contributions. Therefore, their positive assessments often sound unconvincing and forced, lacking in specifics. Like critics, aid supporters cannot easily attribute a successful multilateral bank policy to only one member. It is easier for them to tout the successes of the more visible bilateral aid projects.

Critics and supporters have yet to develop a conceptual framework for the analysis of Japan's multilateral aid policy. The only option seems to be the application of bilateral ODA analytical frameworks to multilateral aid. But the second lesson we learn from the literature is that these approaches do not yield a usable, comprehensive, or convincing framework for the analysis of multilateral aid activism. Neomercantilism, for example, is one-dimensional and limited, ignoring recent developments and the complexities of ODA policy and policymaking. On the other hand, humanitarianism, interdependence, and "fulfilling international responsibilities" are also one-dimensional and overly nebulous, asking us to take a leap of faith and inviting skepticism and derision. The ODA Charter is new, and the conceptualization of the Asian development model is unfinished. It is not easy to transfer bilateral ODA analytical frameworks to multilateral aid, particularly to international financial institutions.

A third lesson we learn is patience. The analysis of Japanese multilateral aid is still in its earliest stages. We noted that ODA literature as a whole has been reactive, a response to policy developments. Multilateral aid activism is an extremely recent phenomenon, and one can assume that observers are only now turning their attention to serious analyses of this dimension.

What do we do in the meantime? We treat ODA not merely as a topic of study in and of itself, or as a technical issue, but rather as a component of Japan's diplomacy that requires a broader foreign policy framework. While ODA literature basically ignores multilateral aid, it can, at least, provide us with the necessary background and understanding of the major issues involved in the study of Japanese aid. In addition, the history of the evolution of the aid policy can suggest areas where ODA intersects with multilateralism: the ODA activism of the 1980s and 1990s, when multilateralism rises to center stage; the aid philosophies of the 1990s, which attempt to provide the foreign policy justification for both bilateral and multilateral aid; and the international financial institutions, where the both activism and philosophizing are played out. Armed with this background, we can now move to a consideration of the foreign policy context of Japan's multilateral aid policy.

2

— ◆ —

REACTION AND ACTION IN JAPAN'S
FOREIGN POLICY: THE ANALYTICAL CONTEXT
OF MULTILATERAL ASSISTANCE

> From now on, Japan will go out into the world, and if there is
> a need, if there is a request from another party, we should not
> hesitate in meeting it.[1]
>
> —Kaifu Toshiki,
> Prime Minister of Japan, June 1990

> Japanese are short people who sit up all night thinking of
> ways to screw the Americans and the Europeans.[2]
>
> —Edith Cresson,
> Prime Minister of France, May 1991

The pronouncements by these two national leaders encapsulate the duality in popular views of Japan by the 1990s. On the one hand, Japan is a timid, hesitant nation requiring the prodding of the world community to induce substantive contributions, especially in the strategic and political arenas. Prime Minister Kaifu's statement seems to confirm the ingrained passivity and reactiveness of Japan's external behavior. On the other hand, people, short or otherwise, who burn the midnight oil thinking of ways to screw others are hardly passive. Japan did prove a proactive military threat in the 1930s and 1940s, and Prime Minister Cresson's opinion reflects a current view of Japan as an aggressive, expansive economic threat requiring tough countermeasures and even containment.

Of the two views, the former holds sway among political scientists and policymakers as the more compelling description of Japan's overall external policy since World War II. Defeat and occupation gave birth to the truncated diplomacy of a passive, reactive state. This course, retroactively labeled the Yoshida Doctrine after the pivotal prime minister who headed five cabinets in the first decade after the war, entailed a three-pronged strategy of emphasizing economic reconstruction and growth, minimal defense efforts, and reliance on the United States. There is little question that the Yoshida strategy led Japan to its current status as an economic great power. But it also yielded an "ad hoc, reactive, and equivocating" foreign policy that "at best . . . is characterized by a shrewd pragmatism and, at worst, by an irresponsible immobilism."[3] It was a minimalist, risk-avoidance diplomacy that seemed single-mindedly obsessed only with economic gain, separating politics from economics, and excessively dependent on and deferential to the United States.

An activist Japanese foreign policy seems a gross contradiction in terms. As Japan faces the next century, however, many of the underlying premises of the Yoshida Doctrine have come under attack both within and without the country.[4] A feeling is taking hold that what worked in the past may not prove appropriate in the future. New imperatives require a move away from minimalist, one-dimensional, and subordinate policies toward more activism, dynamism, and independence. Japan's recent diplomatic behavior reveals considerable reactivity and equivocation, but there are also concurrent indications of greater activism and even hints of leadership, especially since the last half of the 1980s.

If, in fact, Japan is embarking on a new, activist foreign policy that is shedding its reactive cast, we might ask: Is a reactive state theory that excels at characterizing Japanese diplomacy as purely reactive adequate for explaining what appears to be greater proactivism? The theory has strong explanatory power for explaining why Japan has *not* done much in world politics, but can it handle the emerging activist undercurrents? It is a conceptual approach tailored specifically to fit Japan's passive, minimalist postwar foreign policy. It does acknowledge movement in Japanese policies, since the 1970s and especially since 1985, but it denies any fundamental change in the reactive nature of that activity. That is, Japan's recent activism is simply a heightened reaction to developments in the external environment. Therefore, does reactive state theory need to experience the same kind of questioning as the Yoshida Doctrine it explains so well—adequate, perhaps, for explaining the past, but questionable in analyzing future foreign policy?

The answers to these questions are important. The international community expects much from Japan in maintaining a stable international economic and political system and in creating a new world order in the wake of events in East Europe and the Soviet Union. But if the reactive state view is correct, the contributions of a reactive state will be minimal. Its efforts will be focused on adjusting and adapting to its environment, not in shaping or constructing it. Such a view cautions us against expecting much from Japan in the future.

The implications for ODA policy are great. Aid critics lean heavily toward the Yoshida Doctrine depiction of Japan's ODA, while aid proponents would rather view ODA in the context of activism, dynamism, and greater independence. The reactive state conceptualization challenges the proponents by questioning the significance of Japan's attainment of aid great power status. It challenges the assumption that Japan will, in fact, contribute more to the world community through nonmilitary resources, except as a limited and unavoidable response to external pressure. It would characterize Japanese activism in international financial institutions as, at best, an anomaly and, at worst, a fraud, giving the appearance of policymaking competence and a new commitment to the international public good but, in reality, playing bureaucratic games at home and public relations games abroad while pursuing its own narrow national interests.

It is necessary to place ODA policy in its overall foreign policy context, but the reactive state view poses a major obstacle by challenging the very possibility of ODA policy activism and change. We therefore need to dissect the reactive state theory in order to evaluate its continued applicability for analyzing contemporary Japanese foreign policy and, by extension, ODA policy. Its tenets and dynamics require fuller definition and development, and its weaknesses and shortcomings must be addressed. In short, we need to fill in and fill out the reactive state theory and test it with ODA activism. In the end, we will face the question of whether to retain the approach, either intact or in revised form, or to devise a new, more comprehensive framework.

JAPAN AS A REACTIVE STATE

The basic tenets of the passive-reactive state approach are found scattered throughout the literature on Japanese foreign policy, with some stressing the passive more than the reactive.[5] These authors exhibit some differences in their conceptions of the reactive process, but the core tenets are fairly clear.

First, Japanese foreign policy is defined as a response to the external, not the internal, environment. As Donald Hellmann states, "To an extraordinary extent during the past two decades [1950s and 1960s], Japan's international role has been reactive, defined almost entirely by the outside environment. . . . It is to the external environment, then that one should look for stimuli."[6] Any Japanese change requires a redefinition of national purpose and an institutional revolution, but Hellmann has little confidence that Japan can effect such a revolution, thus making "internally generated change unlikely short of a major economic or political upheaval."[7]

Kent Calder states that "The reactive state interpretation merely maintains that the impetus to policy change is typically supplied by outside pressure, and that reaction prevails over strategy in the relatively narrow range of cases where the two come into conflict."[8] Michael Blaker concurs that by arguing that Japan's main modus operandi is to cope:

> Coping means carefully assessing the international situation, methodically weighing each alternative, sorting out various options to see what is really serious, waiting for the dust to settle on some contentious issue, piecing together a consensus view about the situation faced, and then performing the minimum adjustments needed to neutralize or overcome criticism and adapt to the existing situation with the fewest risks. . . .
> Coping is no calculated strategy. Rather, it is an automatic, knee-jerk, almost unconscious pattern in Japan's handling of its foreign affairs.[9]

Or as Funabashi Yoichi argues, "Japan has seldom tried to present itself as a rule-maker in the world community. The rules were already there. . . . [T]he world order is a given, and Japan a reactor par excellence."[10]

At its extreme, Japan is so reactive to external stimuli that it lacks a genuine or conventional foreign policy. The Japanese left asserts that Japan merely kowtows obediently to American dictates. The right questions whether Article 9 of the Constitution robs Japan of its sovereignty, making Japan a "politically castrated" state.[11] Shimizu Ikutaro calls on Japan to acquire nuclear weapons and "be a state" in the conventional sense.[12] Hellmann likens Japan's diplomacy to the overseas activities of a multinational corporation: "Japan was and still remains essentially a passive actor on the world political state, more a trading company than a nation-state, a nation without a foreign policy in the usual sense of the word."[13]

Robert Orr hesitates to attribute Japan's aid policy totally to external stimuli. He delineates routine from crisis situations and identifies some indigenous aid motives, but he ultimately concludes that policy impetus comes essentially from without: "Because Japan's aid program has been almost entirely reactive, most specific aid decisions could be taken only after requests were made."[14] Orr is referring to the technical "request-based" (yosei-shugi) aid process, which leaves project-finding to the recipient government and to the influence exerted by the United States on overall aid policy.

Calder implies that Japan need not be trapped by its reactiveness and wonders why Japan has remained reactive in view of increased proactive opportunities in the 1970s and especially since the late 1980s. Japan should be less reactive because of its enhanced national capabilities, especially financial and technological, and given its "enormous size, its substantial population (more than France and West Germany combined), and its pre-1945 history of pro-activism in the international system." Ohata Yashichi and Tamura Sadao accept reactivism as Japan's nature or fate but argue that "passive adaptability," or the ability to "skillfully utilize changes in the environment," can be transformed into "positive adaptability," or the "power to begin changing the environment in a positive manner."[15] And yet, "the Japanese state has been consistently more cautious in taking international initiatives than most major European governments."[16]

In other words, there is a corollary: A reactive state "fails to undertake major independent foreign economic policy initiatives [even] when it has the power and national incentives to do so."[17] In essence, it is difficult to escape the feeling that Japan does not define its own foreign policy interests or shape its own policies, even with favorable changes in the external environment and enhanced national capabilities. The dynamics of reactive state theory are thus "outside in," but there does seem to be something wrong within.

The second tenet of the revisionists concerns the primary locus of reactivity. The external environment refers essentially to the United States. Hellmann observes that "the American alliance continues to be the critical link for Japan to the global system and the most important outside determinant of Japanese foreign policy."[18] The United States has served "as an international incubator" shielding Japan from "realpolitik" until the 1970s, when the decline of America lifted "the protective screen" and forced a "confrontation for the first time in the postwar period with the realities of world politics."[19] Calder looks beyond the bilateral relationship, touching upon international institutions and European nations, but he concludes that Japan has been "more deferential to pressure from the United States."[20] Funabashi Yoichi states:

> Overdependence on its bilateral relationship with the United States undermined Japan's creative diplomacy by closing off avenues to other foreign policy initiatives. . . . The leadership developed a psychology of dependency—a tendency to view America as a big brother—and failed to assert a distinctively Japanese foreign policy, in effect inviting foreign pressure, or gaiatsu.[21]

For Orr, the rise to aid great power status and American decline have caused only a minor change: "As Japan has emerged as a major donor, the United States impact on Japanese aid has perhaps lessened somewhat, but American approaches remain fairly constant."[22] Orr focuses almost exclusively on American influence over Japanese ODA policy, citing numerous means by which the United States is able to gain Japanese compliance. He refers to the United States as "an unofficial member of the decisionmaking process"; cites increased aid to Egypt and the Sudan and cessation of ODA to Vietnam and Nicaragua as successful instances of direct American pressure,[23] and tied aid and mixed credit as examples of near-coercive American pressure.[24] His study does not document similar Japanese responses to pressure from aid recipient nations. In essence, Japanese aid policy in the 1980s was shaped by Washington, reflecting the three wishes of the Reagan administration: that Japan provide aid to strategically important countries, work with the United States on joint projects, and expand aid beyond Asia to other Third World regions.[25]

American influence may be so pervasive and intrusive that an understanding of American politics is the key factor in understanding Japanese domestic politics. Hellmann argues that "any effort to understand the dynamics of Japan's contemporary domestic politics (as well as its foreign policy) must encompass the international context in which the Japanese live," especially the U.S. factor.[26] At its extreme, the argument seems to imply that understanding American domestic politics—especially the role of Congress and interest groups—is the prerequisite for understanding Japanese foreign policy, at least in the trade arena.[27]

In short, despite enhanced national capabilities and a relative American decline, Japan remains U.S.-centric in its external policy. Hellmann argues that American decline means even greater reactiveness in Japan. In a sense, reactive state theory is just as U.S.-centric as Japan's postwar foreign policy.

While the origin of reactivity lies outside Japan, reactivists do not ignore the internal cause of reactivity. Their third tenet stipulates that the fundamental source of passivity and reactivity is the immobilism that characterizes the policymaking process. For Hellmann, this means the lack of consensus among political parties and the factionalism and weak leadership of the ruling Liberal Democratic Party. From his seminal study of the 1956 Japan-Soviet normalization agreement to his most recent writings, Hellmann finds that "fractious individual rivalries and petty personal ambitions are . . . projected into the heart of the policy-formulation process, thereby complicating the situation and virtually proscribing decisive actions."[28] These "intraparty politics" intrude "deeply into all issues of foreign affairs" and impede "innovations by the prime ministers."[29] Funabashi agrees: "The structural weaknesses of its leadership—highly personalized political allegiances among factions and parties, and the predominance of pork-barrel politics—characterize Japanese political culture and limit the projection of its foreign policy."[30]

Other domestic forces, such as the media, business interests, and public opinion, play almost no role in the policy process. In short, "Japan could not but play a passive role. . . . [P]assivity was assured by the nature of her foreign policy formulation process."[31]

For Calder, the problem of LDP factionalism is compounded by the bureaucracy and the emerging pluralism in Japan's body politic. "The fragmented character of state authority in Japan makes decisive action more difficult than in countries with strong chief executives," he argues, and "the problem of domestic coordination is compounded in Japan by the lack of both a functionally oriented administrative corps and authoritative codification of ministerial responsibilities to dampen bureaucratic disputes over jurisdiction."[32] The bureaucracy can lend an air of

> decisiveness to policy on narrow technical issues . . . but on broad, complex questions of global economic management, or on issues created by emerging technology or economic transformation where bureaucratic responsibilities have yet to be defined, ministerial jurisdiction is often unclear, and internal conflict over how to proceed is often strong. In such cases . . . Japanese policies can hardly avoid being reactive.[33]

Calder acknowledges the increased involvement and influence of politicians in the domestic policy arena in recent years: "Improved expertise, information and staff support, together with the growing ability to control bureaucratic promotions . . . have enhanced the LDP's policy-making influence." However, he concludes that "there are few incentives to propose clear, independent foreign policy initiatives" primarily, as Hellmann would agree, because of the disutility of foreign policy issues in elections.[34] He even dismisses the politician-centric "policy tribes" (zoku) as impediments to decisive policy.[35] Leonard Schoppa's case study reinforces this view by concluding that zoku "do little more than reinforce the sectional character of policymaking in Japan" because "they work with the bureaucrats in the bureaucrats' system."[36] Calder concludes that the "net effect of the party's [LDP] rising influence in Japanese policy making has generally been to intensify the reactive basis of the Japanese state."[37]

Orr also acknowledges the recent rise of politician influence in Japanese politics, but he claims that this phenomenon is restricted to the domestic sphere. In foreign policy, the bureaucracy still reigns supreme, possessing capabilities unavailable to the politicians: "In Japan, the government bureaucracy continues to play the crucial role in foreign policymaking in spite of the emergence of political authority in the domestic arena."[38] He argues that for aid policy, "battles are fought, bargains are negotiated, compromises made, and decisions reached largely within the framework of the administrative structure."[39] In short, "foreign aid largely remains the preserve of the bureaucracy."[40] And it is this decentralized, or pluralistic, nature of the system and process that leads to the jurisdictional conflicts and general immobilism that opens up the system to outside influence. Orr's study illustrates a case where the bureaucracy is vulnerable to immobilism in areas where jurisdictions are clear and not just in Calder's areas where "bureaucratic responsibilities have yet to be defined."

Reactivists downplay the role of societal forces in policy formulation or picture interest groups as hindrances to policy cohesion. Hellmann bluntly discounts significant influence from domestic groups. Calder and Orr note sporadic sectoral involvement under specific or extraordinary situations (e.g., financial interests in economic policy, and engineering, consulting and multinational firms in aid policy), but neither argues for their primacy in the policy process. Orr rejects aid critics' assertions that Japanese companies or consultants shape ODA policy. Calder notes the proactive potential of interest groups and the media but concludes strongly that they actually create incentives toward passive foreign policies.[41]

Hellmann sees change as unlikely in the absence of revolutionary developments within Japan. Funabashi echoes this conclusion, arguing that "Japan must thus examine its own political and decision-making structures to try to overcome these [political] constraints. . . . Future foreign policy success is thus essentially a function of overcoming the immobility of the Japanese system."[42]

Calder seems to argue that activist policies need to transcend the inertia of the policy process; he speculates on the need for transnational linkages between Japanese government and foreign forces to induce activism or change. Orr's study provides a detailed illustration of this process in U.S.-Japan aid relations, where he finds that transgovernmental coalitions between Japanese and American aid policymakers are essential in pushing aid policy through the Japanese policy maze. In fact, of the three methods by which the United States influences Japanese aid policy, transgovernmental bureaucratic coalition-building characterizes the primary means of transcending the standard domestic policy process.[43]

The fourth tenet of the reactivists concerns the scope of reactiveness: ✓ Reactive state theory applies both to foreign economic policy and political-strategic diplomacy. Although seemingly obvious, this point needs to be stated explicitly because of the widespread view of a dual diplomacy—an active and successful foreign economic policy and a passive and questionable political-strategic diplomacy—and because the origins of the theory are found in the political-strategic rather than economic-financial realm. A comprehensive theory of Japanese foreign policy must encompass both political and economic dimensions.

Hellmann bases his theory primarily on Japan's external behavior in the political-strategic arena and makes the classic distinction between a dynamic and relatively effective economic policy and an immobilist and reactive political diplomacy: "The nature of the foreign-policy-making process in Japan has prevented bold leadership not only on security policy, but on all major questions involving political rather than economic matters."[44] He contrasts Japan's track record in these two spheres of activity: "In a basic sense, Japanese foreign policy has been schizophrenic, with a record on major foreign policy decisions involving political considerations as bad as their record in conducting an effective international economic policy is good."[45]

While Hellmann's views reflect a basic concern with power and high-politics international relations, Calder bridges the gap by extending reactive state theory to low-politics and wealth issues. By applying reactive state theory to foreign economic policy, he challenges the popular view of Japan as a proactive, even aggressive and neoimperialist, economic juggernaut. However, in applying the theory to a dynamic economic arena, Calder must grapple analytically with a state that is definitely more active and engaged and less easy to dismiss as passive and simply reactive. He does ask why Japan remains so reactive given opportunities externally and internally to shed reactivity and concedes a proactive potential if domestic forces can get their act together, or if transnational or multilateral processes can take hold. They will not for "an extended period," but Calder leaves an out for Japan: the possibility of a proactive "leadership role that will be technical and sector-specific rather than broadly political," specifically citing energy and finance.[46] In the end, however, Calder remains strongly committed to the reactive nature of Japan's external policy in the economic and financial as well as political realm.

Orr's study bridges the gap in the field of economic aid policy. In contrast to a standard view of Japanese aid policy as strongly purposive (i.e., to promote trade and overseas investment), he depicts a depoliticized policy that lacks clear principles and requires stimuli from a United States motivated largely by political-strategic imperatives. In essence, reactivity in aid policy recognizes no separation of politics from economics.

Reactivists foresee few changes in Japan's behavior. Blaker concludes that "this minimalist style doubtless will go on, despite external pressures and episodic Japanese vows to express its 'leadership' or 'global vision.' Neither rhetoric nor wishing will make it happen. . . . [O]ne can merely wish for—and not expect very soon—a major change in behavior."[47]

Hellmann sums up Japan's probable future as a reactive state: "a passive role for Japan in foreign affairs, at a time when change and uncertainty have come to characterize both the political and economic dimensions of the international order."[48] But doubts about Japan's continued passivity and cracks in the reactive state approach lead us to question the appropriateness of the vision of the nation thrashing helplessly in the swells and whitecaps.

IMPLICATIONS FOR ODA POLICY

Several aspects of reactive state theory raise questions about ODA policy and especially about Japan's future diplomacy. First, reactive state theory tends toward the deterministic; it allows very little room for will or choice. To be fair, there is some room for choice, for Calder does allow for a variety of reactive responses, noting that the reactive state responds "to outside pressures for change, albeit erratically, unsystematically, and often incompletely."[49] But it is choice that is determined not so much by preferences but dictated by external constraints. Choice basically means making marginal adjustments to international developments largely, as Hellmann stresses, beyond Japan's control.

Second, reactive state theory basically dismisses contentions by many international relationists that foreign policy is the outcome of domestic political processes and that the distinction between internal and external has blurred. Some analysts propound "inside-out" approaches as more reflective of a nation's foreign policy. The question raised is: If the Japanese state is reactive, why isn't it equally or more reactive to domestic pressure? In other words, should we go beyond the bureaucracy in analyzing ODA policy?

As for the blurring of external and internal arenas, Calder and Orr find a need to focus on transgovernmental coalitions as the mechanism that links the two. It remains a slim and somewhat awkward link, however. In Orr's study, the transgovernmental dimension is merely grafted onto a bureaucratic politics model that, by definition, identifies the subnational arena as ✓ the origin of foreign policy, not the external environment.

Third, reactive theory is overly selective when looking at the external environment. It is understandable that U.S.-Japan relations should be the focal point of any analysis of Japanese foreign policy. But as we head into the next century, it is clear that Japan's field of vision has expanded and that the country must respond to a diverse number of external influences ranging from nations other than the United States and international organizations to multinational corporations and technology, information and financial flows.

U.S.-Japan relations provided the prototype for the reactive state syndrome. This relationship has been clearly asymmetrical throughout the postwar period. The United States has been the teacher, the mentor, the sponsor, the more powerful; Japan has been the student, the disciple, the beneficiary, the weaker partner. The particular history of defeat in war and occupation has biased Japanese behavior toward dependence and deference. But what about relationships where Japan is on roughly equal or superior footing vis-à-vis another nation? Do we still find that Japan is equally subservient, immobile, and bereft of policy? Would Japan respond deferentially to demands from Myanmar, Poland, or Madagascar? This raises questions about to whom, under what circumstances, and to what extent Japan is reactive. By focusing on the United States, reactive state theory has chosen a case where Japan basically cannot but be reactive. But what must be determined is whether reactivity is a general response to the outside world or a manifestation of a particular kind of response to a particular, unique kind of relationship.

Fourth, reactive state theory reflects Japanese foreign policy at a particular point in time. It is tailor-made to fit diplomacy since 1945. However, if one looks back to the prewar era, we find several similar internationalist themes and conditions but different Japanese behavior. In that environment, Japan chose a proactive course that led the nation through China, the Pacific, and Southeast Asia to Hiroshima and Nagasaki. Back then few accused Japan back then of not doing enough. This fact forces us to question why Japan chose proactivism in one era and reactivism in another. It does not negate the validity of reactive theory for postwar Japan, but it does argue for a broader perspective and implies a need to peer deeper into the national black box not only in this century but back in time in order to understand contemporary behavior. How deeply seated historically is the reactive impulse? If deep, we may assume that a change to proactivism will be difficult indeed.

Fifth, reactivist theory's denial of proactivism is troubling. It explains immobilism and reactivity much better and inclines us to expect activism to be the exception, the anomaly. In fact, it conditions us not to expect proactivism at all, since reactivity is a congenital condition of the postwar Japanese state. The Japanese state is reactive; therefore, by definition, all specific policies are responses to external stimuli. Reactivists are forced to explain instances of decisiveness and activism as merely active forms of reaction rather than purposive, autonomous behavior. Calder acknowledges the "strategic" dimension in economic policy, but he attributes this activism to the reactive imperative. Orr incorporates reactivity into Japan's concept of national interest, but in so doing, he still allows foreign forces to define Japan's national interest. Japan's diplomacy will continue to be merely "derivative," to use Hellmann's term.

In short, monocausal explanations have the advantage of inclusiveness. Reactivism is an all-purpose framework that can explain both past inaction and current activism: Japan is passive because it is reactive, and Japan is active because it is reactive.

The implications for the analysis of multilateral development bank activism are great. We should not expect too much from Japan in these institutions, for behind the activist facade are several qualifications. First, we should look for the causes of MDB activism outside Japan. The international environment should provide the strongest clues concerning the pace and shape of MDB policy, and we should be on a special lookout for the formative influence of the United States. Second, we should not look very hard for an indigenous impetus for activism. We should not be fooled into thinking that Japanese ODA principles or charters originated in the fertile minds of Japanese policymakers; rather, we must look for external models utilized by the Japanese drafters. Nor should we assume that domestic interest groups spur the government into action. Third, we should be on the alert for the bureaucracy and its dampening effect on policy activism because of decentralization and jurisdictional battles. Finally, if we think we have spotted an initiative, we must look again. We can assume that it may be either an exception to the rule or merely activism in response to some kind of external pressure. More than likely, it will be the latter, for any activist policy is designed to cope with something done by someone else.

BEYOND REACTIVITY?

In the 1990s, Japan appears less uniformly passive, low profile, and reactive. Tokyo does not seem to be totally immobile, or else its foreign policy seems to be on the move despite domestic immobilism. Thus we seem to face the prospect not of explaining passivity and inaction but rather of increasing exceptions to the reactive rule. But do alternatives to the reactive state approach exist? Is it possible to broaden the scope of our inquiry of Japan's MDB policy? Proactivism is the most logical alternative conceptual framework. We can begin by arguing that Japan is evolving into a proactive state. Japan, recognizing the inadequacy of its past diplomacy in a new world environment, is shedding the reactive, passive, unidimensional, derivative cast of its foreign policy. It is embarking on a more active, involved, and independent diplomacy more appropriate to the new era, and this requires an activist, rather than reactive, analytical framework.

Some previous studies do question from the outset the reactive, puppet-like depiction of Japanese foreign policy. Martin Weinstein looked specifically at the source of Hellmann's thesis, security policy, and found that Japanese leaders knew all along exactly what they wanted even under the weight of foreign occupation and that they managed to achieve their national goals.[50] Other studies have found that Japan basically followed its own course in its China policy in pursuit of economic and political interests in the 1950s and 1960s, a course not entirely sanctioned by the United States.[51] Japan's initially lone efforts to restore the flow of foreign aid to China after the Tiananmen Square massacre reflects its own deep-seated view of Beijing's importance to Japan, as did its refusal of aid to Gorbachev's Soviet Union.[52]

Other studies find proactivism emerging at various points prior to the 1990s, and several recent cases are ripe for study as proactive ventures. In the 1970s, Middle East policy often is cited as the first instance of a genuinely independent Japanese diplomacy, when Japan followed a decidedly proactive (i.e., decisive and independent from U.S. policy) course toward Arab nations and resource-rich Third World regions.[53] Mike Mochizuki observes that Japan devised its own military defense strategy rather than simply following Washington's lead for the first time in 1976,[54] and several analysts note that Japan formulated a "comprehensive national security" concept that incorporated an indigenous definition of national security, incorporating nonmilitary as well as military threats and countermeasures.[55] In the 1980s there were many more visible instances of Japanese diplomatic activity, including the attempted mediation of the Iran-Iraq war, ODA doubling plans, four debt relief plans, heightened activity in G-7 summits, a new assertiveness in multilateral financial institutions, and financial and personnel commitments to United Nations refugee efforts.

These efforts can, of course, be cast in a reactive light, but one of the appeals of proactive approaches is the necessity to focus on and delineate Japan's indigenous interests. Reactivists can downplay the importance of indigenous motives since Japan merely reacts to others' policies, but perhaps we should give the Japanese more credit by assuming that they can think for themselves and determine their own interests. This is not to say that Japan's motives and objectives are clear, but only that motives and objectives are indigenous and not transplanted.

But problems exist with the proactive view. A major difficulty is the reverse side of a shortcoming of a reactive state theory: It must account better for reactivity. One cannot escape the fact that Japan did mold its foreign policy to the contours of the Cold War, American hegemony, and the liberal economic system. It is difficult to divorce the current activism from an international environment that is witnessing an American decline, the rise of a unified Europe, an emerging Asia Pacific region, a Communist world in turmoil, and a Third World grappling with debt and "low-intensity" conflicts.

Whereas reactivist theory identifies a specific pattern of behavior over time, proactivism still must demonstrate that activist policies are not the exception. It must identify basic national objectives beyond the profit motive or "national interest." Finding articulate Japanese explanations of political and strategic rationales for foreign policy activism remains difficult. The onus is, therefore, on proactivists to demonstrate convincingly that Japan is or can be a proactive state and to identify a core body of behavior or cases that illustrate patterns of proactive behavior.

This task implies the need for an approach that assumes an effective, nonimmobilist domestic policy process. Of course, foreign policy activism can be explained by domestic disarray. For example, it seems clear that a partial explanation for the diplomatic activism of the Nakasone and Kaifu cabinets, despite domestic scandals and factional maneuverings, is the utility of foreign policy in extending the lives of their cabinets through popular appeal. In such cases, it is necessary to explain how activism rather than immobilism resulted.

If proactive approaches pose problems, we can move on to a hybrid approach that may be more appealing to those who acknowledge greater activism in Japanese diplomacy but find it difficult to abandon the idea of a passive and reactive state. Calder acknowledges the "strategic intent of much of Japanese policy making" and "its successful implementation in many cases" but believes that purposive behavior still is clearly subordinate to reactive imperatives.[56] One can, however, conceive of a dual diplomacy model that allows the grafting of strategic behavior onto the old reactive, immobilist approach. In this case, "dual" refers not to the bifurcation of diplomacy into active economic versus passive political spheres but to jousting between passive-reactive impulses and "strategic," "flexible," "dynamic" imperatives across both economic and political-strategic arenas.

This approach must focus more on domestic politics and argue that dynamism as well as immobilism characterizes the policymaking process. In one study, which asks "Why is Japan at one and the same time dynamic and immobilist?"[57] the roots of reactivity are found not in the external environment but in the fact that "the system is much more responsive to domestic political pressures . . . than to foreign pressure."[58] According to Alan Rix

> international pressures are one (albeit highly significant) input to the domestic Japanese policy process. The more important parameters of decision making are domestic: the long-term indicative objectives of government; the diversity of internal processes and the influence of the bureaucratic process itself on policy; and definitions of national interests.[59]

There is, however, also a dynamic side to the usual culprits of immobilism. Rix finds an activist quality in an institution not usually accused of dynamism: "Bureaucracy is not a passive servant of politics, and the institutional process of bureaucratic activity has a life of its own. . . . Bureaucracy can 'energise' like any politician."[60] In particular, "Japan's is a dynamic and aggressive bureaucracy, in maintaining policies or in policy innovation."[61] Aurelia George locates dynamism in the corporatist relationship among interest groups, parties, and government agencies. Interest groups penetrate the parties, which "makes possible the direct exercise of influence by interest groups over party policy, with politicians acting as internal Diet and party lobbyists on behalf of their allied interest groups,"[62] and the bureaucracy, which "enlists the active co-operation of interest groups in the pursuit of government policy objectives by formally incorporating them into the processes of policy formulation, decision-making and administration."[63]

There are problems, however, with a dual diplomacy framework. It must explain more clearly when and how an immobilized policy apparatus can escape immobilism, apparently so easily, and become active and efficient. What allows such flexibility? These analysts' answer illustrates another problem: the continued weight of the reactive impulse. In theory, a dual diplomacy analysis can tilt the scales toward either the active, dynamic or the passive, reactive. In reality, observers ultimately tend to retreat to immobilism and reactivism, for dynamism remains contingent on foreign pressure; it must be triggered from outside. J. A. A. Stockwin asserts that a dynamic domestic arena exists, but only up to a "certain level of intensity," at which point "foreign pressure builds up . . . [and] political and bureaucratic leaders become aware that some response is necessary." That response is typically minimal, designed to "reduce pressure to tolerable levels."[64]

In other words, dynamism is defined in a reactive context. To Rix, dynamism is a reflex to foreign stimuli: "It is the ability that Japan has shown to meet the pressures that require reaction, and to come up with temporary solutions, that has produced what could be called a 'dynamic' response to trade policy problems. Japan has actively developed policies . . . to achieve an easing of pressure."[65] He thus argues that Japan has incorporated the need "to reduce foreign leverage" and to find "a reasonable level of adjustment to external interests" into its concept of national interest, although he stops short of arguing that the country's national interests are defined by external forces: "This does not mean that acceptance of external pressure is automatic; national interest has not been defined as going to that extent, but selective policy adjustments to suit specific . . . concerns appears to be the approach adopted."[66]

Dynamism is a matter of choice within the context of external pressure. This accords with the reactive state explanation of Japanese activism, though less deterministic. In other words, policy impetus still originates outside of Japan. Therefore, while conceptually it is possible to envision dual arenas of Japanese foreign policy—dynamic and reactive rather than economic and political—the escape from reactivity, though not necessarily passivity, proves extremely difficult.

The basic problem in dual dimension analysis is that while it is possible to distinguish two equal arenas or types of behavior, in the end, one usually predominates. For example, neo-realists recognize both power and wealth as state motives and arenas of activities, but in the crunch, states are said to revert to power considerations.[67] In this case, Japan ultimately retreats to reactivism.

In sum, both alternative conceptualizations of Japanese foreign policy activism are problematic. The proactive model is not totally convincing, and the immobilist-dynamic model is too situational and unbalanced. We keep returning to the reactive nature of Japan's foreign policy. The bottom line seems to be that Japan remains reactive despite the new diplomatic activity; activism need not be proactivism. But if we remain skeptical of reactive, proactive, and hybrid approaches, and if we are still convinced of the need for a framework that explains activism without the reactive analytical strait-jacket, we need to continue our search for other alternatives.

A FRAMEWORK

The starting point in our search for an analytical framework that explains Japan's overall foreign policy, not just ODA policy, and incorporates both activism and reactivism is the literature in the field of international relations.

Both the reactive and proactive approaches are derivatives of basic international relations approaches, so we can return to their origins and survey the possibilities.

Of the three basic approaches to the study of international relations—system-centered, society-centered, and state-centered—reactive state theory is a derivative of the systemic approach, while Japanese ODA literature is basically society-centered. The most appropriate approach for the study of bilateral and multilateral ODA activism, however, may be the state-centric approach.

Systemic Analysis

At minimum, understanding the international level of analysis is the "precondition" for explaining state behavior.[68] Kenneth Waltz's assertion summarizes the contention of the reactive state proponents: "it is not possible to understand world politics simply by looking inside states. . . . Each state arrives at policies and decides on actions according to its own internal processes, but its decisions are shaped by the very presence of other states as well as by interactions with them."[69]

All other theories are "reductionist," or theories "about the behavior of parts" in which "the international system, if conceived of at all, is taken to be merely an outcome."[70] In essence, states, regardless of their distinctive histories or sociocultural makeup, are basically alike, seeking similar goals and differing only in their capabilities: "States are alike in the tasks they face, though not in their abilities to perform them. The differences are of capability, not of function....International politics consists of like units duplicating one another's activities."[71]

Stephen Krasner states that

> all states share the same minimalist objectives of preserving territorial and political integrity. . . . The particular strategies adopted by a given state will be constrained by structural considerations—the distribution of power in the international system as a whole, and the place of a given state in that distribution. [72]

This is the anarchic action-reaction world of states attempting to maximize their own power at the expense of others. Differences in capabilities result in a hierarchical system in which the more powerful states deserve attention. Waltz stresses the predominant states and the balance of power. Weak states are just that: "The most usual explanation of the foreign policy of weak states rests on twin pillars: the theoretical concept of power, and the empirical fact that such policy does tend to conform to the preferences of the dominant states."[73]

In other words, there is a causal relationship between power and compliant or subservient behavior. Reactive states are weak states.

There is also a hierarchical distinction between politics and economics, with foreign economic or financial policy only one manifestation of a general effort to enhance or maintain state power: "States only act to structure nonpolitical behavior if this would enhance their relative power capability. Economic policy, for instance, is not an end in itself; it is a device for enhancing the power of the state."[74] Therefore, "the distinction frequently drawn between matters of high and low politics is misplaced. States use economic means for military and political ends; and military and political ends for the achievement of economic interests."[75]

The reactive state approach adopts the core tenet of systemic theory, and therefore the system-centric approach appears as one parent of reactive state theory. Reactive state analysts do not ignore domestic factors, but ultimately, at the core of the approach lies the power of the external environment over national policy. Japan is a comparatively weak state that takes the shape of its environment more than it shapes the system. A critical modification by reactivists is that Japan continues to be reactive even with a relative increase in state capabilities, and this casts doubt on whether Japan, like other nations, is so obsessed with the attainment of "power" as defined by systemic and realist analysts. In any case, international structures, rules of the game, and pressures shape Japan's ODA policy.

Society-Centered Approaches

Unlike systemic analysis, society-centered explanations of foreign policy look within the unitary black box. They view "policy as either reflecting the preferences of the dominant group or class in society, or as resulting from the struggle for influence that takes place among various interest groups or political parties. In either case, this approach explains foreign economic policy essentially as a function of domestic politics."[76]

Society-centered explanations render the system-society nexus flexible, less deterministic, and more situational. They do not discount the importance of systemic factors under certain circumstances and, as Peter Katzenstein implies, in certain time periods:

> Over the last decade the gradual shift from security issues to economic concerns has further increased the relative weight of domestic structures

on foreign economic policy. Everywhere the number of domestic interests tangibly affected by the international political economy is far greater than it had been during the previous era of national security.[77]

From this perspective, a nation-state's international standing provides a less than full explanation of specific policies or general policy courses. Jeff Frieden finds, for example, that America's construction of a postwar liberal international political economy is explainable more by the triumph of internationalist influence within the nations and concludes that

> the national interest is not a blank slate upon which the international system writes at will; it is internally determined by the socioeconomic evolution of the nation in question. . . . The ability to pursue these "national interests" successfully, and the best strategy to do so, may similarly be determined by international conditions, but the interests themselves are domestically derived and expressed within the domestic political economy.[78]

State policymaking organs and policymakers are not autonomous actors but are answerable less to external forces and more to their domestic constituents: "State actors, obliged to their own populations in ways they are not to the rest of the world, will always respond first to demands arising from within. If those demands are insistent or desperate enough, it matters little that they may run counter to the interests of global society."[79]

According to pluralism, the most prominent of society-centered theories, "government institutions essentially provide an arena for group competition, and do not exert a significant impact on the decisions that emerge."[80]

Society-centered explanations can provide good explanations for foreign policy activism. The external environment is not considered only as an omnipresent constraint on national action, thus lessening the determinism of systemic approaches. The spur to activism lies in the dynamism and influence of popular opinion and ascendant interest groups. This suggests the need to identify active sectors of society, whether the electorate or other more politically organized groups.

Society-centered approaches seem well suited to explain a defensive brand of activism in which Japan struggles against foreign trade pressures or involvement in security activities abroad because of domestic interest groups or public opinion. ODA literature identifies specific sectors of the society that shape ODA policy, including the monopoly capitalists, multinational corporations, greedy politicians, and engineering and consulting firms. Their lobbying activities spur Japan's ODA activism. On the other hand, critics in academia and the media push ODA policy toward caution and defensiveness. In any case, the interplay of both domestic beneficiaries and critics shapes ODA and MDB policies.

For reactivists, society-centered explanations provide a better explanation for foreign policy immobilism, although Calder notes the potential for sectoral activism. In general, reactivists present a picture of public univolvement or apathy, or immobilization from competition among interests groups, bureaucrats, and political parties. But for the reactivists, it is really the state that is the ultimate locus of reactivity.

State-Centered Explanations

In contrast with society-centered approaches, state-centered theories postulate a state that is not simply the sum or captive of its domestic parts: "The state is at least relatively autonomous and an active participant in the policymaking or supply process. The government, therefore, does not simply respond to societal demands. Rather, the state possesses interests and makes choices that are central to understanding policy."[81]

The state "is not an empty shell in which social forces compete,"[82] but "in many ways states organize the societies they control."[83] By drawing "upon its unique position between the international and domestic political systems and its ability to mobilize societal actors, the foreign policy executive can achieve its goals despite resistance from society."[84] States thus can play a mediative or leadership role between the external and domestic environments in pursuit of their own interests.

Statist theory challenges society-centered approaches by discounting "mass preferences, political parties, elections, which are viewed as effects rather than the causes of government policy. Interest groups are not autonomous agents exerting the pressure which shapes policy but subsidiary agents of the state."[85] And to the extent that interest groups do shape policy, David Lake points out that their interests are much too narrow and parochial to constitute the state's overall policy even in a specific sector.[86] The state must formulate the national interest.

Government institutions endure and provide continuity in policymaking; they are capable of shaping the private sector in pursuit of their own interests; they are purposive entities that are not only the sum of their societal parts. They also are capable of surviving even after the ideas and coalitions that originally gave rise to them no longer dominate.[87] Therefore, we must look at policymakers and their parochial interests and mind sets. Judith Goldstein stresses the importance of looking at formal, official state institutions and "the belief system of those individuals who enforce the laws."[88] She argues that American liberal economic policies resulted from the ascendancy since the 1930s of the liberal belief system.[89] For example, in Japan, we can imagine institutions still imbued with the Yoshida belief system struggling against new forces pushing for internationalization or nationalistic policies.

In the literature, the definition of state is sometimes ambiguous. The general focus is the foreign policy executives where the domestic and international realms intersect. They constitute "the sole authoritative foreign policymaker and the only national actor mandated to preserve and enhance the position of the nation-state within the anarchic and competitive international system. It is charged, in other words, with husbanding the nation-state's wealth and power, given the interests and actions of other countries."[90]

Some researchers focus on the executive branch, including high-ranking bureaucrats and politicians in charge of defense and foreign policy, while others include the legislature, state-society links (through the electoral process), and "constituent" agencies.[91] Krasner's case study focuses on the American president and secretary of state;[92] Katzenstein looks at the "ruling coalition" (of "dominant social classes with political power-brokers finding their institutional expression in the party system and in a variety of institutions a step removed from electoral competition—government ministries, banks, industrial associations, and large public or private corporations") and "policy networks."[93] The private sector generally is omitted because, according to James Rosenau, it is nonpurposive and uncoordinated,[94] and because, according to Katzenstein, public policies shape private preferences.[95]

In reactive state theory, the Japanese state is not an activist state. Rather, it is deeply divided, infected with excessive or dysfunctional pluralism. The decentralized state is the principal reason for passivity and reactiveness. The theory discusses ruling agents or coalitions, especially the prime minister, the ruling party, and the bureaucracy; it discusses "policy networks," in the form of "policy tribes," or *zoku;* it discusses somewhat belief systems, including the Yoshida Doctrine, neomercantilism, internationalization, new nationalism, and pan-Asianism. But on the whole, the state is neither strategic nor dynamic.

All three international relations approaches are able to explain both Japanese reactivism and activism, though unevenly. The systemic approach can accommodate activism but is heavily weighted toward reactivism given the primacy of the outside world as a catalyst for, or an obstacle to, strategic behavior. The society-centered approach can explain both reaction and proaction—immobilism from rampant pluralism, or sectoral activism—but downgrades the formative function of the international system. The state-centric approach tilts the scales toward proactivism by its very definition of the state and its functions; yet reactive state writers point specifically to the Japanese state as the locus of reactivism.

It is the statist approach that provides an essentially proactive defini-tion of the state. In that approach, the state functions as an arbiter between the external and internal environments with its own, not derivative, interests. It need not be a prisoner of either environment. The state can become "a strategist in the context of domestic and international structures and con-straints."[96] These strategies include creating new institutions, redefining previously domestic issues as foreign policy issues, and mobilizing social groups to offset political adversaries.[97] It can function in both the interna-tional and the domestic environments through offensive or defensive strat-egies that can create new rules of the game, mitigate damage, and adapt to or avoid changes altogether.[98] The state has a mind, and will, of its own.

The statist approach appears most appropriate for the analysis of Japan's ODA and multilateral development bank policy, given what we expect to see in our case studies: (1) the traditional predominance of the bureaucracy in ODA-related and international organization-related policymaking; (2) the sporadic involvement of politicians and the prime minister; (3) a change in mind-set among policymakers as Japan emerged as a global financial power in the 1980s; (4) the peripheral or narrow role of nongovernmental actors; and (5) the amorphousness of public opinion.

Our definition of the state is thus bureaucrat-centric. We expect civil servants to determine national policy in this issue area, with politicians and the prime minister playing secondary, though often important, roles. Specif-ically, we expect to see selective involvement by the former ruling Liberal Democratic Party until its fall in 1993, followed by greater reliance on bureaucrats in the succeeding unstable coalition cabinets. The prime minister's role should not be discounted, but most observers grant the premier little substantive impact on technical issues such as ODA or MDBs. Robert Angel raises the possibility of a dynamic and activist prime minister, but Hayao Kenji reflects the orthodox view of the prime minister as reactive, passive, weak, and boring—a reflection, some would say, of Japanese foreign policy.[99]

The statist approach also reflects our assumptions about state-interna-tional organization relations. International organization literature focuses primarily on state executives and bureaucrats as those "who are most important in determining exactly what policy a state will pursue in an intergovernmental organization."[100] But it assumes the primacy of the bureaucracy. Executives "have the final say . . . [but] many matters are not sufficiently important to warrant their involvement." Therefore,

> usually, the process of formulating instructions [to delegates in international organizations] is confined to bureaucrats. . . . On most issues the bulk of the work of preparing instructions is done by an office in a department or ministry or by several offices working together. . . . The crucial point is that in all governments the process is under the control of, and largely confined to, bureaucracies.[101]

In addition, "delegates are primarily drawn from bureaucracies. . . . [T]he delegate who is not part of her or his state bureaucracy is the exception rather than the rule."[102] Nothing sounds more "Japanese."

The literature is also clear on the role of societal forces. Interest groups participate only sporadically, sectorally, and partially. Public opinion is peripheral:

> Publics seldom have detailed knowledge of the day-to-day activities of international governmental organizations. In most instances, there is a "permissive consensus" among the public that the work of the IGO in question should go on. . . . But it is not often that the public sees its direct interests as being seriously affected by the activities of IGOs.[103]

And the legislative body's "function generally tends to be a matter of setting limits—albeit considerably more precise ones than those established by the public—rather than determining detailed content."[104] Again, this sounds promising for studying Japan's MDB policy.

One final element must be included in our analytical and policy framework—multilateral development banks themselves. How should we view them? What role do they play in Japan's policy process? The answer should be obvious if we adopt a state-centric approach—they should be regarded as an extension, a policy tool, of the state. But international organization literature and a reactive state approach that attributes policy impetus to external actors force us to question the function MDBs play in national policymaking.

Traditional views grant would grant MDBs little freedom of movement. As Ernst Haas puts it, "international organizations exist only because of demands emanating from the environment and survive only because they manage to please the forces there, which also dictate the programs these organizations must adopt to survive."[105] An UNCTAD (United Nations Conference on Trade and Development) study cites its conditional existence: "An international institution cannot prevail against national wills; it depends mainly for its effectiveness on the good will of Governments, on the powers given to it, on its resources and on the response of Governments to recommendations for action."[106] In other words, international organizations are "useful pieces of machinery through which to enhance national policy aims."[107] However, Haas raises the question:

> Must organizations remain the tools their creators have in mind when they set them up—means toward the attainment of some end valued by the creators? Or, alternatively, can international organizations become ends in their own right, become valued as institutions quite apart from the services they were initially expected to perform? [108]

A former International Monetary Fund (IMF) officer testifies that member nations do not, in fact, control the World Bank:

> development objectives and approaches as implemented by the World Bank cannot be usefully viewed as mere manifestations of bargained agreements among nation-states. . . . [T]he practical autonomy and wide discretion of the World Bank make it unlikely that any approach we could identify as representing such an agreement would survive intact if it ran counter to the values and interests of the World Bank as an institution.[109]

We can therefore conceive of international organizations as purposive, interest-driven organic entities in their own right. They too can engage in strategic behavior. They can "use the sovereign-state environment to increase their autonomy" through secretariat action, establishing agendas, legitimizing demands or interests of external actor, and devising strategies against member states.[110] In other words, international organizations "themselves are important units of analysis precisely because they take on a life and character of their own."[111]

This suggests, at minimum, that states face pluralistic environments both at home and abroad. However, we still assume an asymmetric relationship. Robert Keohane asserts that the societal environment exerts the stronger influence on state policy than international organizations.[112] And we still assume the primacy of the state as arbiter of the external and internal arenas. Again, this question responds to the reactive state presumption that since Japan merely adapts to external influences, MDBs constitute one of these influences. Our question at this stage is: To what extent do these institutions influence Japanese thinking and behavior?

If Japan is a more proactive state, however, we need to pay attention not only to the reactive impulse but also to what Keohane refers to as the empowering function of international institutions. That is, "international institutions make it possible for states to take actions that would otherwise be inconceivable."[113] In essence, multilateral institutions can "*empower* governments rather than shackling them."[114] We may find that multilateral banks possess certain qualities and behave in certain ways that actually encourage Japanese proactive behavior. We should therefore be cognizant of the potential dual role MDBs can play in Japan's policy.

Based on our survey of the evolution of Japanese ODA policy, Japanese aid literature, the reactive state approach and its alternatives, and international relations literature, what kind of proactive behavior can we expect from the state? What are the alternative strategies available to the state, and what kinds of behavioral patterns are possible in Japan's MDB policy? We can imagine, in theory, four ideal types of strategies or behavior that incorporate both activism and reactivism: proactivism, acquiescent activism, defensive activism, and anticipatory activism.

Proactivism assumes that Japan has its own ideas, interests, and policy objectives. Its policies are not based solely on the expectations of foreign countries nor in response to direct foreign pressure. Japan is purposive and decisive; its policy process is not afflicted with immobilism. It has a clear conception of its national interests, it knows what it wants, and it seeks to mobilize its citizens and national resources to attain its objectives through the alteration of the external environment. Japan acts rather than reacts.

Proactivism takes two forms. In the real world, we cannot escape the fact that nation-states exist in an environment that compels a certain amount of sensitivity to other actors. We therefore need to distinguish between promotive activism, in which activism is designed to manipulate the external environment and shape domestic interests in line with purely indigenously derived interests (i.e., foreign policy as an extension of state or societal politics), and induced proactivism, which would allow some causative input from outside but does not require Japan merely to respond. Rather, exogenous stimuli are heeded but viewed as obstacles to overcome. Japan still attempts to shape, rather than to take the shape of, its external environment according to its own objectives.

Acquiescent activism implies a purely reactive response to external stimuli, where Japan merely acquiesces to environmental pressures. Japan's policy objectives are exogenously shaped and its policy process is influenced by other actors on the international billiard table. Japan lacks its own vision; its main task is to survive by adapting to a constantly shifting environment. The nation enjoys little autonomy or independence of action. It surrenders to overwhelming pressures from abroad and suffers from a rampant pluralism that it cannot control. It dances as fast as it can to the tune of others. Japan simply reacts.

Defensive activism connotes strong resistance to any external pressure or demand. This is an intransigent type of activism designed to avoid compliance and acquiescence to external pressure. The national slogan may well be "no retreat, no surrender" to external entreaties, demands, or sanctions, either threatened or actual. Defensive activism implies a strong state able to mobilize domestic forces behind its policies; it implies a state that knows what it wants, though not necessarily one that has a vision, and what it does not want. This is either a frightened or self-confident, defiant "Japan that can say no."

Anticipatory activism basically retains the reactive nature of state behavior but allows for some autonomous, purposive behavior that reflects indigenously determined national interests. Activist policies respond not so much to immediate or direct outside pressure but to anticipated future pressure or problems. Anticipated problems may induce spirited and highly active policy measures designed to mitigate potential negative consequences. This activism helps the nation cope with and adapt to the existing system by preempting criticism and calls for change. It implies, again, an involved, highly prescient state in control of domestic forces and capable of better-than-average information gathering and analysis.

Specific case studies will more than likely reveal that these ideal types of behavior overlap, exhibit fluctuation over time or issue area, or require revisions, and there is no guarantee that these are the only possibilities. However, armed with this background information, we are now prepared to proceed beyond the starting line toward the analysis of Japan's multilateral development bank policy.

PART II

THE NEW MULTILATERALISM

3

♦

JAPAN AND THE MULTILATERAL
DEVELOPMENT BANKS: THE SEARCH FOR A ROLE

It is high time that the ideal of success should be replaced
by the ideal of service.

—Albert Einstein

Multilateral diplomacy emerged as a particularly active and conspicuous
feature of Japanese foreign policy from the mid-1980s through the mid-
1990s. Tokyo's activities in the International Bank for Reconstruction and
Development (IBRD, or World Bank), Asian Development Bank, and European Bank for Reconstruction and Development serve as the core of this
activism in the international financial institutions. This chapter begins by
briefly introducing a set of guidelines that may be of help in understanding
Japanese policy toward each of these institutions. Three sets of objectives
define Japan's activism in its MDB policy: institutional, diplomatic, and
development.

Institutional Objectives

Managerial and administrative objectives formed Japan's core priority objectives from the 1970s through the 1980s. These objectives consisted, in turn,
of four primary components: financial contributions, vote share, management presence, and professional staff presence.

Financial contributions have been Japan's traditional focus throughout
the history of its membership in MDBs. Japan consistently strives to strengthen
the financial foundation of each organization and to maintain the standing of
that institution in international financial markets. The government's stated

objective is the smooth and efficient functioning of these institutions, and the hoped-for by-product of that process is the heightening of Japan's stature not only in these institutions but also in the international community.

As Japan's status as a major financial supporter of MDBs rose, Japanese politicians and bureaucrats voiced a concern that their nation's vote shares did not seem to approximate contribution levels. In the 1970s, Tokyo did not push this issue, mainly because Japan was just reaching its take-off stage and because of expected opposition from other donor nations. The attainment of new shares by one country entails the loss of shares by other members. However, the gradual pressure to match vote shares with contributions paid off in the 1980s and 1990s, as Japan sits near the top of the shareholder pecking order in all MDBs.

Japan chafed at the absence, or near absence, of its nationals in top management positions in MDBs, if only for prestige reasons. Japan faced numerous difficulties in attaining or maintaining top positions, ranging from its latecomer status in the older, established organizations, including the domination of upper level posts by long-time staffers and the existence of key "reserved posts" for certain nationalities or regions, to reluctance by Japanese to serve abroad. The problem has survived the 1980s and remains on Tokyo's MDB agenda.

Staffing international organizations, whether the UN or MDBs, is a persistent and vexing problem for Japan. Japan has difficulties filling the positions to which it is entitled by its large financial contributions. The problems include language difficulties, lack of international experience, and personnel policies of Japanese private and public sector institutions that hinder secondment abroad. These roadblocks to effective staffing of international organizations are likely to persist for the foreseeable future.

Diplomatic Objectives

Japan's use of MDBs for a variety of diplomatic objectives became noticeable in the last half of the 1980s, after it became the largest creditor nation and the onset of the debt crisis, and in the first half of the 1990s, especially in the wake of the Gulf and Tianamen Square crises and the collapse of East Europe and the Soviet Union. MDBs served the following eight functions for Japanese diplomacy and domestic politics:

POLICY ARTICULATION. MDBs serve as conduits to articulate and implement national policies. This presumes policies to articulate, which Japan began to formulate from the mid-1980s.

LEGITIMIZATION OF CONTROVERSIAL POLICIES. Japan can share diplomatic risks or blame others by funneling policies through multilateral institutions, a useful tactic both internationally and domestically.

FULFILLMENT OF INTERNATIONAL RESPONSIBILITIES AS A NONMILITARY POWER. This policy use responds to both the strong pacifist sentiment in Japan and to other nations' fears of a growing military role for Japan in regional and perhaps global politics. MDBs call for commitment of monetary, personnel, technological, and moral support, not military resources.

ENHANCEMENT OF INADEQUATE NATIONAL RESOURCES. Japan may be the world's largest creditor nation, but it still struggles with large budget deficits. ODA comes from taxpayers, who have become increasingly restive about public expenditures in the recession-plagued 1990s, and it should be remembered that the private sector possesses Japan's huge surplus.

COMPENSATION FOR DIPLOMATIC AND POLICYMAKING SHORTCOMINGS. Only now is Japan emerging from the neoisolationism of its postwar political-strategic diplomacy, and the large gaps in its knowledge about other countries and regions with which it has had minimal contact are being revealed. MDBs can fill that knowledge gap through the provision of both information and technical expertise.

GLOBALIZATION OF DIPLOMACY WITHOUT SACRIFICING THE PRIORITY GIVEN TO ASIA. Japan can engage in global burden-sharing and division of labor through the World Bank and the regional development banks while, at the same time, continuing to concentrate on relations with Asia (both bilaterally and through the Asian Development Bank).

GREATER INDEPENDENCE WITHIN AN AMERICAN POLICY FRAMEWORK. Japan must chart a course between its traditional dependence on the United States, a new national self-confidence, and the requirements of a post–Cold War world order. MDBs, a pillar in the search for that new order, offer Japan an opportunity to engage in global and regional agenda-setting and rule-making, a task that requires both continued support for and an occasional challenging of the United States.

ENHANCEMENT OF NATIONAL PRESTIGE. This is a core Japanese policy objective in all international organizations, and the opportunities to enhance national status increased when the spotlight fell on MDBs in the post–Cold War era. Japan's MDB activities have a demonstration effect, showing that the nation works for the common good in these international institutions and is thus a good world citizen.

Development Objectives

Despite Japan's willingness to contribute large amounts of money and personnel to MDBs, the question always remained, for what purpose? What did Japan want to do with a larger share of votes or top managers? Throughout most of the postwar period what was missing was a particular development agenda or strategy that Japan pursued through these institutions. Japan remained relatively silent and passive within the MDBs, lacking a particular philosophy or specific formula for development. In short, Japan accepted the orthodox philosophies and strategies articulated by Western nations and reflected in MDBs; it preferred to leave the strategizing to the MDB managements.

By the late 1980s and early 1990s, however, the Japanese began to articulate a preference for an Asian development model. This theme is most noteworthy in the World Bank, but the model's assumptions underlay policy toward all MDBs. Significantly, this model challenged the orthodoxy practiced in MDBs and, by extension, American development philosophy. The orthodoxy, increasingly referred to in Japan as the "Anglo-American" or "Anglo-Saxon" development approach, has been summarized as follows: "The orthodoxy, represented by the IMF, the World Bank, and USAID [United States Agency for International Development], espoused greater roles for market mechanisms and the private sector and prescribed elimination of subsidies to inputs, liberalization of product markets, and abolition of the state-run distribution system."[1]

Japan's policy toward multilateral development banks in the 1980s and 1990s encompasses these three sets of objectives. The early phase of its membership in MDBs is characterized by a preoccupation with institutional concerns, but by the 1990s, a mixture of emergent diplomatic objectives and the promotion of a development strategy worked to make MDB policy more visible, multidimensional, and dynamic.

INTERNATIONAL BANK FOR RECONSTRUCTION AND DEVELOPMENT: THE SEARCH FOR "IDEAS"

Japan's relationship with the IBRD reflects the changes in its fortunes during its rise to economic great power status during the postwar period. The World Bank emerged out of the rubble of World War II as one of the pillars of the new Bretton Woods international economic system. Japan, sponsored by its American ally, entered the bank in 1952 as a defeated Axis nation desperately in need of reconstruction and development. Its entry provided the bank with a major customer during the early years, but Japan graduated from borrowing status in the midst of the economic miracle of the 1960s. Since the mid-1960s, Japan has risen to the status of a major donor member, second only to the United States. In the process, Tokyo, originally a passive and silent recipient, emerged as an active and increasingly vocal contributor. Today Japan is a visible force within the bank, as in the world, searching for an appropriate role.

Japan joined the World Bank as a developing nation. In 1952, its per capita income totaled a mere $200 per year. Borrowings from the bank took the form of two-step loans. The bank funneled funds to official financial institutions, especially the Japan Development Bank, which in turn channeled the funds to specific industries and projects. Government management and guidance was deemed necessary because the Japanese private sector, while increasingly successful, had yet to develop its reputation for creditworthiness or efficiency. The government thus provided the guarantees necessary to secure external funds.[2]

The first bank loan was issued in October of 1953, a two-step loan for a Kansai electric project that became the prototype for succeeding loans. The bank initially was hesitant about granting loans to Japan, but under President Stanley Black, project loans proliferated from 1957, and Japan catapulted to the position of second largest borrower behind India. In 1960, Japan and India shared the status of top borrowers.[3] By 1966, the final year Japan borrowed from the IBRD, it had accumulated loans totaling $862.9 million for 31 projects. Tokyo repaid all bank loans in August 1990 with a $7 million installment by the Japan Public Highway Corporation for a $75 million loan in 1965.[4]

The Japanese funneled IBRD loans to infrastructure projects in core industries. In the 1950s, most projects were in the electric power, shipbuilding, iron and steel, and automobile industries. In the 1960s, the government designated the nation's transportation infrastructure as a priority, with bank loans contributing to the construction of expressways and the famous Tokaido Shinkansen (Bullet Train) that ran between Tokyo and Osaka. However, while bank loans contributed substantially to Japan's industrialization of the 1950s and the "economic miracle" of the 1960s, their role was supplementary rather than pivotal.

Japan officially joined the "rich man's club" of advanced industrialized aid donors with its membership in the Organization for Economic Cooperation and Development and its Development Assistance Committee in 1964. Within the World Bank, Tokyo graduated from its recipient status in 1966, and attained its own seat, which it had shared previously, on the board of directors. Japan, in the midst of this economic take-off period, finally sat among donor nations. However, it maintained a low-key, low-profile stance in the World Bank through the early 1980s. Only from the mid-1980s has Japan gradually reared its head, concentrating first on institutional objectives—namely, issues concerning financial contributions, vote share, and management and staff presence—and moving on to diplomatic and development issues.

Japan's financial contributions to the IBRD have been substantial. Its funds flow to the bank through subscriptions and contributions, bond issues in the Tokyo market, joint financing, and private investors. The World Bank first tapped Japan's financial market in 1969 and the private sector in 1971. The bank issued public bond issues and syndicate loans in Tokyo. From 1971 to 1993, a total of 44 Samurai and Daimyo bonds were floated; syndicate loans started in 1978. In addition, Japan engages in joint financing with the bank, mainly through the Export-Import Bank and the Overseas Economic Cooperation Fund (OECF), which were involved in half of the bank's joint funding projects during the 1982-92 period. Private investors cooperate with the International Finance Corporation (IFC), in which Japanese participated in 36 of 628 projects. Japan also contributed to and participated in the Multilateral Investment Guarantee Agency (MIGA), including the appointment of a Japanese national as its chief.[5] As a result of these activities, Japan attained number-two shareholder status in 1984 in the World Bank Group—the World Bank, International Development Association, the International Finance Corporation, and MIGA—and in the IMF in 1990. And if we add up the figures, Japan entered the 1990s as the largest source of the IBRD's total capital inflow, amounting to some 30 percent of total resources.[6]

In the 1980s, the most visible large-scale Japanese financing of World Bank activities were the three fund recycling programs of 1986-1989, which emphasized the role of MDBs, especially the World Bank, and took the form of subscriptions, special contributions, and expanded joint financing. In addition, Japan created several types of special funds between 1987 and 1990, including a scholarship fund (May 1987); a joint seminar with the IBRD's training institute, the Economic Development Institute (June 1987); a Japanese consultant training fund (August 1987); and an environment fund (July 1989). These separate funds were consolidated in July of 1990 into the Policy and Human Resource Development Fund (PHRD). PHRD emphasizes technical assistance, training and research, graduate training in development, and the environment.[7]

Japan contributes to the IFC by participating in three funds. The Asia-South Pacific Projects Development Fund, which Japan joined in August of 1991, provides technical assistance to find and nurture private sector projects. The Caribbean Projects Development Fund, in conjunction with the Inter-American Development Bank (IADB), the United Nations Development Program (UNDP), and others, was established in July 1986, and Japan joined in December 1990. Japan joined the African Projects Development Fund, a joint effort with IFC, UNDP, and the African Development Bank (AFDB), from its inception in July 1986.

By the mid-1990s, Japan's interest in institutional matters expanded to include administrative and personnel issues within the bank, including the administrative budget, staff salaries, and employment duties. As one example, the Japanese executive director sits on the internal budget committee and was reported to have been influential in eliminating first-class travel for World Bank missions to developing member nations.[8] On the personnel front, the Japanese remain dissatisfied with their presence within the bank, which failed to keep up with the increase in financial contributions. Even though Japan had attained the number-two position, or 6.69 percent of total shares, Japanese staff in 1992 totaled 93 out of 6,961, or a mere 1.3 percent. Japan ranks number 11 among all nationalities, and only Italy has fewer staff members among the G-7 countries.

At the top management level, by the 1990s, Japanese occupied one operational vice presidency, three directorships, and three division chiefs.[9] The World Bank attempted to coax a former Ministry of Finance (MOF) vice minister for international affairs, Gyohten Toyoo, currently chairman of the Bank of Tokyo, to accept a vice presidency, but he rejected the offer. The highest-ranking Japanese currently is the vice president of cofinancing and financial advisory services, occupied by a seconded MOF official. However, the Finance Ministry makes no secret of the fact that it does not consider this vice presidency to be a mainstream management position.[10]

The Japanese blame both the bank and themselves for the personnel situation. The bank finds the recruitment of Japanese staff difficult. Annual recruiting missions are dispatched to Japan, and the bank's Tokyo office engages in campaigns to attract candidates. But Japanese have pointed out that the problem rests in the IBRD home office as well. Job openings are not adequately announced, and, in practice, power regarding personnel decisions rests in the hands of department directors rather than the personnel office since administrative changes in 1987. This practice is thought to work to the advantage of native English speakers, mainly Anglo-Americans, Indians, and Pakistanis. Thus many Japanese feel they have fewer promotion opportunities. Also, in the past, an international financial institution salary may have been attractive to a Japanese; however, as Japan's per capita income surpassed that of other advanced industrialized nations, such salaries have lost this advantage.

For its part, Japan has responded to the problem with a three-pronged campaign designed to make the playing field more level for Japanese candidates. First, the Japanese focused on the bank's efforts. They favored the expansion of the Young Professionals program, which selects approximately 25 people annually. Typically, only one or two Japanese entered the bank through this route, so marginal improvements were pushed to increase the number of candidates considered. Two out of four Japanese candidates were selected in 1991, and three of four in 1992. In addition, the bank introduced a midcareer professional program in 1991 for professionals who have been out of the university for ten years; six of the 26 chosen were Japanese. Finally, Japan worked to strengthen the recruitment system by encouraging the bank to station a high ranking official in the Bank's Tokyo office, and by having the Tokyo office target possible candidates in universities, in foreign firms in Japan, among women who have returned from abroad, among people who studied at noted American universities, and by instituting summer internships.[11]

Second, the Japanese Finance Ministry initiated financial aid to the bank for consultant training and language instruction. One component of the PHRD was devoted to supporting the dispatch of Japanese consultants, who would work at the bank for a one-year term and, if their performance was good, be recruited for a longer term. PHRD also supports advanced language training for consultants when candidates require additional work on their communication skills.[12]

Third, the Japanese government has focused on the private sector, which dispatches the bulk of Japanese staffers to IFIs through the temporary leave system (*shukko*) Under *shukko* practices, employees of Japanese firms are granted leaves of two to five years while they serve in international organizations. There are advantages for the company and its employees, including experience and training in development, Third World regions and countries, and international finance. However, there are also risks and costs for both the individual and the firm. These include delays in one's career stemming from a prolonged absence, lack of language fluency that inhibits promotions in the IFI, and the inability to function in a management system that requires skills not needed or respected in Japanese organizations (e.g., self-promotion, debating skills, etc.). And in recent years, in an age of internationalization and domestic recession, Japanese firms are increasingly reluctant to release their employees even temporarily because they require the very skills needed by the IFI.

The Japanese government has therefore suggested changes in the operating procedures of Japanese firms when selecting *shukko* candidates. These include lengthening the *shukko* period, increasing the number of candidates (usually only one candidate is offered), insuring a successor for the person returning from abroad from an IFI, and weeding out inappropriate candidates.[13] Although these recruitment difficulties are discussed within the context of the World Bank, most of these problems apply to Japanese participation in other MDBs and in all international organizations. World Bank recruitment is one instance of the more general Japanese dilemma of matching international imperatives with domestic organizational procedures. The public sector confronts recruitment difficulties as well, for even as it exhorts private firms to make the necessary changes in their personnel policies, the MOF itself has problems finding individuals for *shukko* assignments abroad. The Japanese will not find this problem easy to solve, but they have become more active in searching for solutions.

Japanese movement in the institutional area is matched by activism in the diplomatic and development arenas. The two are related. Japan began to link financial contributions to its desire for a larger vote share. A greater share presumes a desire for greater say in bank matters, but in earlier periods, the nation's interest in a higher profile and larger vote share can be attributed to its interest in heightening national prestige. The government responded to domestic voices in the Diet calling for more accountability and commensurate rewards for increased financial contributions and to external calls for international burden-sharing from Tokyo. A greater say would come later, after the vote share increase had been attained.

Ogata Sadako, in her study of Japan's World Bank policy in the 1980s, has interpreted this activism within the bank as a power struggle between a Japan attempting to increase its power to match economic resources and a United States attempting to retain its power while reducing financial support. Therefore, Japan's linkage of contributions to the International Development Association, the Bank's soft loan window, with increases in the ordinary capital resources, the basis for determining vote share, became its key strategy designed to catapult itself from the fifth to second position within the bank. Japan's challenge encountered opposition from European members (Germany, France, England) who ranked above the number-five position; from others whose ranking may have been jeopardized by a Japanese share increase (India); from the U.S. Congress and administration, which linked increase shares with demands on Japan to liberalize its domestic financial market; and even from the World Bank President (Tom Clausen).[14]

It is true that Japan began to speak out more in the mid-1980s. The turning points were the attainment of the number-two position within the bank, which placed the onus on it to act like the number-two player; the aid-doubling plans of the Japanese government; the new debt plans; and the

Plaza Accord, which made more dollars available for international contributions. However, Japan's motive for seeking higher status in the first half of the 1980s was not to challenge America's dominant position. The Japanese viewed the IBRD as America's bank and had no intention of displacing Washington. As one MOF official recalled: "Back then, there was no real U.S.-Japan rivalry. This was not Japan's intent. There were difficulties, but since the United States was the major shareholder, it was natural to some extent to have American wishes be accepted." [15]

A U.S. Treasury Department official who worked with the Japanese in the IBRD during the late 1980s reports that the United States and Japan were the "anchor" on many policy issues and worked together closely. He observes that both countries agreed on policies 80 to 90 percent of the time.[16] Neither Japanese nor American policymakers find it easy to characterize Japan's behavior as a power struggle for hegemony in the bank. Rather, as a Finance Ministry official put it, most bank staffers "probably saw Japan as subordinate to the United States, that Japan basically followed America's lead."[17]

The truth lies somewhere between hegemony and subservience. Number two accurately reflected Japan's preferred status in the bank, and this objective brought Tokyo into conflict with Europeans more than with Washington. In a sense, the target was Europe, not the United States. As Japan rose to the status of largest creditor nation, its financial capabilities provided Tokyo with the resources to leap-frog the third and fourth positions in the World Bank. Britain and France were especially adamant that Japan remain number five, but with U.S. support, Japan climbed near the pinnacle in the mid-1980s. The Japanese are currently satisfied with their rank, but their new goal is to consolidate their hold on the second spot by widening the gap between number two and the rest of the pack. In the long run, one can imagine a Japanese government hoping for a position of equality with the United States, perhaps on the Asian Development Bank model, but with the United States being a little more equal. However, it is difficult to imagine Japanese hegemony within the bank.

What is noteworthy here is that Japan's accession to number two was worked out primarily in the context of G-7 negotiations, not just U.S.-Japan consultations and not simply as a U.S.-Japan power struggle within the Bank. Japan reportedly had the support of the developing member nations for the number-two spot, which reflected a growing phenomenon of recipient nations seeking Japan to represent them on controversial issues before the board of directors. To the extent that it is a power struggle, it reflects the global emergence of a competitive and cooperative Japan and a united Europe onto the post–Cold War environment. The ability of the actors to find a solution to the IBRD ranking problem indicates an effort to strengthen and regularize the Japan–West Europe leg of the trilateral structure. This trilateral interaction seems to serve as one of the core patterns of, and even framework for, Japan's recent behavior not just in the IBRD but, as we will see, in other fora as well.

Japan's debt diplomacy inaugurated policy activism in the World Bank beyond the institutional realm. The crisis in Mexico in 1984 and the breaking of the $1 trillion mark in 1985 spurred the United States into action, with IFIs playing a prominent role in U.S. plans. The Baker Plan of 1985 envisioned the IBRD and the Inter-American Development Bank (IADB) increasing financial resources by 50 percent over three years (to $9 billion) and private lending reaching $20 billion. Finance Minister Miyazawa announced Japan's support for the Baker Plan through untied loans from the Export-Import Bank of Japan, including cofinancing with the IBRD.

Tokyo followed suit in the last half of the 1980s with its own multi-pronged debt relief strategy that included: three capital recycling plans, which involved packages of $10 billion in 1986, $20 billion in 1987, and $35 billion in 1989; the Miyazawa Plan, named after the finance minister and announced in 1988 privately at the Toronto Summit and publicly at the World Bank/IMF annual meeting; a new medium-term ODA commitment in 1988 of $50 billion over five years; a plan for Sub-Saharan Africa in 1988; and support for the Baker Plan's successor, the Brady Plan of 1989.

The 1986 $10 billion plan envisioned a loan of $3 billion Special Drawing Rights to the IMF and a Japan Special Fund of $2 billion for the World Bank for technical assistance. The $10 billion package was incorporated with the $20 billion plan of 1987 to form a $30 billion capital recycling package. The World Bank, ADB, IADB, and other MDBs were to receive additional subscriptions and contributions totaling $8 billion, and private capital from the Tokyo bond market. In addition, Exim and OECF were to engage actively in cofinancing with World Bank in particular, to the tune of $9 billion.[18]

The Miyazawa Plan envisioned three prongs, focusing on structural adjustment under IMF auspices, the use of bilateral and multilateral ODA to induce new private flows, and debt-to-bond conversion and debt rescheduling overseen by the IMF. The United States strongly criticized the plan but announced a strikingly similar Brady Plan in 1989. The Brady Plan also emphasized the role of the IMF and the IBRD. Japan quickly expressed support for the plan by announcing an expansion of the $30 billion capital recycling program to $65 billion at the July 1989 Arche Summit. The additional $35 billion included new money to the IMF ($1.6 billion) and World Bank ($2.1 billion) for three SECALS (sectoral adjustment loans) and Exim–World Bank cofinanced loans ($900 million).

The World Bank received the lion's share of recycled capital. The Export-Import Bank, the principal funnel of the capital, committed a total of about $9 billion out of $24 billion in cofinancing (untied loans) by mid-September 1992. The ADB received close to $1.2 billion; the IADB, $918 million; and the IMF, $1.6 billion.[19] As of June 1993, the World Bank had received 41.5 percent of total cofinanced funds for 29 projects, compared with 3.4 percent for IADB's five projects and ADB's 2.5 percent for six projects. The bank's percentage increases to 49.3 percent if projects cofinanced with the ADB and IADB are included.[20]

Critics of Japanese aid policy may attribute this flurry of activity to a desperate effort on Japan's part to reduce its burgeoning trade surplus, which leaped to $86 billion in 1986, when the country began to announce its debt programs. However, this unidimensional explanation of Japanese activism ignores the broader domestic and international environment, Japan's activities within the World Bank, and the changes under way in the Finance Ministry at home. The debt crisis activism reveals a combination of motives, including the economic self-interest visible in all G-7 countries' actions, the reach for heightened prestige as a major actor on the international financial and economic stage, and a genuine search for a proper solution to a problem that threatened the entire world economic system.

In the 1990s, Japanese policy positions within the bank also addressed the historic developments of 1989, namely steps taken toward China after the Tiananmen Square incident, East Europe after the collapse of the Communist systems (to be discussed in the section on the European Bank for Reconstruction and Development), and the Soviet Union's dissolution (the subject of Chapter 5).

In the case of China, Japan trod an intermediate position, between strong condemnation of the massacre and support for the moratorium on loans pushed by the G-7 nations. Japan's campaign aimed at softening sanctions and reinstating the flow of bilateral ODA to Beijing. Japan found its efforts, dating from the 1970s, to forge a close, intimate relationship with China in jeopardy. It feared that the West would isolate China from the international community just when there was a growing momentum within the Chinese economy toward greater openness. The Kaifu cabinet embarked on a particularly active campaign to mitigate the aftershock of Tiananmen Square on China and Sino-Japanese relations.[21]

The Liberal Democratic Party and the Foreign Ministry took the lead on China policy, but because of the role played by the World Bank in Japanese efforts to restore Chinese aid, the Finance Ministry found itself increasingly involved. The Finance Ministry shared the Foreign Ministry's concern with sanctions, taking its traditional position that multilateral aid should not be politicized. Officials found Finance Minister Hashimoto Ryutaro considerably "pro-China" and opposed to sanctions. Hashimoto was a lieutenant in the LDP's Takeshita faction, which had considerable influence over Prime Minister Kaifu. It was the previous Takeshita cabinet that had pledged the aid package that Japan was forced to halt as a result of Tiananmen Square. Hashimoto propelled the MOF to take a more independent line on China in the IBRD (where he served as Japan's representative on the board of governors), and in other international financial institutions.[22] Outside the World Bank, the Japanese government lobbied hard at the Paris and the Houston G-7 summits to restart the bilateral ODA package.

Within the World Bank, Japan may have officially sanctioned the cessation of World Bank loans along with other G-7 nations, but Tokyo also engaged in a simultaneous campaign that designated the IBRD as the opening shot of an effort to restore the flow of yen credits. Japan assumed that if the World Bank, the flagship of international financial institutions, could be induced to reinstitute loans, then its own job to lift bilateral aid sanctions would be that much easier.

Japan's strategy was to find a "motherhood issue" that would soften Western, and especially American, support for aid sanctions. Tokyo assumed that the safest choices would be basic human needs issues or an issue as emotionally attractive as human rights. Japan settled on the environment, an increasingly popular global issue and a major casualty China's rapid growth and, therefore, a logical target of green funds. Thus Japan took the lead on the environment issue and argued that environmental loans should be emphasized in MDBs.[23] At the 1989 Paris Summit, while pushing to soften sanctions against China, Japan announced a three-year, 300 billion yen environmental assistance package slated for both bilateral and multilateral channels. After intense campaigning by Japan, the World Bank proceeded with humanitarian and basic human needs projects in October 1989, only five months after the Tiananmen Square incident and only two months after Japan began to lift its bilateral sanctions. In 1991, Japan embarked on the funding, bilaterally, of a major environmental protection research center—in Beijing. At the Houston Summit of 1990, Japan achieved its objective: Tacit acceptance by the United States and Europe for the resumption of Japanese bilateral ODA to Beijing.[24]

The China factor alone does not, of course, explain Japan's sudden interest in environmental issues, but one wonders about the catalytic effect of Tiananmen Square—especially since Japan took a passive and almost disinterested approach to environmental issues in the January to May negotiations that resulted in the founding of the EBRD just prior to the July Houston Summit. Japan did not merely follow the lead of or respond to American and international pressure on the China issue. Rather, it utilized the World Bank, and the environment issue, to persuade the United States to endorse its own diplomatic objectives. Japan used the World Bank and G-7 summits to legitimize a controversial international policy stance. In other words, Japan pursued its own agenda.

Japan's behavior in the World Bank is therefore neither purely reactive to American pressure nor a "power struggle." It is somewhere in between. Japan tended to side primarily with Washington on most issues, but it also increasingly followed the dictates of its own national interests, often deemed different from American interests. On the debt issue, U.S. and Japanese approaches were compatible, with Japan either bowing to America's borrowing of Miyazawa's plan or Tokyo happily ceding leadership to the United States. On China, Japan exhibited a rare aggressiveness in distinguishing its views from those of other G-7 nations.

The one area where Japan challenged the United States within the World Bank was development philosophy and strategy. The manner in which Japan challenged the United States was indirect—it initiated a bank study—but the target was highly direct—the underlying assumptions of the World Bank's operations. By challenging the bank's development philosophy and strategy, Japan also challenged America's influence on the bank's management and operations without striving for hegemony. It was a show of self-confidence and a bid for greater independence through the contribution of ideas and not just money.

As Japan entered the 1990s, a strong positive assessment of MDBs as a funnel for Japanese funding and a strong feeling that Japan should become more vocal in these institutions converged. According to MOF officials:

> The thinking now is that if Japan is to contribute to the world, then we should do it through international institutions. This applies not just to aid but to foreign policy in general. . . . There is a tendency to favor international institutions, and development aid is no exception.[25]

> There was a feeling that if Japan had something to say, then it should say it. Say it about anything. Not just about debt, but also about any developing nation loan. Speak out about the right and wrong of any issue.[26]

The problem was that Japan lacked an inclination to speak out on anything until the 1990s, when it chose to speak out in particular on development strategy. The tussle between the Anglo-American orthodoxy and the Asian development model was played out in the IBRD from the late 1980s into the early 1990s. In the 1980s, there were three specific catalysts for the Japanese challenge to orthodoxy: the assumption to office of the Reagan administration, with its strong ideological commitment to a universal development philosophy; the intensification of the accumulated debt crisis; and the impressive accomplishments of state-led economic development in Asian countries. These developments had a cumulative effect on the Japanese. In addition, the explosion of the debt crisis in Latin America in particular provided them with an instructive case study of a failure of the orthodoxy. The emergence of an economically successful Asia provided an alternative answer to the question of sustainable development. These two phenomena combined triggered in Japan a reassessment of its own development experience and reinforced doubts about the Reagan administration's seemingly inflexible development approach.

In other words, the Japanese had been handicapped in international financial institutions by their lack of knowledge of development processes. Once the Japanese began to study development in earnest, they discovered the problems and flaws in the accepted wisdom of the day. Within the IBRD, the Japanese challenge to World Bank's neoclassical approach had roots in the bank's adoption of structural and sectoral adjustment loans in the early 1980s. At the time, the Japanese found little to criticize because Finance Ministry officials had little knowledge of the approach. As one MOF official noted:

> The problem was that Japan couldn't understand it [structural adjustment loans] at first. Japan started out with tied project aid and did not apply conditionality. The World Bank would develop cofinanced adjustment loans with conditionality, and this meant that Japan's cofinanced portion would have conditionality attached. Japan brought people to Japan from the World Bank to study adjustment loans. All of this was new, this macro-economics plus conditionality.[27]

However, as MOF officials began to study the approach and to view its effects, they came to question its effectiveness, universal application, and rigidities. As they studied the Asian economic miracles, they found contradictions between their observations of the structural adjustment loan (SAL) track record, especially in Latin America, and the Asian experience. And as confidence in the Asian, including the Japanese, model took hold, Tokyo began to raise questions within the bank about its development approach:

After seeing Asian countries' experiences—Korea, Taiwan, Malaysia, Thailand, Indonesia—there was much stronger confidence in that model as viable and applicable. The crux of that model is the ingenious combination of private and public sector dynamism. Japan feels that Japanese success has something to do with this mixture. When the United States came up with its strong preference for private sector initiative and its clear dislike for the public sector, conflict developed between the two approaches.[28]

This dissatisfaction with SALs came to the fore openly in a document submitted to the bank by the Overseas Economic Cooperation Fund (OECF) questioning several basic tenets of the approach.[29] The OECF document summarizes the main Japanese criticisms of SALs: It casts doubt on overemphasis on deregulation and overreliance on market mechanisms, and stresses the need for a Japanese-type fiscal and monetary policy, with its government guidance and partnership with the private sector. It states that under some circumstances, development finance institutions and subsidized interest rates maximize social welfare. The OECF also cautions against overly rapid liberalization, preferring protectionism for infant industries during the early, formative stages of development. In sum, the proposal concludes that "it is impossible to achieve optimum allocation of resources solely through market principle regardless of the level of development. There are many areas which cannot be handled by market mechanism ('market failure'), and government intervention is necessary to cope with such situations."[30] And it takes a swipe at the apparent universal application of what it feels should be a case-by-case strategy: "We wonder whether privatization is always the solution for improving efficiency of public sector. Various conditions in individual countries must be taken into account very carefully. Unfortunately, the World Bank's approach seems to be almost similar for every country."[31]

Conditionality contradicts the Finance Ministry's principal multilateral aid tenet. The MOF consistently touts the preferability of multilateral aid because of its separation of politics from economics. A former high-ranking official summarizes the ministry's view:

There is always discussion within the Government concerning the optimal allocation of multilateral and bilateral assistance. But on the whole, there is a strong tendency underlining aid—a clear preference for multilateral aid because aid can trigger adverse reactions. The main concern is political pressure. . . . There is a sense that bilateral aid should include these extra-economic issues, or take it a step further, that great emphasis should be placed on promoting these interests in bilateral aid. Japan prefers multilateral agencies because they help Japan escape from politicizing aid.[32]

This separation of politics from economics approach remains one of the main attractions of the World Bank, which forbids political considerations in determining loans. MOF officials are aware, of course, of the American penchant for carrying political issues to the bank, but most officials distinguish Japan's approach from Washington's: "The fact is that the World Bank cannot ignore the influence of the United States. The United States does follow a policy of political conditionality. And the United States tries to transfer the principle of political conditionality (of bilateral aid policy) to the multilaterals. Japan accepts this reluctantly."[33]

The MOF, however, has gradually loosened its strictures against conditionality, including political conditionality. The collapse of East Europe and the Soviet Union had much to do with the reassessment of nonpolitical multilateral aid, and the EBRD's openly political charter reflects the new reality in the post–Cold War world. It became clear that conditions, both economic and political, were necessary if MDBs were to play a role in the transformation of command to market economies and democratic political systems. MOF officials now state that Japan is no longer hesitant about conditionality. The argument today is effectiveness and universal application, though the ministry remains cautious toward political conditionality. As one MOF official states, off the record, "political conditions are okay if done behind the scenes. But, in reality, you can't tell what the situation is in LDCs. What conditions are politically viable is difficult to determine." This official observes that "conditions may be economically viable but not politically viable. What if the government falls?"[34]

The Japanese are now insisting that conditionality should take into consideration a long-term time frame and differences in each country's development stage and economic situation rather than short-term results and universal application. They tend to think that World Bank economists equate developing nation conditions with developed nation experiences. The Japanese focus on World Bank economists is recent but the assessment is harsh. A sampling of opinions yield considerable lack of confidence in IBRD staffers:

> Something may be okay in theory but not in reality. Top management understands this, but the problem are the economists who don't understand this. There are many American academics who are stupid about this.[35]

The United States and Britain speak in loud voices about market mechanisms. This is the Anglo-Saxon way, uttered by American Ph.D.s who talk with strong voices. . . . U.S.-educated Ph.D.s have no experience with government-led economics. Thus they favor laissez-faire.[36]

SALs are easy for staff to apply. All they [bank economists] have to do is follow a textbook.[37]

The attack on SALs was a veiled challenge to what the Japanese considered the Anglo-American orthodoxy, but the irony of the complaints is that in the 1970s, the United States initially had opposed the introduction of SALs. After it was introduced, the United States gradually came to support it. The Japanese complaints are therefore reminiscent of the skepticism voiced by the United States in the introductory phase of SALs. Today, Japan prefers that SALs constitute a lower percentage of bank loans, and it expressed some satisfaction when that figure dropped into the mid-20 percentile range during the early 1990s.

Japan's position reflects many of the conclusions of the 1991 *World Development Report,* issued annually by the World Bank.[38] The thrust of the report acknowledges that "markets cannot operate in a vacuum" and that "the state forms the very core of development."[39] The crux of development is enlightened, selective, and moderate state guidance of the development process. The questions focus on when, where, and to what extent the government intervenes in the economy and forges a close partnership with private sector forces.

While the Japanese could agree with the thrust of this bank report, there were differences of opinion when it came to policy implications. The bank report's conclusions argue for the increased withdrawal of the state from development process in favor of nurturing market forces, a change from the old state-centric development paradigm. The Japanese, while favoring the basic conclusion on partnership between the public and private sectors, read the report as affirming the necessity of state leadership. They regarded favorably the report's use of the development experience of Asian NIEs (Newly Industrializing Countries) in particular in reaching its conclusions. On the other hand, it is also clear that the Japanese saw the report as a corrective to the Reagan administration's rigid, ideological insistence on total reliance on market mechanisms and private sector leadership. Japan noted the report's acknowledgment of cases where market mechanisms were either lacking or inadequate to the task of development and where privatization required caution and prudence. This emphasis on "market-friendly" approaches became Japan's preferred strategy in the 1990s.

While the Japanese favored the report's evaluation of the Asian development experience, Tokyo remained dissatisfied with the bank's tendency to underplay the importance of the Asian alternative to the Anglo-American orthodoxy. At the insistence of the Japanese, and with funding of approximately $1 million from Japan's PHRD fund, the bank embarked on a major study of the Asian economic miracles in 1991. This initiative constituted the strongest challenge to date of the IBRD's orthodoxy and the clearest indication thus far of Japan's intention to contribute "ideas" rather than only money and personnel. Although couched in terms of raising questions about the relevance of the Asian experience for other developing nations, Japan's prime motive appeared to encompass taking a leadership role within the bank on development philosophy. One Japanese government official claims that only Japan and the United States engage in philosophical discussions of development approaches on the board.

The bank's report was completed and published in the fall of 1993.[40] It basically marched down the middle path, endorsing relevant tenets of both the neoclassical orthodoxy and the "revisionist" view. Predictably, it upheld the "market-friendly" conclusions of the 1991 *World Development Report,* which it now deemed a middle ground between the two competing approaches. In short, the World Bank report provided a mixed assessment of the results of Asian development strategies, or else claimed to be unable to establish causality among some of the factors stressed by Japan and other Asian countries.

The 1993 report validated the state's interventionist role, though limited and sectoral, and the superiority of the market, though recognizing its limitations. It placed Japan's development experience in the context of common policies with East Asian NIEs and therefore bolstered Japanese opinions that their experience is neither unique nor irrelevant beyond their own borders. However, the report also was strongly skeptical regarding the effectiveness of state-determined industrial policies, a hallmark of Japan's self-image of its economic miracle. The Japanese could take heart, however, in the report's emphasis on the successes of official export-led growth strategies.

The Japanese were not completely satisfied with the bank's responses to the challenge from Asia, but neither were they surprised by the outcome of these reports, given their basic acceptance of what they term "Anglo-Saxon dominance" in the bank's management, staff, and organizational culture.[41] Some Japanese point out the absence of Japanese among the report's compilers.

The Ministry of Finance's reactions were clear and specific:

First, Japan still believes in the importance of government involvement and guidance in the development process. The 1993 Report argued that the smaller the government, the better, and that prioritizing specific sectors distorts the market, but Japan's experience shows otherwise. Japan's ability to designate priority sectors confirms especially the importance of two-step loans.[42] Market mechanisms must be nurtured and reach a level of efficiency, or else resources will be misallocated.

Second, liberalization must follow a protectionist period that nurtures infant industries: "For a country with a weak external position, its international balance of payments deficits will worsen severely by pursuing trade liberalization overnight, and it would have to borrow unduly from abroad, especially from the World Bank, the IMF, and other countries' foreign aid agencies."[43]

The bank report did not tackle head on the question of whether economic growth strategy is necessary or appropriate, but many Japanese do seem to detect an answer: The report implies that "the neo-classical explanation of the success of East Asia is basically correct. Further, one can interpret [the report as being] skeptical toward the point concerning the necessity of particular developing country strategies for economic development."[44]

However, MOF officials are satisfied that the report at least challenged the self-righteousness of the proponents of the orthodoxy[45] and heightened their awareness and understanding of the role of government in East Asia, pointedly noting that "despite the fact that they majored in economics, this was an apparently new discovery for many World Bank economists who do not have practical experience with either government or the private sector."[46]

The significance of Japan's effort to put the Asian experience on the agenda was, from Tokyo's point of view, that the study was undertaken at all. The Japanese took some satisfaction in breaching the wall surrounding the bank's self-righteous defense of the Anglo-American orthodoxy. They feel satisfied that the Asian development model will at least get a hearing in the bank thanks to their efforts. As a former executive director has written, "Japan's duty is to disseminate to LDCs the experience and development philosophy of Japan and Asian NIEs to developing nations through the World Bank."[47] This has become one of the policy and development missions of Japan in MDBs.

Japan's new interest in "ideas" is neither a power play aimed at the United States nor simply a response to external pressure to give more than money to international financial institutions. In reality, the Japanese find themselves on a parallel course with the United States. Tokyo professes agreement with and support for Washington's direction: privatization, liberalization, reliance on market forces. Japanese hesitation, they contend, is based on two concerns: the idealization and universalization of these principles, which indicates disagreement over methods of implementation more than goals, and America's diplomatic style. Some Japanese feel that the latter is often just as important as the former: The way American spokespersons propound these beliefs causes unnecessary contention. "The United States said things in a strong, severe way, and thus received retorts from all sides. The problem was not the content per se, but the way of saying things. It was a problem of style. . . . It was a problem of nuances."[48]

Diplomatic style, and the underlying influence of the personality of national spokespersons, also may contribute to the image of U.S.-Japan contention and rivalry, though this is an issue that is more applicable to the Asian Development Bank, discussed in the next section, than to the IBRD. However, differences over substance are significant. Although the World Bank presents the Asian development model and the orthodoxy as compatible and supplemental, Japan remains only partially convinced.

The battle lines have been drawn for the next decade, and the outcome of the debate may hinge on the ultimate outcome of the Asian economic miracle and of efforts to resuscitate and rebuild the nations of East Europe and the former Soviet Union. Some Japanese officials consider Russia and its republics the critical test case for the viability of the orthodoxy in the post–Cold War world.

In short, Japan's policy toward the World Bank, more than its policies toward the other MDBs and in tandem with UN diplomacy, symbolizes the arrival of Japan on the global stage. Its rise to prominence within the World Bank is a direct result of its emergence as a global power with global responsibilities. The questions it faces within the bank—about its role, purpose, methods, and principles—are identical to the questions faced by Japanese diplomacy in general. And like Japanese diplomacy, the answers are not yet clear.

ASIAN DEVELOPMENT BANK: THE SEARCH FOR STATUS

Japan's relationship with the Asian Development Bank (ADB) is not the longest among international organizations or most other multilateral banks. Japan joined the World Bank, IDA, IFC, IMF, and United Nations in the 1950s, prior to its 1966 membership in the ADB. However, there is one major difference: Unlike the other institutions, Japan participated in the founding of the ADB, and although the bank's status may arguably have slipped somewhat in Japan during recent years compared with the World Bank, the ADB remains the most intimate and intricate of Tokyo's links with all international organizations. The depth of this relationship that provides both pride and problems and constraints and opportunities for a Japan that is seeking to define its role in Asia and beyond.[49]

The ADB's founding occurred amid a regional organization boom in the late 1960s. Five Southeast Asian nations—Indonesia, Thailand, Malaysia, Singapore, and the Philippines—founded the Association for Southeast Asia (ASEAN) in 1967, and in 1966, South Korea organized the Asia and Pacific Council and Japan founded the Ministerial Conference for the Economic Development of Southeast Asia. Japan's involvement with the ADB began in the early 1960s, when ideas about a regional development bank germinated in both Tokyo and the Asian region.[50] The Japanese effort, spearheaded by influential individuals spanning the private and public sectors, resulted in a full-blown proposal prior to government-level discussions. Japan's strategy had been to await other Asians' formal proposal for a regional development bank, since the Japanese realized the danger of a backlash from former victims of wartime aggression who were strongly suspicious of Tokyo. The Asian proposal came soon, spearheaded by ideas originating in Thailand and adopted enthusiastically by the Economic Commission on Asia and the Far East (ECAFE), the predecessor of the Economic and Social Commission for Asia and the Pacific (ESCAP).

Tokyo sought desperately to be the cite of ADB headquarters, which would have made the ADB the first international organization located in Japan. However, it lost in a bitter struggle with Manila, and Japan settled for its second priority, the ADB presidency. It was telling that Japan initially sought the prestige-raising headquarters rather than what most observers would consider the more substantive presidency post, although the rationale was that Japan could influence the bank without the presidency anyway if it was headquartered in Tokyo. This loss of the headquarters underlined a lesson that Japan did not forget for a long time: Do not take the support of Asian neighbors for granted; the restoration of Japanese respectability in Asia does not depend on economic success alone.

This early shock contributed to Japan's avoidance of a high-profile stance within the bank and a preference for a low-key relationship. Japan avoided political controversies, paid attention to U.S. positions, and empha-sized financial contributions. The government basically followed the ADB management's lead on policy, dispatching executive directors whose main mission was to support the Japanese president. The degree of support varied with the personality and lineage of the president—the second president,

Inoue Shiro (1972-76), received less support because of his Bank of Japan rather than Finance Ministry origins—or with the personality of the executive director—for example, the first director, Fukuda Masaru (1966-71), played an especially assertive role on the board of directors, but his successors did not follow suit—but Japan's general approach dictated that any criticism of management be voiced informally, behind the scenes.

Japan also pegged its ADB policy largely on the American nexus. Tokyo lobbied to ensure bank membership for nonregional nations, using the 1964 exclusion of nonregional members by the African Development Bank as a negative model, and made much of the fact that Japan matched the initial American contribution of $200 million, the first time any country matched a U.S. contribution to an international organization. Tokyo enjoyed the coequal status with the United States and sought to work closely with Washington during the initial years. While the overall bilateral relationship remained decidedly senior-junior, the U.S.-Japan relationship within the bank lent itself to the appearance of equality. As the years went by, however, because of its commitment of financial and human resources, Japan's relationship with the bank appeared stronger. As a result, in the 1980s, the low-key activism began to change, when Japan adopted a high-key approach that sought preeminence within the bank. These developments are visible in the three categories of Japan's ADB policy—institutional, diplomatic, and development.

Even before the ADB's creation, Japan exhibited strong interest in the bank's managerial stability and financial strength. The Finance Ministry has cultivated a relationship that is uniquely close compared with personnel flows to other MDBs. The MOF participated in setting up the bank during the formative years through the participation of ministry officials in both unofficial and official capacities. Watanabe Makoto, director general of the Foreign Exchange Bureau, the predecessor of the International Finance Bureau, was a charter member of the Japanese study group that drafted a suggested articles of agreement for the new bank. The group was headed by Watanabe Takeshi, a former MOF official who had served as Japan's second executive director at the World Bank. Watanabe soon would assume his post as the first president of the ADB. In subsequent years, the MOF nominated a non-MOF old boy for the presidency only once out of six times.

Once the idea for a regional bank reached the level of intergovernmental discussions, the MOF further contributed to the ADB charter drafting process by dispatching two young officials to ECAFE headquarters in Bangkok in 1964-65 to work specifically on the charter. These officials, sent by Watanabe Makoto, were Chino Tadao and Nakahira Kosuke, both of whom rose in the 1990s to the pivotal positions for Japanese MDB policy—director general of the International Finance Bureau and vice minister for international affairs. After the ADB's inauguration, Nakahira served as special assistant to President Watanabe, succeeding Gyohten Toyoo, a premier "internationalist" in the ministry who also rose to vice minister for international affairs via the International Finance Bureau (IFB) in the 1980s. The MOF also assigned Chino to head the Osaka tax bureau in 1987, when Osaka hosted the twentieth anniversary of the ADB's founding.

In the bank's early years, yet another MOF official, seconded to Manila, was in charge of drafting the bank's by-laws, recruiting staff, and managing the budget. This person was Fujioka Masao, who, upon his return to the ministry rose to director general of the International Finance Bureau and then returned to Manila in 1982 as the fourth president of the ADB. The MOF claimed the Administration Department (now called the Budget, Personnel and Management Systems Department) as its "reserved post." The MOF considered this department the pivotal focal point of bank foundation-building in the early years because of its impact on the formulation of bank by-laws, budget outlays, and the recruitment of quality staff members. MOF-seconded personnel held the directorship for two decades before losing the "reserve post" in the late 1980s, though they regained the position in the 1990s.

The MOF continues to view the Budget, Personnel and Management Systems Department as key to the maintenance of the bank's administrative foundation. It therefore continues to pay close attention to administrative matters, as seen, for example, in the issue of "capping" staff salaries in the late 1980s. Unlike the World Bank, which uncapped salaries, ADB staff salaries cannot exceed the salary of the executive directors. Japan argued that "if the cap were lifted, there would be a loss of financial discipline. The ADB must maintain financial discipline—it takes pride in this—and capping is one way to do this as part of an overall policy."[51]

In other words, the Finance Ministry was intimately involved from the earliest stages of the ADB's conceptualization and establishment. The pattern of dispatching officials to the ADB and utilizing their experiences upon their return to the home ministry was visible from the beginning and institutionalized in the 1970s. This pattern took on added significance in the late 1980s and early 1990s. In 1985, the MOF began dispatching division director-level (*kacho*) personnel to Manila to serve as Japan's executive directors. The significance of this move for the ministry is that these officials are relatively young and return to the ministry to finish their careers. This contrasts with the EBRD and World Bank. EBRD executive directors come from the ranks of deputy director-generals of a bureau (*shingikan*), and IBRD directors come from the director-general level (*kyokucho*). These individuals are near the top of the ministry's career ladder and either leave the ministry upon their return to Tokyo, or serve in only a few more positions before retiring. ADB executive directors, on the other hand, bring their experiences and expertise back to the ministry's key MDB policymaking units. The relationship is so close that a former executive director stated, "I didn't consider the ADB appointment as any kind of great honor. I considered it as my fourth division director (*kacho*) post in the International Finance Bureau's Manila branch."⁵²

A look at the MOF's lineup in 1993 will illustrate the significance of the ADB for Japan's overall MDB policy. ADB veterans are conspicuous in the vice ministry for international affairs post and in the International Finance Bureau. Through the first half of 1993, Chino Tadao held the vice ministership for international affairs, the top international post and number three in the ministry, while Nakahira Kosuke directed the International Finance Bureau. Nakahira then succeeded Chino in July 1993 as vice minister. Among ADB executive directors, Kato Takatoshi, executive director from 1985 to 1987, served as Nakahira's IFB assistant director general and succeeded Nakahira as IFB director general; Mori Shoji, ADB executive director from 1987 to 1990, served a stint as director of the IFB's Coordination Division before being sent to Washington as financial attaché; Yagi Ken, ADB executive director from 1990 to 1992, served as director of IFB's Development Finance Division, which oversees bilateral ODA.

Among other ADB veterans, Ikawa Motomichi, who served in the Budget, Personnel and Management Systems Department from 1986 to 1989, returned to the IFB's International Organization Division, to the Development Policy Division, and then to the Coordination Division; a former special assistant to the ADB president, Sugisaki Shigemitsu, served in the IFB as deputy director general before moving on to the Tokyo Regional Tax Bureau; and Asakawa Masatsugu, special assistant the ADB president from 1989 to 1992, returned to the Financial Bureau, which oversees the Fiscal Investment and Loan Program, a major source of ODA for cofinancing with MDBs via the Export-Import Bank of Japan and the OECF.

This ADB-based lineup on the international side of the MOF structure contributes to the ministry's 1990s reputation as Asia-oriented. This "Asia Mafia" has roots in the IFB personnel's secondment experience at the ADB or in ADB-related activities. Vice minister Chino did not serve at the ADB, but his involvement in the Economic Commission for Asia and the Far East's (ECAFE) charter drafting activities, his stint in Osaka during the twentieth anniversary celebration, his strong support of the Central Asian Republics of the former Soviet Union, and his ministry's support for Chinese and Vietnamese aid were also catalysts for this "Asian" identity.

The reputation is perhaps exaggerated, for the ministry still focuses heavily on domestic issues and on its relationship with the G-7 nations, especially the United States. However, it may be no coincidence that the ministry began to speak out on Asian development issues in the World Bank and elsewhere with greater knowledge and self-confidence than in the past when this lineup came into existence. And it may be significant that many of these individuals served at the ADB at a time of great turmoil and contention with the United States, to be discussed shortly. The Asianist tinge does raise questions about whether the ADB was a major source of Japan's advocacy of the Asian development model and of Japan's increasing willingness to challenge the United States in the World Bank.

On the issue of professional staff presence, the ADB offers the most favorable environment for Japanese of all MDBs. Japanese occupy the presidency, possess their own executive director seat, and oversee the administration department. And unlike other MDBs, the Japanese staff is relatively numerous, often constituting 10 percent of the total professional staff (for example, 62 out of 600 staff in 1989). In addition, many Japanese staffers have committed their lives and careers to the bank, serving long years, with several of them having risen to top-level management positions. In 1992, Japanese nationals held the positions of assistant general counsel, four directorships (treasurer, the Programs Department, the Private Sector Department, and the Budget, Personnel and Management Systems Department), and two resident offices (Indonesia and Pakistan).

This situation, however, does not necessarily mean that suitable Japanese are easier to find and send to the bank. Usually filling the presidency is very difficult for the Japanese. Few Japanese are qualified for the position. Only a handful can be considered experts on Asian development, international finance, development issues, completely fluent in English, and comfortable living abroad. In addition, the location of the ADB is a major deterrent to prospective presidential candidates as well as to potential professional staffers.

As for professional staff, the same obstacles to easy recruitment of Japanese in the World Bank apply to the ADB. These problems tend to be ones applicable to Japanese participation in all international organizations. Yet the ADB poses a few additional problems, besides its locale. For example, the bank's focus on Asia is both a positive and negative recruitment inducement. The Japanese private sector's heightened interest in Asia at a time of creeping protectionism in the West enhances the ADB's utility as an information source. On the other hand, Japanese businesses are far more educated about Asian economies, societies, and cultures than in the past. Therefore, their need for the ADB is reduced. And even procurement of bank projects offers a mere fraction of profits earnable through the businesses' regular operations throughout the region.

On the whole, however, the Japanese find it much easier to dispatch staff to the ADB than to any other MDB. Proximity to Asia, a feeling of cultural affinity, an "Asian" versus "Western" or "Anglo-Saxon" atmosphere and management style serve as inducements. In recent years, one-third of Japanese personnel at the bank is seconded from Japanese government ministries, one-third from private sector firms, and one-third from individual recruitment efforts. Younger staff members are more conspicuous, as well as those who hope to make the ADB a career. Among staffers seconded by private firms, many are now staying at the bank longer, from three to five years rather than the previous average of two to three years. The ADB is one international forum where Japan does not complain much about staff or management presence.[53]

Japan's financial commitment to the bank, the other major institutional concern, is not questioned. Japan provides 16.435 percent of resources for the ordinary capital resources (OCR; as of December 31, 1992), usually at least one-third of Asian Development Fund (the soft-loan window) contributions (47 percent in 1989), and over half of total contributions to the Technical Assistance Special Fund (reaching $47.7 million, or 56.9 percent, in 1988). In 1988, Tokyo established a Japan Special Fund and a $700,000 ADB-Japan Scholarship Program for one to three years of graduate training at 11 institutions in nine member countries. In May 1990, Japan proposed a new environmental preservation fund, offering to contribute $4 million out of the $59 million allocated to the Japan Special Fund. Japan's private sector also supported the establishment of the ADB's Asian Finance and Investment Corporation (AFIC), offering to contribute 40 percent of total funds but scaling the offer back to 30 percent when some quarters expressed fears of Japanese domination. In the 1990s, Japan has responded to the bank's needs by focusing on poverty eradication programs through contributions to the ADF (37.7 percent of contributions). In 1992, Tokyo pledged to double contributions to the Japan Special Fund for environment programs and private sector activities. In addition, it created a scholarship fund for human resources development to set up seminars for top-level officials from financial institutions of developing countries.[54]

The government has contributed all that was asked of it by the bank, and, in fact, actually has wished to contribute even more. The major constraint has been an American refusal to agree to an increase in Japan's share. OCR contributions determine votes, and while Japan fulfills its commitments, the United States does not contribute its full share each year. Japan would therefore catapult into the number-one position if it increased OCR contributions. It has managed to bypass this problem through additional contributions to non-OCR funds, including the Asian Development Fund, the Technical Assistance Special Fund, and the Japan Special Fund. Contributions to these funds have no effect on vote shares. The United States thus manages to maintain nominal parity, with Japan holding 13.533 percent of total vote shares and the United States maintaining 13.105 percent (as of December 31, 1992) despite Japan's de facto role as principal financial pillar of the bank.

This facet of the U.S.-Japan relationship received renewed attention in the late 1980s, as Tokyo designated the ADB as one of the outlets for its recycling plan and strongly supported the ADB's periodic calls for capital increases and replenishments. As in the World Bank, Japan linked support for larger contributions to a special capital increase (SCI) to an increase in vote shares. In the ADB, Japan revealed a willingness to shed the coequal status with the United States in favor of predominance. The Japanese waged a campaign through most of the 1980s, and, in the end, the SCI, though smaller than desired, was approved. But, unlike the World Bank, Japan's status remained unchanged, as its bid for sole number-one status failed in the face of American (and other) opposition.

The Japanese strongly felt that the United States sought to maintain its speaking rights without paying for them, while Japan had to play along by showing restraint in its funding at a time the ADB required a large infusion of new capital. However, Japan had not intended an unfriendly takeover of the bank. Its goal had not been to humiliate the United States but merely to gain recognition for one of its major contributions to the international community. U.S.-Japan cooperation remained the priority: "When Japan sought top status with SCI, Japan raised the issue but the United States wanted [to maintain] equal shares, so Japan couldn't go it alone. Japan had not been thinking of leaving a reluctant United States behind."[55]

At the time, Japan did not have a policy agenda in mind in seeking the top spot, which raises the question of why it sought an increase in vote shares. Japan had not utilized its coleader status to push its development agenda openly. At this stage, studies of the Asian experience had not yet coalesced into a "model" or policy proposals. That would come after the 1986 SCI, and it would be manifested in the World Bank in the 1990s. In the meantime, at the ADB, Japan choose to rely on the twin pillars of its policy: support the management and cooperate with the United States. As MOF officials re-marked at the time,

Japan's general policy is to support the ADB president. MOF doesn't have specific things in mind to promote. Japan contributes, but it doesn't have knowledge of Asia. It does support concrete policies, like the environment, but it doesn't say much. It doesn't push anything that is opposed by DMCs [developing member countries].[56]

Japan and MOF don't know Asia, but the ADB management does. The board makes policy; it sets the general direction. Japan doesn't know Asia very well, so why make trouble on the board?[57]

However, both of these pillars were shaken in the 1980s. Both the bank management, especially the president, and the United States made life extremely difficult for Japan. Tokyo found itself hard-pressed to provide unqualified support to an independently minded Japanese president, and it found the United States increasingly eager to use the bank for its own diplomatic agenda and increasingly intransigent in its development approach. In response, Japan developed its own policy agenda in the region while attempting to mitigate the clashes within the bank.

On the policy front, Japan increasingly sought to use the ADB as a diplomatic instrument during the late 1980s and 1990s despite American obstacles. On China, Japan supported sanctions in the ADB after the 1989 Tiananmen Square incident. Its apparently contradictory stance—efforts to lift sanctions in G-7 fora, to restore World Bank loans, and to cease ADB loans—reflected its multiple objectives in the ADB: to renew Japanese ODA to China by avoiding open clashes with G-7 nations, to maintain friendly relations with Beijing, to repair damages to U.S.-Japan relations caused by clashes within the bank and by the overall escalation of trade and financial friction, and to retain close relations with Asian nations that opposed harsh sanctions against China. The World Bank restored BHN and humanitarian aid flows to China, but the ADB could not follow suit easily since Beijing was not allowed to draw from the ADB's soft-loan window. Only ordinary capital resources, or non-BHN aid, could flow to Beijing, and Washington frowned on resumption of any aid to China.

Japan also hoped to restore economic aid to Vietnam. Tokyo froze its bilateral aid package after the 1979 Vietnamese invasion of Cambodia. Japan has increasingly considered Vietnam important in structuring a viable peace in Cambodia, in balancing China to the north, and in tapping natural resources and developing a potentially huge domestic market. The peace and stability of the region also depends on the promotion of closer relations between Hanoi and the ASEAN nations, a Japanese concern since the 1978 Fukuda Doctrine.

Japan sought to restore aid to Hanoi through the ADB by utilizing the Japan Special Fund (JSF), which it established in the ADB in 1988. Donor nations set up special funds to be administered by the bank, and they are allowed to specify uses of these resources. Japan, with the support of the ADB president, sought to open the door to Vietnamese aid through this route. The United States, however, objected strongly to the use of the JSF. The Japanese were aware of the impact of the missing-in-action issue in American domestic politics, but they still considered the use of the fund legitimate and justified. As one MOF official complained, resources in the JSF were "100 percent Japanese. They had nothing to do with American taxpayers."[58] However, Japan would have to await the decision of the Clinton administration to allow limited contact with Hanoi through the World Bank in 1994. In the meantime, however, Tokyo did proceed to lift the bilateral aid sanctions and restore ODA flows in November of 1992.

On the issue of the Central Asia Republics (CARs), Japan took the lead in getting these five nations—Kazakhstan, Uzbekistan, Tajikistan, Kyrgyzstan, and Turkmenistan—on the DAC list in November 1992. This step was necessary to justify Japanese allocation of ODA to the region. Japan also initiated a move to have the CARs inducted into the ADB as regional members. The step would be unprecedented, for the CARs were already members of another regional development bank, the EBRD. The United States initially questioned the inclusion of the CARs on the DAC list (reportedly concerned that their inclusion meant Israeli exclusion) and strongly opposed the suggestion of dual membership. After intensive lobbying by Japan and others, the United States supported CAR inclusion on the list, and, within a year, the Japanese noted with satisfaction the nearly unanimous support for the idea of dual membership.

In the 1990s, Japan supported the entry into the ADB of new members that hold special significance for Japanese diplomacy. Mongolia and Turkey, for example, became members in 1991. Japan has practically adopted Mongolia as a prototype for its assistance for economic and political reform. Tokyo chaired a multinational donors meeting for Mongolia and provided technical assistance to promote economic and financial restructuring and briefings on the requirements of democratization. Turkey is one of the reasons for Japan's heavy involvement with the CARs, since Tokyo views Ankara as a moderate Islamic force that is vying for influence in the region against fundamentalist Islamic regimes, especially Iran. Japan stepped up bilateral aid to Turkey after President Suleiman Demiral's visit to Tokyo in late 1993 and considered a novel aid arrangement: The Japanese Export-Import Bank would provide funds to Turkey, which would, in turn, distribute it in the CARs.

Iran, perhaps Turkey's main competitor for influence in the CAR region, would like to join the ADB. Its efforts have met with strong opposition, especially from the United States, which considers Iran a terrorist state. Japan has not taken a public position on this issue, but one can surmise that Tokyo, though supportive of Washington's stance, eventually would prefer to see Iran enter the bank. Tokyo views the opening up of Iran as a necessary step toward encouraging greater moderation in its external policies. Japan took its first bilateral step in this direction by restarting ODA flows to Tehran in 1993 after an 18-year hiatus despite American unease.

Russian membership also may be a future possibility, since Russia has dispatched observers to recent ADB annual meetings. However, Japan can be expected to oppose such membership unless Russia enters as a nonregional—that is, nonborrowing—member. Japan remains wary of Russia's huge capital needs, preferring to maintain the bank's focus on traditional Asian borrowers and CAR nations. The Japanese are less than enthusiastic about Russian aid, given unresolved bilateral issues such as the Northern Territories, which are claimed by Japan but occupied by Russian military forces, and Russian dumping of nuclear waste materials in waters surrounding Japan. Russian aid will be analyzed in the next section on the EBRD and as a case study in Chapter 5.

Clashes within the ADB proved more vexing for the Japanese. Problems with both the president and the United States involved policy differences, which are expected between sovereign nations and between states and international agencies. Within the ADB, unlike within the World Bank, the added dimension of personality clashes within exacerbated U.S.-Japan relations and U.S.-ADB relations in the 1980s. Again, Japan found itself caught between its two policy pillars—support for the president and cooperation with the United States often became a contradiction in terms.

After the 1981 inauguration of the Reagan administration, U.S. executive directors embarked on an especially assertive promotion of values it deemed universal, applicable to all regions and MDBs. The administration's emphasis on private sector development and private flows rather than public sector guidance and official aid was filtered through the strong voices of executive directors whose knowledge and expertise of Asia and Asian development were, among the Japanese, suspect. The strong insistence on the correctness of the American view of development also came, in the view of many Japanese officials, from representatives of a country that assumed a right to make demands without paying its full share to the bank's coffers. American officials may retort that the United States contributes mightily to the region both economically and especially in the realm of security commitments, but, as one MOF official observed in the 1990s, "That was during the Cold War. The Cold War is over."

MOF officials compared statements by the ADB American executive directors with those emanating from executive directors' offices at other international institutions. They concluded that the policies expressed were consistent across MDBs but that the personal style of the American directors at the ADB differed greatly. The combination of American assertiveness of universal principles and the strong personality of American representatives influenced two of the most notable developments in Japan's ADB and MDB policy: the increasing uneasiness with the American development approach, which culminated in Japan's call for the World Bank to study the experiences of Asian nations, and the appointment of younger, more assertive Japanese executive directors to the ADB. The Japanese, fearing irreparable damage to the ADB's reputation and operations, found cooperation with the United States more and more problematic in the 1980s.

During that time the Japanese had few complaints about the American emphasis on the importance of market forces, privatization, and liberalization. Discussions in the ADB echoed these themes. However, Japan increasingly questioned the neoclassical model and its appropriateness for the Asian experience or for regional needs. The Japanese resented what they saw as inflexible, arrogant American efforts to apply these principles universally, in textbook fashion, to Asian countries that often lacked a strong private sector and depended on strong government guidance and a degree of protectionism for infant industries. These themes emerged in the ADB crucible of the 1980s and carried over to the World Bank in the Japan's call for a study of the East Asian miracles. Many of the arguments heard in the IBRD originated in the ADB. In other words, Japan's experience in the ADB during the 1980s may have served as the testing ground for its challenge to the United States and the orthodoxy in the IBRD.

Japanese arguments in the ADB, as expressed by the MOF's ADB policymakers, are similar to later assertions in the World Bank:

> Privatization must fit the appropriate conditions; for example, it may be appropriate in Thailand, Indonesia, Malaysia, but questionable in Bangladesh and Nepal.[59]

> America's support for policy dialogue was tough. This is the Anglo-Saxon approach, the World Bank approach. But the ADB should take an Asian approach. The World Bank deals with the world and does not especially understand Asian thinking. It has a Western philosophy: yes–no, give–not

give. They have brilliant young economists, but they don't understand Third World societies or psychology at all.[60]

Policy dialogue is important, but you must base it on Asian experiences. Then it's okay. But nonregional countries look at Asian development in a textbook fashion, with textbook knowledge. The United States asks Japan to cooperate on this basis, but Japan takes a lukewarm attitude.[61]

The United States emphasizes program lending. That's not a bad direction, but the question is, what kind of policy dialogue do they want? U.S. policy dialogue is based on the belief in the market, liberalization, private sector. That is, if only countries liberalize, everything will be all right. But developing countries are in different stages, especially in Asia. Each has distinctive characteristics. This should be the basis of policy dialogue.[62]

It is not good to do what the United States does by pressuring DMCs based on ideology. Asia is not Latin America. There the United States acts as a consultant or doctor and intervenes in a country's management—and look what happened. Latin America followed U.S. philosophy, and it has become the world's baggage.[63]

The Asian development model did not constitute the focal point of the clash of views. In the 1980s, it was too early for that, since Japan's conceptualization of a model had not yet matured. That would occur around the turn of the decade, when Japan would carry the model to the World Bank. From Japan's perspective, the ADB's approach, not the IBRD, accords well with its preferred development strategy. The ADB focuses on project loans, recognizes the importance of infrastructure, allows for state guidance and two-step loans, and recognizes uneven levels of market efficiency and private sector development in the region. The MOF strongly supports specific ADB policies and direction: the eradication of poverty, economic reform aimed at strengthening market economies, support for privatization and inducing larger private flows, and special concern for the environment.

In other words, the "Anglo-American orthodoxy" is not as strong in the Asian Bank, and, therefore, Japan has little need to emphasize the Asian development alternative. Japan's advocacy of Asian development tenets was designed primarily to provide a counterpoint to the American executive directors. In Manila, the United States was pushing against the "Asian" orthodoxy, while in the IBRD, Japan pushed against the "Anglo-Saxon" orthodoxy. Again, Japan's defense of an Asian-type development strategy in the ADB provided the testing ground for its later foray in the World Bank. At that earlier stage, Japan's own development experience provided the main source of its "ideas." In the 1960s and 1970s, Japan's model was a rather simple view that developing nations should follow the sequence it followed in its rise to economic great power status: solidification of the nation's agricultural base, a shift to light and then heavy industries, followed by a shift to tertiary industries. In the early years, Japan felt that Asia was in too much of a hurry to industrialize before its agricultural base had been solidified.[64] Japanese awareness of the Asian development process throughout the 1980s led to updating, revising, and perhaps the merging of Japan's concept of development with the lessons of the Asian experience.

During this crucial period in the late 1980s Japan focused on the role of the state in economic planning, developed a cautious attitude about rapid privatization, saw the utility of protectionism at early stages of development, and questioned the viability of a purely unregulated market mechanism. It developed a sense of its "mission" as the source of technology and knowledge for Asia, just as the advanced Western nations had served that function for Japan in the past. This is especially notable on issues such as the environment and financial mechanisms such as two-step loans. Japan began to cite its experience in successfully taming the environmental pollution engendered by the high growth of the 1960s; it began to stress government leadership in forging a private and public sector cooperation that mitigated the most egregious cases of pollution. And the Japanese, aware of their own experience with World Bank loans, referred approvingly to the ADB's two-step loans that funneled capital to the private sector through public agencies as the "traditional operations" of the ADB.[65]

In sum, personality and policy differences accentuated difficulties in U.S.-Japan relations throughout the 1980s. Japanese officials downplay the policy differences and play up the personality factor. However, it seems clear that both played an equal role in causing a rift between Tokyo and Washington. Personality clashes may have exacerbated the policy differences, but there is no denying the emergence of a gulf between American and Japanese conceptualizations of development strategies and philosophies. Personality, however, does seem the primary cause of difficulties between Japan and the bank president.

During the Fujioka Masao (1982-89) era, Tokyo found itself increasingly mired in intra-bank matters. Fujioka's tenure presented an especially vexing problem for the MOF. He was one its own, a former director general of the International Finance Bureau who worked on the ADB's establishment process and was seconded to Manila during the early years as Administration Department director. He therefore understood both the MOF and ADB well. The MOF considered Fujioka as what Japanese refer to as a "one-man" president, someone who tended toward unilateralism rather than the traditional Japanese management style of consultation and consensus. "Fujioka thought of the ADB as his own bank," according to a knowledgeable MOF official. "Fujioka wanted to do things his own way, on his own—even if it meant collision."[66] Fujioka, a product of the most conservative and traditionally "Japanese" of Japanese ministries, proved to be a singularly "un-Japanese" president who adopted a "Western," top-down management style.

He actually played a dual role for Japan. On the one hand, he spearheaded policy changes favored by Tokyo, engaging in consultation and cooperation. The agreement to allow the People's Republic of China membership in the ADB without ousting Taiwan was a example of Fujioka's shuttle diplomacy that carried him to both Beijing and Taipei via Tokyo.[67] He also requested that the Japanese government second a China expert to the bank; the Foreign Ministry eventually sent an official, though not a China specialist. Some MOF officials consider Fujioka's successful handling of the China-Taiwan controversy as his greatest accomplishment.

In such cases, the Japanese could follow their traditional policy of supporting the president. In this context, the MOF felt that a Fujioka-type chief executive was just what the ADB needed:

> International organizations are a world of power. Fujioka was capable and able to issue orders and keep a tight ship. If you don't have leadership from the president, then the vice presidents will exert power. That's what usually happens. The president must exert power, or else even the managing directors will start taking power.[68]

The MOF appreciated Fujioka's ability to run a tight ship, as many ADB and ex-ADB staff members noted that vice presidents under Fujioka played a restrained role in bank affairs. Fujioka was said to have instructed vice presidents to acquiesce in favor of presidential initiative and leadership, prompting, according to many observers, the incumbent vice president to leave the bank soon after Fujioka assumed the presidency. Since the mid-1980s, the ADB has had three vice presidents, in charge of Projects, Operations, and Finance and Administration, with none of them wielding the power and influence of their predecessors of the 1960s and 1970s.

On the other hand, the president did not hesitate to sidestep or bait the MOF. According to one MOF official, "Fujioka's attitude was: I am the president of the ADB. I am an international civil servant, not an MOF official."[69] Fujioka was even quoted as saying "In the end I can go [directly] to the Ministry of Finance. They are my boys; I trained them."[70] For example, Fujioka complained bitterly about the MOF seconding an official he considered too young to the Budget, Personnel and Management Systems Department, and he terminated the ministry's hold over a position occupied by MOF officials since the bank's founding. Instead, he appointed a close non-Japanese associate to the post. In general, Fujioka was viewed as highly involved in personnel selection matters: "Fujioka never accepted recommendations on staffing from others. It was a kiss of death to be recommended to him."[71]

The creation of the ADB's Asian Finance and Investment Corporation resulted from the president approaching the Japanese private sector directly, ignoring the MOF and forcing an initially skeptical ministry to approve the president's initiative. The MOF was "neutral to slightly positive, but didn't discuss the idea much. The idea was good, but it was not done in the Japanese style. In the end, MOF supported it because private flows were necessary as the basis for future Bank activities and because Fujioka's plan was already underway."[72]

From the perspective of the MOF,

Fujioka was a forceful person. He had ideas and would try to push them through. However, he did not do much groundwork (*nemawashi*). Things would have been smoother if he had done more *nemawashi*. This applies to Japan. He didn't do much *nemawashi* in Japan either. He would think up an idea by himself, come up with a concept, and then move on his own.[73]

Fujioka's defiance of Japan went only so far, however. Japan's policy of supporting ADB presidents provided him, to some extent, with the leeway to be forceful, especially against the United States: "Fujioka had the support of the Japanese government," according to a former non-Japanese board member. "With that support, he could take the lead and try to do things. He had the will and the power to try things, but the United States would come and put roadblocks in the way."[74] And despite his habit of taking Japan for granted, Fujioka often seemed to give it special consideration. For example, he reportedly criticized the seconding practice for all nationalities except the Japanese, arguing that Japan's case was different, and that *shukko* was therefore justified.[75]

However, Fujioka did understand the limits of his power: "Fujioka looks at each country and doesn't follow the U.S. lead. He always cites the

Charter. But he would acquiesce if the United States and Japan said no."[76] In fact, his reliance on the Japanese government constituted the main restraint on his actions. As tensions between the "one-man" president and the board of directors increased, the MOF came to serve as the intermediary between the warring factions. According to a former non-Japanese executive director, "The only way to get to Fujioka was through the Japanese government. The United States, Australia, and others would go to the MOF in Tokyo at a high level and get the MOF to influence Fujioka."[77] This is confirmed by a former Japanese executive director: "The United States would come to Japan and ask if something could be done about Fujioka. The MOF would then try to smooth things over with Fujiioka."[78]

Fujioka won reelection to a second five-year term with Japanese support, but retired in 1989. In the end, the rancor and bitterness in the bank, accompanied by charges of mismanagement, forced the Japanese to ease him out of office. Fujioka greatly complicated Japan's preferred policy course of supporting the ADB president. Despite his influence over the MOF, in the struggle between the president of an international organization and the MOF, the Japanese government prevailed.

The MOF replaced Fujioka with a more consensual, traditional "Japanese-style" president. The result has been a softening of Japan's policy in the 1990s. With the problems of Fujioka and cantankerous American executive directors behind them, the Japanese sought to restore the pre-Fujioka status quo. Its appointment of Tarumizu Kimimasa was based on a lack of candidates for the position plus a hope that Tarumizu's management style would bring tranquility back to a troubled bank. Tarumizu was considered a typical "Japanese" leader with his willingness to listen to others and his preference for consensus decision making rather than unilateralism. The MOF considered him a strong antidote to Fujioka's "one-man" rule.

The Tarumizu era, however, provided the MOF with another set of problems. Tarumizu had little international experience. He had served a stint at the Washington embassy, in the International Finance Bureau, a decade before leaving for Manila, and directed the Customs and Tariffs Bureau. His MOF career had been domestically oriented, with very little exposure to international finance, Asian affairs, or development issues. As one means of compensating for these weaknesses, observers had assumed that Tarumizu would rely heavily on ADB vice presidents. However, he was hit with a major crisis involving a vice president at the beginning of his presidency, a crisis from which he would not recover.

ADB presidents choose their own vice presidents based on recommendations from member states. In Tarumizu's case, however, he initially refused to accept what appeared to be a fait accompli by the United States, which nominated and strongly insisted on only one candidate, a long-time ADB hand from the U.S. Treasury Department. Tarumizu faced an adamant United States, and attempted a delaying tactic by extending the incumbent vice president's stay for six months. But in the end he was forced to accept Bill Thomson, especially when the MOF, Tarumizu's former home, failed to support his objections. Japan supported the United States rather than its own old boy. Tarumizu then attempted to shift vice presidential assignments, moving Thomson from the operations vice presidency to the administration vice presidency. This too failed, and Tarumizu's defeat was complete, leading to reports that he would serve out Fujioka's remaining term and resign.[79]

The image of a bullied, powerless president, coupled with his own personal management style, set the stage for what resulted—an administration that had difficulty gaining the respect of the board and the bank staff. Even MOF officials privately acknowledge problems resulting from Tarumizu's management style:

> Tarumizu was not the type to pull the bank along, nor was he a reformist. He would discuss, lose his way, and not make decisions. The United States would therefore try to get the ADB to go its way. Fujioka would have pulled in the opposite direction. Tarumizu, however, would not move. He would not consent to or approve a move. Japan would then try to get him to move a certain way, but he would not move.[80]

Even on the Thomson issue, the MOF found Tarumizu difficult to fathom: "Tarumizu was puzzling because you couldn't tell whether he said yes or no. He said he was just asking about Thomson, but in reality, he opposed Thomson." This comment about Tarumizu's "inscrutable" Japanese management style, learned at the MOF, comes from a Japanese MOF official.[81] Ironically, the MOF had problems dealing with the traditionally "Japanese" Tarumizu as much as the "un-Japanese" Fujioka.

Tarumizu served the remaining two years of Fujioka's term and was reelected in 1991 for a full five-year term. But, unsurprisingly, he announced his intention to retire, citing health reasons. The MOF felt that someone in between Fujioka and Tarumizu's personalities and management styles would be the ideal candidate, and the name of Vice Minister Chino emerged as a likely candidate. However, Chino refused the assignment, as did all other candidates approached by the ministry, including all recent vice ministers for international affairs. A candidate at the vice ministerial level would be highly qualified to address the feeling that the ADB drifted directionless the past few years, but there is a widespread assumption in Japan that vice ministers consider the ADB presidency a step down in status. The MOF eventually nominated another MOF old boy as Tarumizu's replacement. Sato Mitsuo assumed the presidency in November 1993, leaving his post as vice president of the Tokyo Stock Exchange. Sato's background resembles Tarumizu's, with a stint abroad (though at the IMF rather than the Washington embassy), director generalship of the Customs and Tariffs Bureau, and a stint in the IFB about a decade before going to Manila. Sato, however, is considered more of an internationalist than Tarumizu, although descriptions of his type and personality are strikingly similar to Tarumizu's heard in 1989.

Of course, the MOF thinking resembles the adage that it is fighting the last war, merely responding to the previous president's personality and record. The Ministry understands that the problem rests not just with the president but with the quality of vice presidents, the particular makeup of the board of directors, and the (overly) strong upper echelon of the staff. But the MOF also realizes that problems happen on a specific president's watch and sought to address the problem in 1993. However, the paucity of candidates proved an insurmountable obstacle, and some observers attribute the quick announcement of Sato's nomination to the MOF's desire to continue to appoint old boys in the face of a challenge from the Bank of Japan.[82]

In the 1990s, the MOF maintains its traditional policy of supporting the ADB president, but on the whole, it seems to be putting greater weight on the other pillar of its ADB policy—U.S.-Japan cooperation. Japanese policy in the ADB reflected efforts to mitigate the rising tensions between the United States and Japan on trade and financial issues outside the bank. In Manila, with the passing of Fujioka and the abrasive U.S. executive directors, and the ascension of an MOF vice minister considered strongly pro-American (Utsumi Makoto), the opportunity seemed ripe to restore closer ties. U.S.-Japan relations cooled down considerably in the 1990s, with differences focused more on policy than personality. The president became less of a contentious issue between Tokyo and Washington, and entreaties to the MOF to restrain the president ceased. This seems to confirm the statement by an MOF official that "the president is the key factor in U.S.-Japan relations within the ADB."[83]

Ironically, with the president less of a contentious issue in bilateral relations, Japanese activism was now spurred by the opposite problem from the 1980s: America's apparent indifference toward the bank. From Tokyo's perspective, after the intense, almost intrusive participation in bank affairs under Reagan, successive administrations downgraded the ADB. In the waning years of the Bush administration, the MOF noted less activism on the part of the United States and disarray in the American ADB policymaking apparatus, notably the lack of communication between the U.S. executive director's office and the Treasury Department. In the early months of the Clinton administration in 1993, the Japanese received the impression that the United States had downgraded the ADB because Under Secretary of the Treasury Lawrence Summers failed to attend the 1993 ADB annual meeting (but appeared at the African Development Bank meeting) and because the delegation that did go lashed out at the proposed capital increase for the bank. Also, the new administration left the executive director position unfilled until November, in the meantime entrusting the office to a youthful surrogate. Clinton tried to signal renewed commitment to the ADB by appointing an Asian-American woman to the post immediately after the Tokyo Summit of 1993, but it is clear that America's perceived lack of interest, rather than intrusiveness, provides a major impetus to Japanese activism.

On the other hand, one could perhaps accuse Japan of downgrading the ADB as well in the 1990s. It did not spend the time or exert the energy necessary to recruit a big-name presidential candidate suitable for the requirements of the ADB presidency. Nor has Japan articulated its own vision for an ADB that is obviously sailing into a future Asia in the throes of historic changes. Therefore, as the ADB prepared for a changing of the presidential guard, neither of the two major forces in the bank is credited with exhibiting any leadership or direction: ". . .even the Japanese seemed unsure of the direction in which the institution should be headed. As for the Americans, their attendance was low level and barely coherent. The Clinton administration has yet to develop a policy for multilateral institutions in general, let alone for the ADB."[84]

Also, some MOF officials consider the switch to division director-level appointments to the executive directorship a considerable downgrading of the bank. Traditional directors tended to be senior MOF officials prepared to make the ADB their final ministry assignments. The younger directors often found it difficult to confront an ADB president who happened to be a senior old boy. The task of challenging the president, never easy for even senior MOF officials, was softened by Japan's practice of raising objections and points prior to, not during, board meetings, in private and not in public. One MOF official, in an interview with the author, referred to Fujioka as *sempai* (a senior or mentor), while one of the younger ADB executive directors had been reportedly criticized for referring to Tarumizu as "boss."

On the other hand, the time and age differences between the *kacho* class and MOF old boys is significant, diluting the interpersonal ties between virtually two generations of MOF officials.

However, the MOF's main reason for relegating the director to a division-level appointment had been to bring assertiveness and visibility to Japan and to act as mediator among the warring bank factions. The *kacho* class in the MOF is instrumental in policy formulation and implementation, and one of the primary skills necessary to be an effective division director is the ability to mediate and coordinate personnel and policy. These were the very skills necessary for a country that decided to play an intermediary role in the bank, and the contentious situation between the United States and Japan and between the United States and the president seemed to cry out for such skills.

One wonders how effective this strategy had been, or whether the departure of Fujioka and the American directors was the main reason for the ensuing détente. Japanese directors did seem able to hold the line, preventing any significant deterioration in U.S.-Japan relations, and did appear to calm the waters between the president and the United States. But one also wonders about the possible negative effects of these difficult mediation efforts on Japanese executive director attitudes toward the United States once they returned to the ministry. Did the unpleasant experience in the 1980s dealing with what they viewed as inflexible and universal U.S. policy positions espoused by what they saw as young, naive, and obnoxious American representatives influence the ministry's decision to challenge the U.S. development orthodoxy in the World Bank in the 1990s?

In sum, Japan's relationship with the ADB remains intimate. The crux of its policy remains the financial and managerial health of the bank, and the U.S.-Japan partnership on the board. Because of the bank's Asian focus, and because of its particular history with the ADB—which links Japan's reputation with that of the Bank's—Tokyo may have felt that the stakes were higher and the opportunities greater. Japan was perhaps more willing to challenge the United States with what it might have considered home field advantage. Unlike the World Bank, Japan did not consider the ADB an "Anglo-Saxon" institution but rather an Asian institution that should respect Asian sensitivities, including those of Japan. Therefore, while carefully taking into account American sensitivities, and unlike its behavior in the World Bank, Japan strove for nominal hegemony and de facto partnership with the United States in the ADB. While its attempt to attain top shareholder status proved abortive, most observers would agree that Japan is, de facto, the leading shareholder.

The lesson Japan learned in the ADB is the same as in other MDBs, and in its foreign policy in general: Enhanced national status requires more than money, positions, and staff. It also requires "ideas" and deeds. Japan also learned a second lesson: Japanese ideas and deeds can trigger resentment and opposition. The ADB may have been the training ground for later ideas and deeds in the World Bank and other international fora, including the EBRD.

THE EUROPEAN BANK FOR RECONSTRUCTION
AND DEVELOPMENT: THE SEARCH FOR RELEVANCE

The EBRD sprouted in the fertile soil of the political and economic hothouse of post–1989 Europe. It was the first international institution created in the post–Cold War era, following the collapse of the political and economic systems of East and Central European nations and embracing the dissolution of the Soviet Union. The bank is a European idea, the president is French, its location is England, the United States is the largest shareholder, its target countries are East and Central Europe plus the nations of the former Soviet Union, and its mandate is overtly political rather than purely developmental. Its history and this configuration explain Japan's active yet relatively peripheral role in the new bank.

The dedication to the idea of a regional financial organization by the founders and the utilization of the existing MDBs as models largely explain the speed with which the bank came into existence. European founders were motivated by the significance for their future of the sudden collapse of East Europe and the Soviet Union. The resulting instability held significant implications for regional security interests, and some West Europeans worried about the potential influx of refugees from their eastern neighbors. The historic and strategically critical developments in neighboring countries also came at a time of economic difficulties in West Europe, especially in a Germany wrestling with the unexpectedly mushrooming expenditures associated with the unification of East and West. No nation alone could meet the tremendous needs of the Second World for economic, financial, and technical assistance. Multilateralism, however limited, offered the only escape from bilateral and regional burdens.

The EBRD was conceived in France as the offspring of a marriage between the organization and values of the existing MDBs, the new themes and imperatives of the post–Cold War era, and French concern about Germany's economic might in Europe.[85] The European Community (EC) endorsed the idea at Strasbourg during its annual meeting in December 1989. Negotiations ensued in three plenary meetings between January and April of 1990, with the signing of the Articles of Agreement on May 29. Operations commenced in April 1991.

The EBRD is unique among MDBs, mainly in its overtly political mandate and its emphasis on the private sector. Its Articles of Agreement clearly state that the purpose of the bank is to promote the principles of multiparty democracy, pluralism, respect for human rights, the rule of law, and market economies. Other MDBs expressly forbid political considerations when making economic decisions, but the EBRD requires a commitment by recipient nations to political and economic reforms as a condition for funds (and holds the right to deny or withdraw funds in the event of noncompliance or a violation of these conditions).

Unlike the World Bank and like the ADB, Japan was present at the creation of the EBRD, participating in the establishment process, though as a nonregional charter member. But unlike the ADB, Japan did not take any initiatives in conceptualizing or planning for the bank, nor did it contribute much to the establishment of the bank's bylaws, management, or organization. And yet, because of the unique character of the institution, the EBRD calls on Japan to play the most openly political role of all MDBs in a region Japan understands little. The bank thus tests Japan's pledge to play a formative role in the creation of a new world order, but it also may symbolize the limits, both domestic and external, of Japan's global diplomacy.

Japan's participation in the bank's establishment activities can be characterized best as an invitation to participate. Japan basically responded to Europe's initiative-taking. Like the United States, Japan had no role in the initial conceptualization of the idea for a new regional bank, but unlike the United States, the MOF viewed the new proposal favorably when announced. Officials felt that the bank would play a major role in aiding the transition to market economies in East Europe. For Japan, the bank would be especially useful because "East Europe was distant geographically, in human relations, in historical relations. Japanese cooperation efforts would be difficult. And some Europeans feared a Japanese [economic] invasion of East Europe as well as West Europe, so an international financial institution was a positive factor."[86]

A few in the ministry argued in favor of maintaining some distance from the new bank, but most officials recognized its potential role as a source of information for a region they knew relatively little about: "MOF did not possess much knowledge about East Europe, or the former Soviet Union; therefore, the EBRD could be used to find out what was going on. There was a strong desire to find out through the use of the EBRD."[87]

There was also the practical reason for supporting the new bank: The Japanese questioned "whether we can channel economic assistance to these countries most effectively solely through bilateral means. Consequently, making the bank a central core of our support for this region seems both the most efficient and most useful means of our contributions to this region."[88]

In contrast, the United States strongly opposed the new bank initially. "The United States thought it was not a good idea," according to a Treasury Department official. "The United States hoped it would go away." The Treasury Department opposed a perceived proliferation of regional development banks, leading to unnecessary overlapping of duties and foci. If new funds were necessary to service East Europe, Treasury officials preferred the establishment of a new fund in the World Bank.[89] However, "the Bush administration's initial doubts about the need for a new bank were overcome by the conviction that the EC would create the EBRD with or without U.S. support."[90]

Once it was clear that France would push ahead with the idea, the United States decided to join the establishment process in an effort to shape the bank more to its liking. On the other hand, Japan had relatively little to say. For Tokyo, it was clear from the start that this was to be a European, especially French, show,[91] and this colored its attitude throughout the talks. Japan found this understandable and largely acceptable, while the same realization spurred the United States into action. The United States and Japan thus entered the establishment process with different perspectives, and throughout the proceedings that led to the signing of the Articles of Agreement, Japan, with few substantive demands of its own, chose a middle course between the Americans and Europeans, often playing a mediatory role.

If we look at our three policy arenas—institutional, diplomatic, and development—we find that the diplomatic context of the EBRD overshadows the other two categories. Japan's institutional interests were specific and limited, its diplomatic interests paramount, and its development strategy for the region rooted deeply in Japanese assumptions about the nation's own development experience.

Japan's institutional and organizational status within the bank resembled the traditional form of its MDB policy—financial contributions without many management or staff positions and without a loud say in bank business.

During the founding negotiations, Japan discussed the level of its shares primarily with France, which suggested that Japan, as a G-7 nation, enter the bank on a par with West European members. The MOF had decided that if each of the major European members held an expected share of 10 percent, Japan should seek either 6 percent or an equivalent 10 percent.

Japan thus found the EC suggestion of parity, at 8.5 percent, satisfactory. The Americans pushed for top shareholder status, at 10 percent, and while there were rumors that Japan desired parity with the United States, MOF negotiators deny this was ever Japan's intention.[92]

The United States obtained the largest shareholder status and the second most powerful management position, vice president for merchant banking. Europeans, however, hold the majority of management positions and control 51 percent of bank votes, which enables them to push their agenda forward on a daily basis if votes are taken. Japan is entitled to its own executive director, whose office houses four people, but no Japanese national sits in a top management seat and few have joined the professional staff (some 14 out of approximately 700 by the middle of 1993). The United States (10 percent) and Japan (8.5 percent) together do hold a veto power on certain significant issues that require 85 percent of the total vote, but this is largely symbolic since, as in other MDBs, consensus is the preferred decision-making method.

Japan's financial contributions are unsurprising and unexceptional. At 8.5 percent of the total share, Japan's OCR subscription comes to ECU (European Currency Unit) 851,750 (about $1 billion), with ECU 355,520 to be paid in. The initial capitalization was $10 billion (ECU $12 billion). The Japanese report that France originally proposed $20 billion, America countered by suggesting $5 billion, with $10 billion the compromise. The United States then fought for the right to contribute in dollars rather than just ECUs, to counter exchange rate fluctuations, and Japan followed suit for yen payments. For Japan, the uniqueness of the EBRD lies not in Tokyo's financial contributions per se or the low level of management and staff presence, but in the fact that the EBRD is the only MDB that accepts subscriptions and contributions in Japanese yen.

As in the case of other MDBs, Japan has contributed additional funds to supplement its ordinary subscription. The EBRD, unlike the World Bank and ADB, lacks a soft-loan window, but in July 1991, Japan created the Japan-Europe Cooperation Fund (JECF) to be administered by the EBRD. Japan contributed ECU 5.6 million ($6.75 million) to the JECF in 1991 and increased the 1992 contribution by 80 percent, reaching nearly ECU 10 million ($12.4 million). JECF funds are designed to serve as technical assistance to find, prepare, and execute loans to projects, and to support the recruitment and training of Japanese consultants.

Japan participated in the drafting of the EBRD charter, but those involved can point to no major input, except perhaps for the wording of some clauses. In some ways, the EBRD Articles could be expected to meet with Japanese approval since many of the organizational articles were borrowed from the World Bank and especially from the ADB charter.[93] The French, pressed for time in drawing up a draft bank charter, relied heavily on the ADB because of its reputation for good management, its inclusion of nonregional members, and the fact that it was the last of the regional development banks, which implied that the ADB had been able to include the best features and avoid the pitfalls of its predecessors.

One provision that the EBRD did not borrow from the ADB, or any other international financial institution, was its overt political mandate. As mentioned, the EBRD conditions loans on the acceptance of political conditions by the potential recipient. During the negotiation phase, Japan was one of the two participants that "expressed doubts" about political conditionality, citing the ADB and IBRD Articles of Agreement as examples of the separation of politics from development. Negotiators recognized the need for political conditions in the case of Communist nations moving toward democratization and free enterprise systems, but Japan had problems with statutory conditions and questioned whether the board of directors was the proper forum for these kinds of political questions.[94]

Japan ultimately supported the general consensus that favored political conditionality and the sanctions allowed the EBRD in cases of noncompliance. In many ways, EBRD conditionality spares Japan from establishing its own political conditions, something the MOF is reluctant to do bilaterally or on its own. Japan simply is not experienced or knowledgeable enough about East Europe to begin dictating conditions. It can follow the policies of the EBRD, entrusting the Political Department to lay down the line to the recipients. The EBRD thus serves as a buffer to direct involvement in political conditionality; it is the EBRD that engages in political conditionality, not Japan.

Subsequent to the bank's opening, the Japanese remain conspicuously silent on political matters on the board. According to a former executive director,

> European directors' comments get caught up in political thoughts. Japan is a "nonregional country" in the EBRD. Therefore, [Japan] assiduously comments by sticking to logic, even when painful, without being swayed by politics. That is what others desire from Japan. . . . If Japan's director can contribute in that way as well [politically], his influence in the bank would probably strengthen. It may be in Japan's national interest. However . . . if anyone ever says that Executive Director Fujikawa [Tetsuma] did so, it never, ever happened."[95]

The MOF is aware that Europe basically welcomes Japan's funds without its "ideas," and Tokyo accepts the EBRD as a European world. Besides, few issues in the EBRD touch upon what Japan would consider its critical national interests: "There are cases where it is necessary for the executive director to represent the national interest, narrowly defined, but those instances are rare. Discussions that involve Japan's national interest are rare."[96]

Japan remains silent even on the Russian aid issue, which is politically controversial in Japan and anathema to the majority of policymakers in Tokyo. Japan did focus on Russian aid during the founding process, but since the bank's opening, it has never raised the issue at board of directors meetings. The MOF has maintained the separation of politics from economics approach to the EBRD by leaving the politics to the bank while focusing on the technical issues of loans. A former director points out that there is no need for Japan to mention the issue since all participants are well aware of Japan's position.[97]

Perhaps management style also contributes to this behavior within the bank. After all, the Japanese find the IBRD uncomfortable because of its American, or "Anglo-Saxon," management style and the ADB uncomfortable because Anglo-Saxon representatives seem to have difficulty respecting the "Asian" management style. In both institutions, Japanese directors have spoken out or lobbied actively for Japan's interests, often against Anglo-Saxon influence. Theoretically, this should not be much of a problem in the EBRD because of its "European" rather than "Anglo-Saxon" management style. However, listen to a former Japanese executive director:

> In reality, an international organization is an Anglo-Saxon world. In the case of the IMF and the World Bank, they were established under the leadership of the United States and Britain after the war. In the case of the EBRD, it was under French leadership. Even so, operations are conducted in English and it thus remains an Anglo-Saxon world.[98]

Anglo-Saxons cannot seem to win. However, Japan does not seem motivated to criticize or counter "Anglo-Saxon" dominance in the EBRD to the extent we have seen in the IBRD and ADB, and one suspects that this is because the stakes are not as high in the EBRD.

Tokyo had no significant involvement in the selection of the president and his staff. Rather, the MOF was resigned to the selection of Jacques Attali as the founding president and spent the initial years attempting to cope with his management style. A close friend of François Mitterrand who served as the president's special aide, Attali is considered the originator of the EBRD concept.[99]

Attali's operational habits created discord and dissatisfaction on the board of directors and in home governments of the member states. The Japanese were concerned especially, as were other members, with his unilateral—some would say autocratic—decision-making proclivities.[100] For example, a Japanese delegate to the 1992 annual meeting felt compelled to counter Attali's unilateral proposal that the bank set up a separate facility, with concessional lending, for the conversion of military to civilian industries in Russia.[101] Vice Minister Chino Tadao argued that the facility should be discussed further by the board of directors and viewed from a broader, global perspective, which would argue for concessional funds being reserved for the poorest nations.[102] Japanese delegates noted with satisfaction that Attali did not mention the facility directly in his closing comments but referred the matter to the board by the end of the year.[103]

By the summer of 1992, Attali was involved in a series of scandals that put the bank into the spotlight. The EBRD had spent twice as much on itself ($300 million) than on East Europe during its first year. The president stood accused of spendthrift habits on his travel arrangements via hired aircraft or first-class seating, on the acceptance of honoraria and double compensation for travel expenses, on the redesigning of the bank headquarters, and on the establishment of a bank office in Paris without clearance from the directors.[104] Attali resigned in July 1993 and was replaced by Jacques de Larosiere, governor of the Bank of France and former managing director of the IMF.

The Japanese may have had some justification for concern over Attali's selection. A prolific writer on a wide range of topics, he was known to have regarded Japan as a threat to Europe in the post–Cold War world. Just prior to assuming the post of EBRD president, he wrote:

> It is possible that Japan will decline to pursue the political role of the economic center, choosing instead to limit its influence to the western nations of the Pacific. But such a decision is redolent of its disastrous dream earlier in the century of establishing a "greater co-prosperity sphere." . . . Japan is unlikely to be able to restrain its desire for power. . . . Perhaps its current reluctance to trumpet such an ambition is disingenuous, a deliberate strategy to confuse its competitors. Perhaps it only pretends to play with the idea that it does not wish to be the center—and tells us this so that we will mistake its insistence for its intention—just so that Tokyo has a better chance to triumph over all rivals.[105]

Attali's two-pronged antidote for Japan's challenge is 1) to strengthen the United States and bring it closer to Europe as an ally against Japan[106] and 2) to foster unity between East and West Europe: "If Western Europe progresses toward political unity and East Europe succeeds in democratization, if the two parts of Europe can invent audacious ways of joining together, of aiding each other, then it is not impossible to imagine a European triumph over its Asian rival."[107] This was Attali's mission for the EBRD. The bank's projects

> will [themselves] cause a continual economic and cultural homogenization of what will one day become a European sphere. For the creation of a European confederation, for the entry of all European countries into the existing European Community, for the construction of a European "common home," the bank will play a similar role to the European Coal and Steel Community of the 1950s as the cornerstone of today's European Community.[108]

Upon his election as EBRD president, Attali addressed the 1991 inaugural meeting of the board of governors. It was clear that his comments were aimed at the European members more than the nonregional nations in attendance:

> As the first institution of a united Europe, the Bank is the first institution of which all European countries are full and equal members. I hope that it will help to bring into existence what some call the "Common Home" and others call the "Confederation." In any event, it will provide the natural framework for learning continental solidarity and a focal point for designing, organizing and financing the major physical, financial and intellectual infrastructures which will make the convergence of member countries irreversible. In this way the European Bank will become the natural forum for the great debates that will lead up to the formation of a continental economic space.[109]

Therefore, while Western nations joined the Bank for the primary purpose of reconstructing a collapsed Second World, the president harbored an additional personal vision of a bank that strengthened Europe against an Asian, especially Japanese, threat. The irony is that the recruitment of Japan as a coequal shareholder with West European members within the bank, for strengthening Europe against Japan, apparently requires Japanese money and participation.

When Attali resigned, the Japanese remained notably silent. Japan remained quiet during the search for Attali's successor as well. The name of a former MOF vice minister, Gyohten Toyoo, surfaced briefly in the media as a possible Japanese nominee,[110] but the government maintained a posture of benign neutrality. Again, the EBRD was considered Europe's bank. It was not the ADB, and Attali was not Fujioka.

In sum, Japan entered the bank in the number-two position, which it found acceptable and inevitable. Tokyo did not have to struggle to achieve number-two status nor, as it did in the World Bank, find it necessary to leap above the European founders. Neither did Tokyo wish to challenge America's number-one slot. Japan also resigned itself to a minimal role in the management, especially in view of the absence of qualified individuals who were knowledgeable about East Europe and Russia. The lack of expertise on the region also restricted Japanese staff recruitment. In many ways, despite the fact that Japan entered the bank on the ground floor, the EBRD provided it with an environment that was already a given. Japan did not leap into the EBRD's founding with the same concern and enthusiasm as it did with the ADB's administrative and institutional foundation-building. But then East Europe is not East Asia, and Russia is not China.

As for the diplomatic imperative for membership, Japan was not interested in the EBRD per se but in the broader implications for its global and regional role. During the establishment process, Japan's main concern rested with the implications of the founders' decisions on its extrabank policies. Japan joined the bank amid a flurry of diplomatic initiatives designed to symbolize Japan's entry into the realm of political and strategic diplomacy in areas outside of Asia. Some in Japan considered Japan's East European activities as, in the words of a Foreign Ministry spokesperson, "our first move in meeting the real challenge of our global role."[111]

The centerpiece of this diplomatic push was Prime Minister Kaifu Toshiki's European visit in January 1990 and the use of financial aid packages to East and Central European nations to demonstrate commitment to reform in the region. As Kaifu stated in Europe, "I am convinced that Japan . . . as a leading member of the industrialized democracies is expected to play a major role not only economically but also politically."[112] He stressed political objectives in Japan's new diplomacy toward East Europe. Japan's stated goals paralleled the EBRD's charter mandate: democratization, multiparty political systems, respect for the rule of law and human rights, market economies. Kaifu extended political conditions on aid to all of Japan's ODA policy, which foreshadowed the ODA Charter that would be adopted by the succeeding cabinet two and a half years later.

Japan had multiple diplomatic objectives in its East Europe diplomacy: It sought to strengthen its ties with West European G-7 partners through support for a matter they considered top priority; it endeavored to deepen relations with East and Central Europe, a region with which Japanese had little contact or interest historically, culturally, politically, and even economically; it hoped to contribute to the historic changes in the region by aiding the transition from command to market economies and from socialism to democracy; it sought to secure a foothold that would allow Japan to avoid European protectionist policies after the expected 1992 unification; and it sought to cooperate with a United States that, while not as enthusiastic as Europe, became more active in its support for East Europe and Russia. Japan's overarching intention was to contribute to the world community beyond Asia in a manner consistent with its pacifist principles and in a way that transcended national economic interests.

Membership in the EBRD could respond to each of these objectives and was therefore part of a larger diplomatic scheme. Aid to East Europe fits Japan's aspiration well: involvement beyond Asia, in political as well as economic dimensions, through the use of economic and financial resources desperately needed in the region, and through a multilateral mechanism in partnership with Europe and the United States, nations that cannot meet these needs easily.

EBRD membership coincided with bilateral and multilateral (especially G-24) aid initiatives from Tokyo. In late 1989, Japan rescheduled $402 million worth of Polish debt and announced $200 million in ODA to Poland and Hungary, of which $150 million would go to a G-24 currency stabilization fund for Poland. On Kaifu's January 1990 trip to Europe, he pledged $1 billion in Export-Import Bank loans for Poland and Hungary ($500 million each); $350 million in trade insurance for Polish exports to Japan; a $200 million increase (to $400 million) for trade insurance for exports to Hungary; and $25 million in technical cooperation for both Poland and Hungary. Japan's pledges of aid elevated Japan to second place in East European aid, second only to West Germany, and was twice the amount of the United States.[113] Japan also extended aid to the other East and Central European nations—Czechoslovakia, Yugoslavia, and Bulgaria—under a G-24 framework established at the Paris Summit of 1989.

The one issue that did trouble the Japanese and galvanized their diplomatic activities during the founding process concerned Soviet membership in the EBRD. Japan's early endorsement of the EBRD idea assumed that the target countries of the new bank would be East and Central Europe. Only during the negotiations in early 1990 did it become clear that the Soviet Union, with European backing, intended to become a borrowing member.

Foreign Ministry officials felt that Russian membership should have been discussed in the G-24 forum and assumed that Mitterrand produced a fait accompli during his visit to Moscow and through a letter of invitation to join the previous year.[114]

Japan joined the United States and Australia in efforts, first, to oppose Soviet membership and then, when that battle was lost, to impose limits on Soviet borrowing. Japan's position reflected the harsh feelings toward the Soviets among the political elite at home, and it reflected the strong feeling that aid to the Soviets must await a favorable settlement of the Northern Territories issue. But the greater concern in the MOF was the fear that the Soviets would absorb the bank's limited capital, given the Soviet Union's limitless need for financial assistance, thus depriving the original East and Central European beneficiaries of EBRD assistance. Japan had little confidence in Soviet capabilities in utilizing foreign assistance, which, according to a Japanese foreign minister, "would be no more than money down the drain."[115]

The Japanese considered East and Central European capabilities and commitment to political change and economic reform much higher and stronger than the Soviets. As one MOF official observed, East Europeans show greater perseverance (*gaman-zuoi*) than the Soviets when it comes to democratization because they first had to liberate themselves from Soviet rule, and they are more realistic about the efforts needed to achieve economic reform. On the other hand, the Soviet people do not have a strong feeling for democracy because they had not liberated themselves from authoritarian rule with their own hands, and because they expect economic reform without much political and social change. They are not prepared to bear the cost of change.[116]

When the United States and Japan lost the first round on Soviet membership, Japan moved to a fallback position—observer status for the Soviets. But that failed as well. The United States then insisted that Soviet borrowing be severely restricted. France proposed the compromise that the United States and Japan endorsed: Russia would limit its borrowing to the amount of its paid-in capital for the first three years, after which this arrangement would be reassessed. The Japanese recognized the incongruity of allowing a country to borrow only up to the amount it contributed to the bank, but Tokyo's assumption was that the limited amount would be supplemented by private sector flows and by cofinancing with the Japan Export-Import Bank.[117] In 1991, the Export-Import Bank signed a cofinancing framework agreement with the EBRD.

The main Soviet concern was the danger at home of appearing to acquiesce to Western demands and conditions. The extension of a face-saving formula to the Soviets—in the form of Article 8(4) of the Articles of Agreement, which allows any member to limit its access to bank funds voluntarily—was accepted by the head of the Soviet delegation, Victor V. Gerashchenko, in a letter to the negotiating committee.[118] The Japanese wanted this compromise agreement put in writing. As a result of this arrangement, the Soviets would borrow only up to the amount they paid into the bank and would not borrow funds for public sector infrastructure projects. This would amount to a maximum of $216 million.

An agreement was also reached that any change in Soviet borrowing limits after the three years must be agreed upon by at least three-fourths of the board of governors representing not less than 85 percent of the total vote shares. This allows the United States and Japan a veto power over any such changes, since together these two nations hold 18.5 percent of total vote shares. The Europeans sought to raise the limit on Soviet borrowing at the July 1991 G-7 summit. France sought to raise the limit to 15 percent from the allotted 6 percent; Italy suggested 20 percent; Germany supported some increase; Britain gave tacit agreement. However, the United States and Japan refused.[119]

With the dissolution of the Soviet Union into more than a dozen independent republics in 1991, this compromise solution became inoperative. Japan's immediate concern became the method by which the former Soviet Union's shares would be distributed among the republics. Tokyo favored reapplication for membership by all 15 republics as independent states, and of these, Japan began to devote special attention to the five Central Asian Republics in particular.

U.S.-Japan cooperation constituted the core of Japan's negotiating approach on Soviet membership and borrowing arrangements. Japan solidly supported American hesitancy toward the Soviet Union. Because of Japan's bilateral problems with Moscow, in public Tokyo adopted the hardest line of all negotiators in public. Its main objective was to moderate the European insistence on shifting the EBRD's original focus to include the Soviet Union as well as East Europe. And as the United States moved toward greater willingness to provide assistance, Japan still held back. At the Houston Summit, Kaifu sought to convince the United States and other G-7 members not to invite Gorbachev to participate. The Soviet president had previously visited Tokyo, only to be given the cold shoulder in economic assistance commitments, and Japan lobbied to limit assistance at Houston. It is reported that German Chancellor Helmut Kohl angrily cancelled a scheduled meeting with Kaifu because of Tokyo's opposition to Soviet aid. During the conference, France and Germany led the European push for greater Soviet aid, while the United States and Britain urged caution. Japan stood on the periphery, with the toughest position toward Moscow, and therefore supported the more cautious position of the United States. In private negotiations, however, Japan's hard line positions did not translate into intransigence. Japanese negotiators chose a middle course between domestic hostility toward Russian aid and the need to accommodate G-7 wishes, and between the United States and Europe. Its policy stance reflected the makeup of its negotiating team, which reflected, in turn, complementary ministerial interests. The Foreign Ministry handled Kaifu's European trip and was the main advocate of Japan's activism in the region; it raised the sensitive political questions, including the Northern Territories issues. The Finance Ministry was in charge of EBRD negotiations and preferred the nonpolitical mandate embodied in the charters of the other MDBs. The MOF looked at Russia's suspect capacity to use foreign aid effectively, focused on technical issues, and remained silent on bilateral politics. In the end, the Northern Territories and other bilateral difficulties in Japanese-Soviet relations did not rule the day, as the MOF's viewpoint on the preferred role of MDBs prevailed. This can explain the apparent irony of Prime Minister Kaifu's loud call for political activism in the region and the EBRD negotiating team's focus on technical and legal concerns and the nonpolitical statements of the executive director. The juggling of the technical and the political reflects the makeup of the executive director's office: The MOF appoints the executive director, someone at the level of deputy director-general of a bureau (*shingikan*), and the MOFA appoints the alternate director, thus far from the division director level (*kacho*). This unprecedented cooperative arrangement between two competing ministries seeks to meet the needs of the post–Cold War era.

While Japan stood with the United States on the Russian membership and borrowing issue, on other issues it functioned as a moderator of American positions, siding more with European members. The Bush administration brought its rigid, strident belief in market mechanisms to the negotiating table. For example, it urged that 100 percent of EBRD funds go only to the private sector, thus effectively shutting out any funding for the public sector: "In fact, the Bush administration initially pressed in negotiations to prevent even one penny of EBRD funds from going to support East Europe's public sector, arguing that this would amount to subsidizing failed socialism."[120]

This also would distinguish the EBRD from the World Bank: "The United States insisted that the EBRD not be a carbon copy of the World Bank. It must have a different mission; that is, it should have a private sector orientation."[121]

The Europeans favored some financing of the public sector, an important feature of their own economies. Their view of current needs in East and Central Europe convinced them of the importance of public sector support because of the region's undeveloped private sector, the importance of government participation in the transition processes, the lack of an adequate physical infrastructure that could support sustained development, and the lack of financial infrastructures in these countries, and the need for government initiatives in cushioning the expected social impact of the transition and in cleaning up the environment.[122]

The Articles of Agreement embody the compromise worked out among the founders: The EBRD shall not go beyond 40 percent of its funding for public sector projects. Sixty percent of the both the EBRD's total and country-specific annual loans and investments shall be earmarked for private sector projects. Any public sector loan must be restricted to state enterprises in the process of shifting to private ownership.[123] However, the chairman of the negotiating committee's report made clear that, by the end of deliberations, all participants recognized the difficulty in anticipating private sector projects.[124]

Like most Europeans, the Japanese, while endorsing privatization, felt uncomfortable with the extremity and inflexibility of the U.S. position. An MOF negotiator referred to the American insistence on only private sector lending as "rigid" and "theological," and felt that what the United States wanted was "pure distilled water."[125] Tokyo sought a mediatory role of "trying to mitigate dogmatic [American] policies toward greater pragmatism."[126] Therefore, Japan positioned itself between the United States and Europe. It argued against the total focus on the private sector, because of the expected difficulty in finding these kinds of projects, but at the same time it supported the 40 percent limit on public sector funding, out of a fear that the needs of public sector projects would drain bank resources.

Tokyo's views reflected both its own development experience as well as Asia's development model, in which the state served a constructive and active role in guiding the economy to growth and prosperity. This was the debate that had raged throughout the 1980s in the ADB, which may have prepared the Japanese for what came in EBRD negotiations with the United States. It was a debate that Japan was just about to introduce in the World Bank through its proposal for a study of the East Asian miracles. Japanese experiences with the EBRD, and their exposure to the development needs of East Europe and Russia, provided another instance, in addition to the Latin American record, of the inadequacy of the Anglo-Saxon orthodoxy. Some MOF officials maintain that the East European and Russian cases provided final confirmation that the World Bank report erred in concluding that the Asian model was inapplicable elsewhere.

It becomes increasingly clear that Japan's own development experience provides the foundation and framework for its EBRD policy in both the diplomatic and development spheres. Tokyo's reliance on its own development model as its policy guide was on display at the 1991 inaugural board of governors meeting. Japan's governor, Finance Minister Hashimoto Ryutaro, noted the parallels between Japan's past relationship with international financial institutions and East and Central Europe's future transition:

> Looking at the difficulties that the Central and Eastern European nations now confront, I cannot help being reminded of our own situation immediately after World War II. Until then, neither a democracy in its true sense nor a market economy driven by real entrepreneurial spirit can be said to have existed in our history. Therefore, advice and support from the international institutions as well as the United States and other industrialized nations played a key role in effecting the necessary political and economic reforms amid the post-war turmoil and in achieving our present prosperity.[127]

In discussing Japan's "basic thinking" toward the EBRD at the first annual meeting in 1992, the vice minister of finance revealed the extent of the nation's reliance on its own experience as its EBRD policy framework. His statement covered the major themes, either directly or implied, including nurturing human resources, entrepreneurial spirit and management know-how, industrial policy and the role of the government and public sector, and concentration on small and medium-size companies[128]:

> First, fostering competitive industries. . . . Japan's own experience suggests that the first key to success will be to identify industries that possess comparative advantage. The countries concerned would focus their policy measures in order to bring up such industries.

> Second, effectively utilizing policy-oriented financial institutions of the recipient countries. Where these institutions do not yet exist, the EBRD can assist in establishing such institutions.

> Third, developing human resources with a strong entrepreneurial spirit. . . . In encouraging these countries' transition to market economies the EBRD can play an important role in providing technical

assistance to facilitate the transfer of management know-how and other business expertise. [129]

In addition, the MOF found many of the EBRD's emphases compatible with its own ODA policy preferences. For example, the bank emphasizes technical assistance, which the MOF feels critical in developing the private sector and a market economy through the transfer of know-how and management skills; infrastructure, which Japan has traditionally felt to be the key to sustained development, and especially so in a region that does not require BHN funding; and the environment, which Japan did not stress during the founding negotiations but which became a major ODA policy emphasis after the 1989 Paris Summit and, especially, following the 1992 Earth Summit. And the EBRD funds only projects, not balance of payments loans. The EBRD explicitly eschewed World Bank–type SALs. According to the chairman's report, "Delegates described the precise form of programme lending in which the Bank could become involved as "projects, whether individual or in the context of specific investment programmes", so as to make clear that fast-disbursing policy based lending is not included."[130]

What is striking about Japan's East European diplomacy in general and EBRD policy in particular is the underlying presence of Asia in Japanese calculations. The government took special pains throughout the formative activities of the EBRD to assure traditional Asian aid recipients that Japan was not turning its attention to Europe at Asia's expense. Kaifu, on his European trip, sought to secure European support for the resumption of Western and Japanese aid to China in the wake of the Tiananmen Square massacre. And he justified Japan's involvement in East Europe in part on its importance for Asia: "The moves toward reform in East Europe will affect not only the European scene but the basic structure of the current international order as well and thus will have a significant impact on the stabilization of the Asia-Pacific situation."[131]

After the 1990 Houston Summit, he also reiterated that "By not just extending funds, Japan's positive cooperation in ways such as personnel, technology and cultural exchanges will directly contribute to peace and stability not only in Europe, but also in Asia, the Pacific region and the world."[132]

Japan's most active efforts to date within the EBRD are efforts to champion the cause of the Central Asian Republics—by supporting CAR wishes to loosen their ties with the EBRD in favor of the ADB. CAR countries face bleak prospects in the EBRD, whose founders are focused more on the needs of East and Central Europe and Russia. The EBRD sought to chair the

Consultative Groups on CAR multilateral aid, but this fell under the World Bank's jurisdiction. The private sectors of CAR nations require nurturing before funding can be used effectively, thus making it difficult to meet the EBRD's private sector requirements for loans. By mid-1993, loans had not flowed to the region.

While the Northern Territories issue clouds Japan's relations with Russia, it does not affect relations with CAR nations. Japan took the initiative in November 1992 in placing CAR nations onto the DAC list of developing nations, thus making them eligible for ODA. Tokyo championed CAR membership in both the EBRD and the ADB, against strong initial American opposition. Some of these nations, now freed from direct Soviet rule, have begun to identify more with Asia than with Europe, and Japan has welcomed CAR peoples to the Asian fold enthusiastically. Tokyo feels that the ADB's emphasis on public sector loans and infrastructure better suits the needs of the CARs. The ADB also has a soft-loan window, and some CARs qualify for soft loans, but the MOF views even ordinary credits as relatively soft.

In conclusion, the EBRD is the most distant of the three MDBs geographically and in terms of Japan's interest. And yet it has propelled Tokyo into the most overtly political of all its relations with MDBs. The historic developments in Europe, the response by Western nations, the particular mandate of the bank, and Japan's search for a global role converged to make this almost inevitable and unavoidable. Japan's movements were largely reactive, but so were those of Europe and the United States. No one foresaw these historic changes, and everyone was caught off guard and forced to cope with a new world.

Japan's path through this unfamiliar territory led between the United States and Europe, leaning to and fro but following its own national interests and development philosophy. Japan had found its niche in this environment, and it was not a leadership niche. But then, Japan never considered the East European and Russian region its backyard; it viewed these regions as West European and American turf. Whatever leadership role it assumed was reserved for those countries newly deemed Asian, the Central Asian Republics. Japan emerged as an advocate of Asian constituents both within and without the EBRD. On the whole, Japan never seemed as invested in the EBRD as in the ADB or even the World Bank. Its stamp on the bank appears light, and its actions give the appearance, still, of searching for a role.

4

— ◆ —

THE NEW MULTILATERALISM:
A COMPARATIVE ANALYSIS

The man who goes alone can start today; but he who travels
with another must wait till that other is ready.

— Henry David Thoreau

You will be safest in the middle.   — Ovid

Japan's bilateral ODA activism preceded multilateral aid activism. Bilateral aid began its journey from the periphery to become a central pillar of Japanese foreign policy in the 1970s, while movement in MDB policy came to the fore only from the mid-1980s. Japan's involvement in the establishment of the Asian Development Bank (1966) may be an exception, but ADB activism remained low key until the 1980s and was not duplicated in other MDBs. In the 1990s, multilateralization constitutes one of the main trends in overall ODA policy, along with diversification of objectives and uses of aid, politicization both regionally and globally, and philosophizing about new "ideas."

Japanese policies toward the World Bank, ADB, and the European Bank for Reconstruction and Development have been cumulative and mutually reinforcing, over time and across banks. Activism began with institutional concerns and rapidly spread to diplomatic interests and development strategy and philosophy. Japan's interests started in Asia but spread to other Third World regions and, in the post–Cold War era, to the Second World. By the mid-1990s, the major institutional goals were either attained or "satisficed," the diplomatic agenda legitimized, and a development philosophy and strategy underlaid overall MDB policy.

Japan's new multilateralism cannot be explained simply as a search for economic gain or as a power struggle with the United States. Nor could Japan be accused simply of reacting to American demands or to events beyond Tokyo's control. All of these objectives play some role in Japan's actions, but none of them provides a compelling explanation of the nation's foreign policy motives or behavior. The picture is not that clear. We have introduced numerous policy strands and themes, and we now need to consolidate them from a broader, comparative perspective. Japan's policy is tailored to each bank's particular history and character, but there are also certain commonalities across institutions and regions in three areas: policy objectives, policy patterns, and the policymaking process.

POLICY OBJECTIVES

Japanese activism began in the area of institutional policy objectives. Japan always had been concerned with the financial foundations of all MDBs. The ADB case was especially noteworthy because of Japan's involvement in its founding process and management. Until Japan's subscription parity in the ADB, no nation had matched an American contribution to an international organization. From the beginning, Japan accepted its duty to play the role of largest coshareholder in the ADB. As the years passed, increased contributions to nonordinary capital resources rendered Japan the larger coshareholder nominally and the largest shareholder de facto. To Japan, the World Bank was America's responsibility, the EBRD was the prime responsibility of the United States and European nations (with Japan playing an important support role in both institutions), and the ADB was its own principal responsibility. Throughout the postwar period, Japan's role in MDBs had been defined narrowly as financial.

In the 1980s, Japan utilized its financial power to solidify more than just the banks' financial footing. Tokyo set its sights on its own footing by lobbying for higher status within MDBs through increased financial contributions, at first through increased subscriptions to extra-OCR funds that do not affect vote shares and then to capital increases that do determine shares. By 1990, Japan achieved its objectives: elevation from number-five to number-two status in the World Bank and IMF, recognition that it occupies a de facto number-one position in the ADB, and assignment of a number-two position in the EBRD equal to that of the West European powers.

One may argue that the Japanese raised their status the old-fashioned way: They bought it. However, the process was untraditional in that Japan

TABLE 4.1

Profile of Japan's Subscriptions to the IBRD, ADB, and EBRD

Bank	Shares	Total Amount	Paid in	Callable	% of Total	% of Vote	Rank
IBRD*	93,770	11,311,944	703,452	10,608,492	8.3	7.89	2
ADB*	276,105	3,792,468	455,335	3,337,133	16.4	13.52	1
EBRD+	85,175	851,750	153,315	596,225	8.5	8.5	2

*Thousands of US Dollars.
+European Currency Unit.

Sources: *The World Bank Annual Report 1991; Asian Development Bank Annual Report 1993;* and *European Bank for Reconstruction and Development Annual Report 1992.*

was willing to use its financial strength openly for political purposes within the banks and thus risk the ire of those nations it leap-frogged. West Europe fought Japan's accession to number-two status in both the IBRD and IMF for years; the United States initially linked higher status within MDBs to Japan's commitment to domestic financial liberalization and refused to cede coleader status in the ADB; and Japan attained a number two-position in the EBRD, but without commensurate management positions. Previously, Japan would have avoided rocking the boat, especially if it entailed contention with the United States and Europe.

Also in the 1980s, Japan focused not only on shares but also on management positions. Once again, entrenched interests and national pride made this a difficult task. Japan's efforts in the World Bank were especially difficult because it was not a founding member and did not stake out its claim to posts early on. As a latecomer, it either had to outmuscle entrenched European and American personnel and interests, or it needed to collar newly created positions, which it managed to do in the form of a vice presidency. However, this position did not fully satisfy the Japanese in terms of status and mandate. A few Japanese were able to rise up the ranks to operational directorships, but this is a rare phenomenon in an institution where promotion and positions often are said to rest in the hands of well-established nationality constituents or old-boy networks.

Japan was a founding member of both the ADB and EBRD, but only in the ADB did it manage to obtain top positions, since the organizational

TABLE 4.2

Japan's Rank in All Multilateral Development Banks
Compared with Other Major Donors (as of September 10, 1992)

Bank	JAPAN % of Shares	Rank	U.S.	% of Shares Germany	England	France
IBRD	6.2	2	17.4	4.8	4.6	4.6
IDA	16.7	2	25.6	11.4	8.5	6.7
IFC	6.1	2	24.8	5.6	5.3	5.3
MIGA	5.1	2	20.5	5.1	4.9	4.9
ADB	16.3	1	16.3	4.5	2.1	2.4
ADF	47.1	1	12.2	6.8	3.2	3.7
EBRD	8.5	2	10.0	8.5	8.5	8.5
IADB	1.1	1*	34.7	1.0	1.0	1.0
FSO	2.1	1*	54.8	2.0	1.9	1.9
MIF	39.8	1*	39.8	2.4	—	1.2
IIC	3.1	1*	25.5	3.1	—	3.1
AFDB	4.8	2*	5.9	3.6	1.5	3.3
AFDF	13.9	1	12.7	9.0	3.7	8.1

*Among nonregional members.

Source: Ministry of Finance, "Kokusai Kaihatsu Kinyu Kikan no Gaiyo" (September 1992).

structure had not yet solidified and since President Watanabe and Administration Director Fujioka engaged in personnel recruitment efforts. In the
early years, Japanese were conspicuous in several important positions, and
although several "reserved posts" attained early on dropped by the wayside,
Japan still managed to retain the presidency, the special assistant to the
president, and the budget, administrative, and personnel directorship. In
addition, a number of Japanese staff members climbed up the ranks to
occupy manager-level positions, although this resulted from their own career
commitment to the bank rather than to home government influence. For
careerists, Japanese nationality, in fact, often was cited as a negative factor.
On the other hand, the EBRD has virtually no Japanese management person-

nel, due to both the European nature of the institution and the lack of Japanese candidates or of will to lobby forcefully for posts (unlike the United States, which did lobby successfully for its citizens). In contrast to its financial clout, Japan's presence in the management of these banks is weak, except for the special circumstances in the ADB.

The lack of Japanese professional staff members is another common feature in all MDBs. Japanese staffers make up no more than 1 percent of the staff in the World Bank and IDA, and can be counted on one hand in other agencies. In 1990, Japanese staffers totaled 71 out of all IBRD and IDA staff, both professional and support. In the IFC, five Japanese served out of 604 total staffers, and in MIGA, three out of 38 were Japanese.[1] The ADB is again the exception, but even here, the Japanese note that they are underrepresented (64 Japanese out of a total of 1,670 staff in 1990) given the size of Japan's financial contributions. The Japanese fare even worse in the other regional development banks: three out of 1,694 staffers in the Inter-American Development Bank, and none out of 1,030 in the African Development Bank and African Development Fund.[2] All MDBs share the same recruitment problems in Japan, rooted in the organizational structures and personnel policies of corporate and ministerial structures plus difficulties in recruiting suitable unaffiliated candidates.

In sum, by the mid-1990s, the net effect of Japan's efforts in the institutional arena was a successful raising of its profile in MDBs to reflect its general standing in the world community. As IFIs turned to "Japan money," Tokyo began extracting concessions in the form of shares, votes, and management positions. Japan is temporarily satisfied with its gains in vote shares; it feels it is currently where it should be in the three Banks. Its goal of management presence has not been an overwhelming success, but the movement is in a forward direction. In the area of professional staff, Japan feels that more should be done on both sides in recruitment efforts, with it taking the lead in the World Bank.

By the late 1980s and especially in the 1990s, Japan moved beyond institutional concerns, a fact that becomes clear when we take a comparative look at the other arenas—diplomatic and development—of policy activism. Beginning in the late 1980s, Japan gradually recognized the usefulness of MDBs for pursuing diplomatic objectives. Its role is no longer restricted only to contributing money without a voice. We can identify eight specific diplomatic uses of the three MDBs:

1. Articulate policy.
2. Legitimize controversial policies.
3. Fulfill international responsibilities as a nonmilitary power.

4. Enhance national resources.
5. Compensate for diplomatic and policymaking shortcomings.
6. Globalize diplomacy without sacrificing Asia.
7. Pursue greater independence within an American framework.
8. Enhance national prestige.

We will discuss each point individually.

ARTICULATE POLICY. This is perhaps the most obvious use of MDBs as international fora, but in the past, Japan had few policies of consequence to articulate. Recently, these banks serve a useful purpose in implementing policy or standing as symbols of foreign policy themes.

The most obvious example is the EBRD as a demonstration of Japan's new determination to participate as a good world citizen in the remaking of East Europe. Tokyo signaled an intention to play a global role in a region beyond Asia, far from home, about which the Japanese knew little, and beyond a purely economic role. The EBRD became a symbol in what appeared to be Japan's departure from its traditional nonpolitical and pragmatic foreign policy to a new commitment to political principles and ideology. Japan would now condition aid on a commitment to democratization, respect for human rights, a multiparty political system, the rule of law, and open market economies. The EBRD served as a means to strengthen relations with West Europe by showing solidarity and by supplementing the EC's scarce financial resources for the East.

The World Bank and ADB also served a similar purpose. Japan uses its IBRD activism to signal its coming of age as a global nation ready to accept international responsibilities by participating in the pressing tasks of the day: the political and economic transformation of East and Central European and the former Soviet Union, the international debt crisis, and the global environment. Also, Japan signaled its willingness to challenge the prevailing orthodoxy in development thinking in the bank. This challenge served several purposes, including indicating a determination to serve as Asia's spokesperson and perhaps defender, to demonstrate Japan's independence from the bank's Anglo-American dominance, and to articulate Japan's newly found development strategy, or "ideas."

From its founding days, the ADB has stood as a symbol of Japan's commitment to Asian economic development and growth and solidarity. Japan's push for preeminence signaled a new self-confidence, and the Asian development experience has given the nation a model to advocate beyond the bank. Tokyo recognized the diplomatic utility of the bank for its Asia policy, especially for its policies toward China, Vietnam, ASEAN, and the

Central Asian Republics. Japan has gradually incorporated the bank into its Asia policy, something it avoided during the politically and ideologically contentious Cold War era.

LEGITIMIZE CONTROVERSIAL POLICIES. Multilateral institutions serve as buffers that may shield the government from domestic and international criticism for taking unpopular steps. The most striking example in recent years has been the dispatch of Japanese military forces abroad for the first time since World War II under a UN peacekeeping banner to Cambodia and the dispatch of minesweepers to the Persian Gulf after the Gulf War. Multilateral banks played a similar function for aid to Russia and China.

MDBs deflected strong domestic opposition to Russian aid: Neither the Japanese elites nor the public support assistance for Russia. The Northern Territories provide the immediate political obstacle to Japanese aid, but this unwillingness to aid Russia is rooted deeply in history and in the perceived insults and cruelties toward Japan. Japan never shared the world's excitement with Mikhail Gorbachev's glastnost or Boris Yeltsin's reform efforts. The government did, however, recognize the historical significance of events in Russia and acknowledged the imperatives for providing some aid to Moscow, especially under strong pressure from Europe and, eventually, the United States. The IMF, the World Bank, and the EBRD provided a necessary multilateral cloak to send a limited amount of Japanese aid to Moscow under the guise of a united G-7 initiative. In addition to following the lead of the G-7 nations, Japan pushed for special attention to some of the Russian republics, namely, those it could define as "Asian." Its means were multilateral—consultative groups in the IBRD and dual membership in the EBRD and ADB. We return to this topic in the next chapter.

MDBs also served as a buffer against strong foreign opposition to Japanese resumption of economic aid to China after the Tiananmen Square incident. Japan sought multilateral support for softening sanctions against Beijing and for resuming a bilateral ODA package. It turned to G-7 summits, especially those in Paris and Houston, for tacit agreement on resuming bilateral aid to Beijing. The Japanese turned to the flagship of MDBs, the World Bank, in an effort to convince the bank to reinstate multilateral aid. After months of campaigning by Japan, the IBRD resumed BHN funding, and the ADB resumed OCR lending. Japan's aid resumption thus appeared part of a general international softening of aid sanctions against China.

Vietnam is another case of Japan's utilization of an MDB to legitimize the lifting of economic sanctions. In this case, Tokyo attempted to use the

ADB as a foot in the door to Hanoi. Here, the United States opposed any softening of sanctions, due to Vietnam's 1979 invasion of Cambodia and the domestic political issue of MTAs. In 1994, however, the Clinton administration decided to allow American firms to participate in multilateral procurement projects in Vietnam. Ironically, the administration utilized the World Bank to spearhead that softening.

MDBs also can be of use in legitimizing changes in popular ODA approaches. Japan's traditional preference for request-based procedures and the separation of politics from economics gave way in the 1990s to the acceptance of political conditionality in both bilateral and multilateral aid. But it was the shift in MDB willingness to articulate politically based conditions that allowed Japan to support political specifications and requirements. The EBRD is the most obvious example, with democratization written into the Articles of Agreement, but in the 1990s the World Bank also took up the issue of "good governance" and the relationship between development and military expenditures.

FULFILL INTERNATIONAL RESPONSIBILITIES AS A NONMILITARY POWER. None of the three MDBs makes military demands on Japan. MDBs became nonmilitary weapons in the war against the debt crisis of the 1980s and catalysts for change in the Second World after 1989. In these banks, military contributions are not required to obtain a vice presidency or greater vote shares, a situation different from the United Nations, where questions are raised about Japan's commitment of troops to peacekeeping operations as a quid pro quo for a permanent seat on the Security Council.

MDB mandates accord well with Japan's conception of its own security needs. Tokyo considers nonmilitary threats just as likely and deadly as military ones. In the current world, nonmilitary threats—including instability in the international economy, disruption of natural resource flows, protectionism in foreign markets, and stoppage of energy resources to Japan—are actually more likely for Japan. These dangers require nonmilitary countermeasures, and MDBs serve as one mechanism to preserve the nation's comprehensive security.

The World Bank was conceived by its founders as a means to forestall war by preventing the kind of economic chaos of the 1930s that resulted in World War II. Japan credits the ADB as a contributing factor in the rise of the Asia Pacific region to prominence as the fastest-growing area of the world, and the EBRD's underlying goal is to bring stability to a region in flux through political and economic reforms. For pacifist-minded Japan, desirous of contributing substantially to world affairs utilizing nonmilitary resources, MDBs provide an ideal forum.

ENHANCE NATIONAL RESOURCES. Outsiders view Japan as a wealthy nation, but insiders are less sure. The quality of life in Japan is below levels in other industrialized nations, the national budget is often in the red, and the nation's huge surpluses are in the hands of the private sector. In addition, in the 1990s, Japan's bubble economy burst, sending the economy into a deep and persistent recession. The government has three concerns: Maintain public support for continued ODA spending despite the economic slowdown at home; make sure that limited official funds, or taxpayers' money, are spent effectively; and coax the trade surplus out of the private sector and into the global economy.

MDBs thus function as a means of supplementing scarce official resources and enticing private flows to developing nations. They allow Japan to get more bang for their ODA buck. Japanese funds, the argument goes, will be used efficiently because of the MDBs' knowledge of the developing world and technical expertise. MDBs also level conditions on borrowing governments and public and private institutions, something Japan finds difficult to do because of its request-based aid procedures and dislike of conditionality. Japan thus argues for MDB capital increases and expansion of soft-loan windows, promotes cofinancing between the Export-Import Bank and MDBs, establishes special funds within MDBs, and takes a more positive view of donor coordination than in the past.

The Japanese realize full well that even their ODA levels are inadequate for meeting the insatiable needs of the developing worlds, which now have expanded to include East and Central Europe, the Russian republics, and Russia itself. And it is clear to Tokyo that as fellow donors continue to labor under economic difficulties and restrict or reduce their financial flows to developing nations, Japan will be called upon to contribute more despite its own economic problems. The resources of the multilaterals thus begin to look even more attractive to Japan.

COMPENSATE FOR DIPLOMATIC AND POLICYMAKING SHORTCOMINGS. MDBs have become essential not only for compensating for financial shortages of donor nations but also for supplementing their technical expertise and manpower shortages. Japanese diplomacy faces a complex and diverse world in flux without a long, deep foreign policy experience. Its history has been dominated by an isolationist impulse, and its emergence onto the world scene since 1945 has been hindered by the drag of the anchor of wartime aggression. Japanese civil servants and politicians cannot compete with the experience and knowledge attained by corporations that engage in business throughout the world. MDBs can help close this knowledge, expertise, and manpower gap.

The EBRD educates policymakers about East and Central Europe, where Japan's ties, even economic relations, are shallow. Effective aid policy implementation requires regional and country expertise, and the EBRD's professional staff can provide this. The World Bank, with its international scale, offers the same benefits on a global basis. In many ways, as the oldest and most experienced development institution, the IBRD serves as a training ground for Japanese public and private sector personnel seconded to Washington. Even the ADB is essential in assisting understaffed and overworked bureaucrats to understand regional issues. Japan may consider itself Asian, and therefore knowledgeable about its neighborhood, but MOF officials are neither regional nor development experts.

MDBs can alleviate, to some extent, the manpower shortage that plagues Japan's ODA policy. There are only hundreds of foreign aid policy implementers throughout the Japanese government, compared with some 5,000 people in the U.S. Agency for International Development alone. Japan, the largest aid-giving country in the world, thus finds it difficult to disburse over $10 billion a year. In the MOF, the Development Institutions Division of the International Finance Bureau has a staff of fewer than 15; yet they are expected to oversee and follow the goings-on of all MDBs. MDBs help them disburse about $3 billion worth of aid. They do not have much time to sit around and debate the merits of neoclassical versus Asian development models when they are barely able to follow developments within all of these institutions.

GLOBALIZE DIPLOMACY WITHOUT SACRIFICING ASIA. An Asian undercurrent runs through Japan's policy toward all MDBs. Japan's ties with the ADB are the deepest of all the MDBs and its policy activities the most active. Japan is involved in all its aspects, from organizational problems and recipient nation conditions to relations with fellow donor nations and attention to Central Asia and China. This interest precedes the ascent of the "Asia Mafia" in the MOF and extends back to the very founding of the bank. The emphasis accurately reflects a basic Asia-centric pillar of Japan's foreign policy.

In the IBRD, Tokyo watches out for the interests of Asian borrowers and cautions against an overemphasis on Russia and East Europe, and its major initiative sought to put the Asian development model on the agenda for discussion. In the EBRD, Japan took a leadership role in promoting Central Asian interests, and Prime Minister Kaifu clearly incorporated concern for the Asia Pacific region in his explanation of an active policy in East and Central Europe. The Asian development model provides a framework within which Japan judges progress in the EBRD's mandated regions.

In some ways, Japan appears to be fostering a division of labor among the MDBs: It would take primary responsibility for Asia, especially through the ADB; the United States, as a global power, could focus on the World Bank and the IADB and Latin America; and Europe could take care of Africa and the AFDB as well as the EBRD and Russia and East Europe. Each major trilateral partner would assist the principal nation or nations in each bank and region, and these banks would foster greater cooperation through joint planning and operations while avoiding duplication and bolstering each other's scarce resources. The core nexus for Tokyo of such an international burden-sharing approach is Japan-Asia relations.

PURSUE GREATER INDEPENDENCE WITHIN AN AMERICAN FRAMEWORK. U.S.-Japan relations serve as the cornerstone of Japanese MDB policy. On the whole, Japan strives to cooperate with the United States on management and operational policy issues. This is evident in a broad range of issues, such as opposition to Russian membership and borrowing in the EBRD, channeling recycled funds through the World Bank in support of the Brady Plan, and siding with the United States rather than the ADB president on the American candidate for vice president. In all three banks, Japan and the United States have a close, consultative working relationship.

Yet this support role does not translate into submissiveness to Washington's dictates. Japan gradually has begun to develop its own "ideas" and policy approaches, and these often contrast with those of the United States. Dissatisfaction with the United States is widespread within Japan, increasingly expressed openly within policymaking circles and in international fora. In the 1990s, Japan consciously strives to promote an image of independence in its foreign policy, which is often measured by distance from U.S. policies and positions. This is evident in bilateral ODA policy, where Japanese positions and initiatives often clash with Washington's. The most notable examples are resumption of aid to post-Tiananmen Square China, the end of the 18-year-long aid freeze to Iran, the resumption of aid to Vietnam, an almost carte blanche aid commitment to Alberto Fujimori's Peru, and resistance to providing stronger aid to Gorbachev and Yeltsin's Russia.

Japan's independence is reflected in multilateral institutions as well. Tokyo sought preeminence in the ADB, breaking with the traditional policy of maintaining coequal status with the United States despite America's expected opposition, and complaining about American arrogance and ignorance of Asia. Japan challenged the development orthodoxy of the World Bank by suggesting that the neoclassical approach was inferior to a new, well-tested Asian development model. In the EBRD, Japan clearly found the American insistence on 100 percent private sector emphasis naive and unrealistic.

To some extent, this new attitude reflects a growing sense of nationalism in Japan, but it is perhaps more accurate to attribute it to greater self-confidence in the field of development and economic assistance among a new generation of elites, especially bureaucrats. The attitude sometimes borders on arrogance, especially when Japanese voices suggest that Americans tend to be naive, ignorant about Asia, and textbookish in their approach. This feeling of superiority is reminiscent of the pride felt in some quarters during the 1970s toward the Western recognition of the virtues of the Japanese management style. An increasing number of Japanese have begun to assume that their nation has discovered the true path to economic development in the developing world, a path that cuts through the Japanese and Asian experiences.

It is not totally accurate, however, to label Japanese behavior as a power struggle with the United States. Japan is generally content with its new status within these banks. Its challenges to the United States have been indirect and incomplete, if power is the goal. Its attempt at preeminence in the ADB seemed aimed more at compensating for a perceived American downgrading of the bank and its inability or unwillingness to contribute its share of funds. Japan pulled back once it was clear that the United States and others opposed Japanese preeminence. In the World Bank, Japan's challenge focused on the West Europeans who occupied the number-two to four positions, ahead of fifth-ranked Japan. Japan's insistence on the East Asian miracles study was not intended to replace the neoclassical orthodoxy but to point out its weaknesses and inadequacies and thus to initiate a discussion or debate. In the EBRD, Japan did not challenge America's position as the largest shareholder, nor did it chafe at the fact that Europeans held the majority of total votes. The EBRD was, after all, Europe's bank. Japan's role had been to moderate what it considered the extreme, unrealistic American positions and to mediate American-European differences.

ENHANCE NATIONAL PRESTIGE. The struggle for status in the world community constitutes one of the strongest impulses of Japanese foreign policy. This search extends back to the nineteenth century but gained increased importance with the tarnishing of the Japan's reputation as a result of World War II. One of the most effective ways for Japan, as a defeated nation, to return to the world community was membership in international organizations. Upon attaining UN membership in the mid-1950s, Japan designated UN diplomacy as one of the three pillars of its foreign policy, and it struggles today to obtain a permanent seat on the Security Council, even without a veto power.

MDBs also play a critical role in raising a nation's stature. They serve as a visible indication of a nation's standing in the international system. Japan's number-two position in the World Bank and EBRD and its number-one standing in the ADB come close to representing the nation's self-image with respect to its standing in the world community and the Asian region. The World Bank remains perhaps the most prestigious of the MDBs, a symbol of the Bretton Woods old world order. In recent years, its focus on debt and Second World issues has catapulted its standing as a pillar of an emerging new world order. The standing of the EBRD, the first institution of the post–Cold War era, is still ambiguous, but Japan desperately wanted to join the developed nation effort to assist the historic developments in that region. Japan's active stance parallels its bilateral activities in the regions covered by both institutions.

Japan's prestige has been tied most closely to the ADB's fortunes and reputation because of the intimate history that extends back to the founding years. But its status might have slipped in recent years. Japan intervened actively when the bank's reputation seemed in danger from internal difficulties in the 1980s, but that intervention seemed to take place for defensive reasons. Since that time, Japan has failed to present a vision for the bank's future despite the appearance of aid and development debates and an ODA Charter at home. While the World Bank and the EBRD are rising to meet the post–Cold War challenges in East Europe and Russia, the ADB seems somehow uninvolved in the new world order, failing to articulate even the merits of the Asian development model it in part bolstered. While focused on the traditional borrowers and needs of the region, which remain critical since poverty remains widespread in Asia, the ADB has not presented a vision that responds to the graduation of some borrowers, the future of China and Indochina, questions concerning Central Asian membership, and other issues of the 1990s.

Japan, of course, does not deserve sole blame for the apparent plateau reached by the ADB. Observers also can point to the absence of strong direction from the bank president and vice presidents and from the board of directors. But one could expect "ideas" to emanate from a nation that desires to become the sole number one nation in the bank, especially ideas about an area Japan considers its own neighborhood. Given the energy with which the Kaifu cabinet leaped into an relatively unknown East and Central Europe, and given the challenge to orthodoxy mounted in the World Bank,

Japan's apparent lethargy in the ADB is puzzling. Perhaps it is resting on its laurels since the ADB is widely considered to be the best managed—and most successful—of the regional development banks, or perhaps Japan finds taking the lead tougher in an area that still harbors suspicions against a former conqueror. Outside Asia, Japan does not face those constraints and, in that sense, is more able to exercise freedom of action. Japan's prestige in Asia is tougher to enhance and maintain, which may explain in part the nation's cautious and low-key activism in the ADB.

Japanese activism on the development as well as the institutional and diplomatic front is a distinguishing feature of the 1990s. The advocacy of philosophies, principles, ideas, charters, and development models now constitutes an integral part of Japan's multilateral diplomacy. However, the application of these principles and models has been asymmetrical, uneven, and often contradictory across MDBs. In the ADB, the Asian development model seems to undergird Japan's policy line, while the ODA Charter's political principles seem to get in the way. In the EBRD, the political principles of the ODA Charter parallel the political mandate and conditions of the bank's lending policy, while the assumptions of the Asian model seem to shape Japan's specific positions on technical issues. In the IBRD, Japan seems to prefer a middle course, somewhere between support for condition-ality (such as "good governance," with its political implications) and the market-oriented orthodoxy, and for the Asian model that it pressured the bank to study as a counterpoint to the orthodoxy.

Critics of this policy approach may complain of incoherence, schizo-phrenia, and the ultimate absence of solid principles. The dominant impres-sion is that of a clash between Western political principles and Asian development principles. Supporters may praise Japan's flexibility, pragma-tism, and move away from drift through the adoption, finally, of principles. Most observers focus on one of these philosophies, either the charter or the Asian model, as the main Japanese approach, but one needs to view them in tandem even though this will cause problems, for they are both comple-mentary and contradictory. However, because of the basic ambiguity of both philosophies, which allows a great deal of leeway in interpretation and application, they seem contradictory in substance and complementary in implementation.

The Foreign Ministry compiled the 1992 ODA Charter as a means of responding to politicians' calls for an official aid philosophy, presenting a coherent explanation for ODA to a Japanese populace increasingly suspicious of aid for foreigners in a time of recession, and answering foreign critics of Japanese ODA who complained about the ambiguities in Japan's motives and objectives. Many of the principles embodied in the charter are explicitly political, reflecting what many may say are the prevalent "universal" Western values propounded especially by the United States:

(1) Environmental conservation and development should be pursued in tandem.

(2) Any use of ODA for military purposes or for aggravation of international conflicts should be avoided.

(3) Full attention should be paid to trends in recipient countries' military expenditures, their development and production of mass destruction weapons and missiles, their export and import or arms, etc., so as to maintain and strengthen international peace and stability, and from the viewpoint that developing countries should place appropriate priorities in the allocation of their resources on their own economic and social development.

(4) Full attention should be paid to efforts for promoting democratization and introduction of market-oriented economy, and the situation regarding the securing of basic human rights and freedoms in the recipient country.[3]

These "Western"-sounding principles seem to depart significantly from Japan's traditional ODA policy approach of separating politics from economics and eschewing political conditionality. They seem to challenge especially the Finance Ministry's multilateral aid policy as well as the nonpolitical strictures of the IBRD and ADB's articles of agreement. It would be easy to picture this situation as a clash between differing philosophies emanating from two rival ministries. However, there is common ground that allows these ministries to coordinate and implement.

First, the charter does not carry the weight of law, and it does not specify implementation conditions and procedures. The charter is a policy statement, a cabinet resolution, not a legal document passed by the Diet. MOFA officials stress that these principles need not be applied in knee-jerk fashion in any predetermined manner. For example, a human rights violation in China need not trigger an immediate and automatic economic sanction by Japan. Rather, the charter allows for a long-term, step-by-step application of any type of sanction after bilateral and multilateral negotiations. Japan thus retains flexibility in the charter's application.

Second, the charter itself has built-in loopholes. In the paragraph before the listing of the four principles, conditions are established on when to apply the charter: Japan will take "into account comprehensively each recipient country's requests, its socio-economic conditions, and Japan's bilateral relations with the recipient country. Japan's ODA will be provided in accordance with the principles of the United Nations Charter (especially sovereign equality and non-intervention in domestic matters). . . ."[4]

The charter can, therefore, justify the avoidance of sanctions or any response to specific violations of its provisions. Here there are at least three escape clauses that allow Japan to do nothing if it so chooses: a reaffirmation of Japan's request-based approach; consideration of each issue on a case-by-case basis, taking into account the current state of overall bilateral relations; and adherence to the international principles of respect for national sovereignty and noninterference in the domestic affairs of other nations.

Finally, upon closer look at the charter's tenets, it is clear that few contradict MDB principles. In fact, they echo MDB policies adopted in the post–Cold War era. All MDBs have prioritized environmental issues, with the EBRD unique in its inclusion of environmental concerns in its charter. Military expenditures, weapons of mass destruction, and arms sales are currently within the purview of MDB loan decisions, with the IBRD having taken up the issue in 1990. And democratization and market-oriented economies are the accepted orthodoxy in all three of the MDBs, with the EBRD incorporating these principles in its charter as preconditions for loans.

From this perspective, the issue for Japan becomes selectivity and means rather than ends. The charter allows selective application of its principles. For example, the MOF may be skittish about placing conditions on a recipient nation's military policies but enthusiastic about guidelines for environmental projects. In addition, Japan's differences with the American version of the orthodoxy may lie in the realm of how, not whether, to achieve "universal" goals. Both nations can agree on democratization and marketization, but Japan may incorporate in its development strategy the role of the state and limited protectionism and gradualism over shock therapy.

Japan has managed, therefore, to retain maximum flexibility in its policies across MDBs: a nonpolitical "Asian" approach in the ADB, with necessary concessions to the political demands of nonregional members consistent with the ODA Charter; advocacy of "Western" political principles and universal values for East Europe and Russia in the EBRD, while utilizing the Asian experience as a guide to judging the bank's effectiveness; and adherence in the World Bank to a hybrid course, applying the charter principles when politics rears its head while touting the Asian model during discussions of technical development issues.

As long as Japan's charter does not strictly define its terms nor specify conditions for their application, the Finance Ministry is allowed considerable leeway in implementing—or not implementing—the charter. The MOF can continue with its bottom-line preference for the Asian model as the foundation of MDB policy rather than the charter, which is identified more with the Foreign Ministry anyway. In short, Japanese now prefer the Asian development model in its multilateral aid policy and the ODA Charter in its bilateral ODA policy. The overall impression is that of an ODA policy that reflects both the basic features of Asia's economic miracles and the universal political principles espoused by the West.

Japanese policymakers readily admit the ambiguities in these "ideas." Foreign Ministry officials candidly acknowledge the difficulty in operationalizing charter principles and Finance Ministry officials openly acknowledge the amorphousness of the Asian development model. Both the charter and the model are still in the process of development. This is a transitional era. Policymakers' mindsets have undergone change, but they are bureaucrats, and bureaucrats prefer pragmatic, incremental change. Based on our case studies, Japan's "ideas" will continue to evolve on a case-by-case, trial-and-error basis in which the nation will continue to attempt to integrate the charter and Asian model tenets. But the core of that effort is likely to shift more toward the lessons learned from Japan's own development experience.

POLICY PATTERNS

By the 1990s, Japan moved beyond its institutional gains as increased shares, votes, and management presence demanded commensurate policy contributions. Therefore, Japan began to respond in both the diplomatic and development arenas. It is now time to consolidate Japanese activities in our three MDBs into seven general underlying assumptions and patterns of behavior.

First, the U.S.-Japan nexus constitutes the pillar of Japan's MDB policy. The few analyses of World Bank policy ignore the context of Japan's push for a larger vote share, and this omission leads to the conclusion that Japan's motive was to challenge the United States. However, the United States was not the prime target. If anything, Europe filled that role. Japan did not seek to displace the United States as the leading nation in these banks. Rather it sought to work closely with the United States, and its challenges took the form of suggestions, often strong, for revising thinking or policy approaches. Japan remains a strong supporter and mild challenger of the United States. Tokyo did not consciously strive to establish Pax Nipponica in any of the MDBs. If anything, Japan would settle for Pax Ameripponica, an equal partnership between the two largest economies in the world. Japan strove for status more than power.

Second, Japan's MDB policy is formed within a trilateral framework. Tokyo may consider relations with the United States central, but Japan looks beyond Washington to the weaker European leg of the triangular relationship. Its policies within specific MDBs often reflect policy frameworks previously determined by the G-7, especially at its annual summits. Debt relief programs, Russian membership in the World Bank, aid to East and Central Europe, and resumption of ODA to China were policies worked out by the industrialized world at the summits in Toronto, Paris, Houston, London, Munich, and Tokyo.

Within these banks, trilateralism also may extend to recipient nations when countries, hesitant to voice complaints against the United States and Europe directly, request that Japan serve as an intermediary. However, Japan interacts most closely with the major donor nations within these institutions. The patterns seem clear: In the ADB, trilateralism takes the form of U.S.-Japan predominance, with Japan the de facto number-one nation and Europe in a weaker support position. In the EBRD, trilateralism takes the form of a U.S.-European partnership, with Europe the major force, and Japan playing a support role. In the IBRD, trilateralism takes the form of the United States and Europe at the core, with the United States predominant, and Japan somewhere between America and the West Europeans.

Third, Japan's MDB policy is Asia-centric. We have noted Japan's persistent concern for Asian interests in its participation in MDBs. Japan strongly believes that its main means of contributing to the global community is through attention to its own region. This is evident in its bilateral ODA policy and is reflected to a great extent in MDBs. Japan's policy toward international financial institutions reflects the strong emphasis on Asia found in Tokyo's overall foreign relations.

In the 1990s, Japan's policies toward all MDBs have become infused with a new theme—the clash between an Asian-type development model and the "Anglo-Saxon" development model. Japanese increasingly refer to "Anglo-Saxon" thought processes, which they usually consider mistaken, and criticize MDBs as "Anglo-Saxon" institutions. The racial, as well as cultural and ethnic, connotations of this particular usage of the term may signal a disturbing dimension in future Japanese policy toward international organizations (which many non-Western nations do view as Western-dominated), especially if Japan chooses to designate itself as a leader of the non-Anglo-Saxon forces in Asia.

Fourth, Japan thinks of its MDB policy in terms of an international division of labor. Consultation and coordination with the United States and West Europe provides an almost natural regional division of labor and bur-den-sharing arrangement for taking care of the world's development needs.

This coordination could avoid overlapping and duplication among donors; it could help troubled donor economies better target scarce financial resources for the maximum good abroad; and it could utilize the knowledge and expertise of each donor in its respective regions or technical areas for best effect. Division of labor for Japan is functional as well as regional. Japan would confine its commitment to nonmilitary national resources. Tokyo, with its constitutional restrictions on the use of force and deep-seated pacifist sentiment among the populace, would contribute money, nonmilitary personnel, technical assistance, and materiel. The United States could then take the initiative and primary responsibility for military assistance and peacekeeping operations throughout the globe, assisted by Europe. On the other hand, Japan, along with Europe, could take the lead, especially in Asia, in providing economic aid, consisting of ODA, other official flows, and private flows. This vision was shaken recently when Japan was criticized for its reluctance to provide little but money for the Gulf War effort, when it dispatched military personnel to Cambodia and Mozambique, and when its bubble economy burst. Despite these setbacks, Japan's policy still reflects the aspiration to establish some kind of regional and functional division of labor in multilateral as well as bilateral aid.

Fifth, national prestige constitutes a major objective of Japanese activities in all MDBs. Arguably, status concerns constituted the whole of Japan's MDB policies prior to the 1980s. It is difficult to identify pressing Japanese priorities, policy initiatives, or challenges to the established order or orthodoxy—except for issues that visibly improved its standing in the institution, namely, financial contributions and vote share. Activities in the World Bank symbolized Japan's general foreign policy interest in matching its status with its economic power; the EBRD enhanced Japan's global status by including Tokyo in the number-two club; and the ADB was considered the anomaly, with some Japanese considering it "their" bank.

Japan's MDB activism reflects a lesson learned in the 1980s—that national prestige no longer depended on the attainment of wealth but on how that wealth is used for the public good. It depends less on money and more on ideas and deeds. However, another pattern is also visible: An increase in Japan's prestige seems to imply the diminution of someone else's status. The attainment of larger shares by one nation automatically entails the loss of shares by others. Japan's rise in the IBRD and EBRD seemed to symbolize the decline of American power and European status, and America's effort to forestall Japan's predominance in the ADB seemed the rear-guard effort of a country desperately seeking to maintain top status but not willing to pay for it.

The corollary is that prestige-raising can engender opposition and resentment. It is clear that fellow MDB shareholders welcome Japan's rise grudgingly, especially the Europeans in the IBRD and Americans in the ADB, or that they prefer Japan to play only a certain specified role: Contribute money but not ideas. The IBRD East Asian Miracles report diplomatically but clearly discounted the applicability of the Asian model elsewhere; the EBRD, especially under Attali, viewed Japan suspiciously and preferred its financial role; and the ADB's American and European delegates, on the whole, opposed Japan's willingness to shoulder greater financial burdens in exchange for sole number-one status. In the 1990s, Japan has cited external criticism of its MDB policy of giving money but not ideas as a justification for greater activism. But what Japan finds, in reality, is that such uninvolvement is exactly what many foreign partners want.

Sixth, Japan's primary role in MDBs is that of mediator. Tokyo seems more interested in mediating incompatible interests and ideas in order to maintain general harmony and stability. It seems less interested in defending its own interests by forcing its own ideas onto others. Tokyo's behavior during the EBRD's formative period is a striking example of this behavioral pattern, especially in mediating the differences between the United States and Europeans on private sector lending. Japan mediated the problems that existed between Fujioka and the United States in the ADB; it sought to fashion a mutually acceptable compromise on Central Asian membership in both the EBRD and ADB; it represented China against the United States and Europe in the IBRD; it represents Asian nations against the board in the IBRD and ADB. In general, Japan increasingly seeks to act as intermediary between G-7 nations and between Asia and the West.

The role of "bridge" is a standard metaphor in Japanese foreign policy pronouncements. In the past, Japanese have often argued that Japan could serve as a mediator between the United States and Communist China, the United States and the Soviet Union, Iran and Iraq, ASEAN and Indochina, or the Third World and the First World. The concept is alive and well in the 1990s. It has become a pillar of Japan's MDB policy.

Seventh, and finally, this study also raised the question of whether MDBs were simply extensions of the nation-state or autonomous, organic entities capable of shaping state behavior. The reactive state approach alerted us to the latter possibility since it asks us to consider MDBs as components of an external environment that determines Japan's foreign policy.

We found that MDBs did exert influence over Japan prior to the mid-1980s, when Japan's policy was passive, fiscally-oriented, and lacking in ideas. It was greatly influenced by the dominant member nations, especially the United States, and it followed the lead of MDB managements. This included the ADB, even with—or because of—its Japanese president, large staff presence, and dominant share. In this earlier stage, MDB operations, policies, and philosophies provided the framework for Japan's policies. Tokyo basically lacked either the power or the will to exert power, or, perhaps more accurately, a reason for exerting power.

From the mid-1980s, as Japan's relative influence increased and activism came to distinguish its approach, MDB influence over Japan waned. The Japanese are in the process of establishing their own agenda, challenging some of the long-established rules of the game, while fashioning uses of the banks for broader diplomatic purposes. It is more willing to speak out and to exert influence. It has gained leverage over MDBs and, most important, it is willing to use it. This is not to imply that Japan totally disregards the banks' wishes or opinions, but it indicates that Tokyo is content to let the banks lead on some issues, especially on technical development issues, but that it no longer does so unquestioningly.

We have found numerous examples of Japan exerting its new found weight in these banks: Japan used its funds in the IBRD to initiate a study of the East Asian economies in hopes of stimulating consideration of a new perspective on the bank's development orthodoxy; it joined the United States in placing restrictions on Russian borrowing in the EBRD and took the lead on dual EBRD-ADB membership for CAR nations; it made a power play of sorts in the ADB by seeking to take sole possession of first place.

Japan's role in forcing the resignation of a strong-willed Japanese ADB president illustrated two basic points: MDBs can best exert influence over Japanese policy if Japanese nationals occupy top-level management positions, but even then, MDB influence is conditional on Tokyo's acquiescence. This may be a lesson to keep in mind as more Japanese emerge at the executive levels of international organizations and as Japan gains knowledge, experience, ideas, and self-confidence in the 1990s. Based on the ADB case, Japan acquiesced for a time, but it also took back the helm.

THE POLICYMAKING PROCESS

In our study of three MDBs, we have seen that the promise and problems of Japan's policy rest squarely on the shoulders of the nation's civil servants. Bureaucrats make and implement MDB policy. Other forces play a peripheral role: Interest groups participate in the implementation phase but do not constitute an influential policymaking presence; the media virtually ignores

MDB policy (as opposed to bilateral ODA); and the public remains ignorant and unconcerned about international financial institutions. All of these forces are more interested in multilateral aid policy funneled through the United Nations, primarily because of the higher status enjoyed by the UN and also because of the recent controversial involvement in peacekeeping operations. In the last decade, the debt crisis and the Russian aid issue have focused more attention onto MDBs, but even so, few laypersons closely follow the complex and intricate debt relief strategies or Russian aid arrangements. As a result, multilateral bank policy is made outside the limelight, and this works to the benefit of the bureaucrats. In other words, the state makes MDB policy.

Politicians play a sporadic, limited—but sometimes important—role. Their participation should not be ignored, but neither should their involvement be overemphasized. Most politicians remain ignorant about the details of MDB policy, though some have taken more of an interest in ODA policy of late. Younger politicians (those elected between two and five times) of the former ruling Liberal Democratic Party are notable for their interest in ODA policy. They have formed study groups, invited speakers, and fashioned policy proposals. Many of them served on the LDP's Special Committee on External Economic Assistance and followed aid policy developments. But ODA and MDB policy garner few votes in Japan, and the technical aspects of this complex issue area creates a dependence on the bureaucrats for information and understanding. And many of those interested focus on the public relations and prestige aspects of Japan's performance as the world's largest aid donor. Their greatest impact on MDB policy has been the demand that ministries get something in return for Japan's hefty contributions, namely, more votes and management positions.

The future impact of politicians remains unclear in the wake of the LDP's loss of power in 1993 and return to government in a coalition in 1994. Some of the younger LDP politicians joined the splinter parties, Shinseito and Shinto Sakigake. The shifting coalitions among these parties, the LDP, and the traditional opposition parties pose almost insurmountable problems for concentrated attention to ODA policy. The Hosokawa coalition government (1993-94) incorporated into the cabinet the most strident critics of ODA, the Socialists and Komeito. These critics were in a position to introduce foreign aid legislation or to urge restructuring of the aid policy process as ruling, rather than opposition, parties. Critics have vociferously called for both aid reforms. Yet nothing much was accomplished on their watch. Rather, the coalition parties singled out the bureaucrats, the caretakers of ODA policy, for criticism during the election campaign that brought them to power, and they joined in the American bashing of bureaucrats in the spring of 1994, shortly before the fall of the cabinet. Aid reform efforts came to naught, and with the collapse of the Hosokawa government and the advent of the LDP-Socialist-Sakigake cabinet in 1994, it remains to be seen if these critical attitudes will translate into policy. Given the past record, the advantages enjoyed by the bureaucrats will not only remain intact but be enhanced as Japan faces an extremely fluid and chaotic era in party politics. The prime minister can be a major actor in MDB policy. Prime Ministers have stepped into the policy process at key moments to initiate or serve as catalysts for policies. Nakasone Yasuhiro supported MOFA efforts to devise a debt relief proposal in 1986, ordering a reluctant MOF to get to work and produce a plan before the next summit. Kaifu Toshiki articulated Japan's political objectives in East European aid. Miyazawa Kiichi, who had an impact on MDB policy with his own debt plan as finance minister in 1988, spurred Soviet aid as chair of the 1993 Tokyo Summit despite strong misgivings at home. Prime Ministers have focused attention on the importance of both bilateral and multilateral aid, and they have defined the policy context of specific MDB policies. They have raised multilateral aid above the immediate, technical, and standard operating procedure level to a longer-term, political, and national priority status. This is one way of transforming bureaucratic politics into national priorities and ordinary measures into policy initiatives.

Yet the record of prime ministers since the fall of the LDP has been questionable. No articulation of ODA policy initiatives or principles has emanated from Japan under Prime Ministers Hosokawa, Hata Tsutomu, or Murayama Tomiichi. ODA policy initiatives do not seem to fare well under coalition governments. Bureaucrats, however, do.

The main locus of Japan's MDB policy remains the Ministry of Finance, which jealously guards its jurisdictional hold over MDB policy. Without movement in this bastion of bureaucratic tradition and conservatism, MDB policy cannot budge. The Budget Bureau controls the general budget, which includes economic cooperation allocations. The ODA budget is disbursed each year primarily through specific ministries. MOFA and MOF receive the lion's share of Japan's ODA budget each year. The Financial Bureau oversees the Fiscal Investment and Loan Program (FILP, or *zaito*), often cited as the "second budget." FILP receives approximately 80 percent of its resources through postal savings accounts (via the Trust Fund Bureau) and is the source of much of Japan's multilateral aid, especially through the OECF and the Export-Import Bank.

Of the seven bureaus in MOF, the International Finance Bureau (IFB) plays the key role in MDB policy. IFB holds jurisdiction over Japan's external financial affairs, everything from foreign exchange and balance-of-payments issues to foreign investment in Japan. In reality, restricting IFB activities to "external" affairs is difficult since it is increasingly difficult to maintain the distinction between "international" and "domestic" in an economically interdependent world. The director-general (*kyokucho*) of the IFB administers the operations of the entire bureau, though he does not necessarily come from within the ranks of the bureau, given the ministry's personnel policy of rotating generalists from post to post. He is assisted by an assistant director-general and two deputy director-generals (*shingikan*), one in charge primarily of administrative matters and the other in charge of international financial issues, including MDBs.

The IFB is comprised of several divisions that handle economic aid and multilateral diplomacy. The main divisions for MDB policy include: the Development Finance Division, which monitors bilateral ODA (yen loans) and Export-Import Bank loans; the International Organizations Division, which handles the IMF, OECD, and the G-7 summits; the Development Policy Division, which coordinates planning and the aid budget, and oversees technical issues such as the global environment; and the Development Institutions Division, which directly supervises the operations of the World Bank group and all regional development banks, including the ADB and EBRD.

At the top of the ministry's hierarchy are the minister of finance (*Okura daijin*), a political appointee; the administrative vice minister (*jimu jikan*), who occupies the highest career post in the ministry; and the vice minister for international finance (*zaimukan*), the third-ranking ministerial post. The finance minister serves as Japan's representative on the board of governors for all MDBs, with the governor of the Bank of Japan serving as alternate governor. The administrative vice minister is responsible for the entire operations of the ministry but concentrates on domestic matters. The vice minister for international finance, who has recently come from the ranks of the director-generalship of the IFB, is the principal official in charge of external policy, including MDBs. The *zaimukan* office also selects the executive directors (and alternate directors except for the EBRD) on the boards of directors of all MDBs, with candidates coming from various ranks within the ministry, depending, as we saw, on the specific MDB.

The MOF is believed to be the preeminent ministry, the elite of the elite, with its officials often accused of sharing this assessment. If money is power, then one understands why the MOF, with its strong grip on the economic cooperation budget, is blamed often for ODA policy immobilism. Likewise, Japan's MDB policy of "silence, smile, and sleep" is laid at the

MOF's doorsteps because of its power over the appointment of representatives to international financial institutions. The MOF's reputation rests on its adherence to bottom-line considerations as guardians of the national purse strings and on its preference for the status quo. How, then, did Japan's MDB policy move toward greater activism in the 1980s and 1990s amid this theology of frugality and conservatism?

The roots of a new MOF willingness to move are found in five developments from the mid-1980s.

First, MOF officials recognized the need to liberalize their thinking toward international issues as foreign and domestic pressure demanded the liberalization of the financial markets. By 1985, the ministry had taken steps to open domestic markets to foreign entrants and to liberalize restrictions on foreign operations in Japan. And Japan's new status as the world's largest creditor nation focused attention on how it could reduce that surplus, or how the surplus could be put to use for the betterment of the world economy. In other words, MOF officials were caught up in the themes prevalent in Japan at the time. The MOF foresaw the impending focus on Japan's financial resources and international responsibilities, and in this context, the potential utility of international financial institutions, over which the ministry had direct jurisdiction, became clear.

Second, the MOF strengthened its capacity to deal with international financial and especially development issues. Personnel policy changes were central in this effort. The MOF recognized the need for better-trained personnel in international finance and development. The ministry is considered a "national" ministry, focused primarily on domestic rather than foreign financial affairs. Its officials' career opportunities seemed enhanced if associated with the domestic more than the internationalist ladder. Therefore, the ministry revised its personnel training policy. For example, since the 1970s, about half of each year's entering class of officials was dispatched abroad early in their careers for periods ranging from a few months to two years. Popular destinations were Princeton University and Cambridge University, and one can find Princeton and British "mafias" in the ministry today. In 1994, the ministry began to dispatch all of its newly hired officials abroad as a regular rotation in their careers.

The MOF found MDBs increasingly useful for personnel policy. Upon the return of these officials to Tokyo from abroad, some are selected for secondment to international financial institutions for a two-year tour of duty. Some are dispatched to the African Development Bank or the Inter-American Development Bank; others are seconded to the IMF and IBRD to work in the financial departments; and some are sent to the ADB to serve as special assistant to the Japanese president. In other words, the ministry expanded its pool of personnel qualified for assignments dealing with external affairs.

Also, up to the 1980s, the ministry dispatched MDB executive directors who reflected the low-key, low-profile characteristics of the diplomacy of silence, smile, and sleep. The seniority system dictated that executive directors come from the old school, or those near retirement who are given an MDB post as their final MOF assignment. In the 1980s, however, the MOF began appointing younger executive directors to some MDBs, notably the ADB and IADB, or senior officials who were more assertive than those of the old school. The selection of younger officials resulted partly from a shortage of senior personnel to send, but it also reflected a desire to send younger, more articulate and assertive representatives to international institutions perceived to be in flux. The long-run effect of this policy shift may be the emergence of a cadre of more internationally minded and experienced officials who will return from the MDBs to take up influential positions in the International Finance Bureau or in positions that touch upon the ODA budget. They bring back to the MOF foreign language skills, expertise on development issues, expanded personal contacts abroad, knowledge of foreign financial markets, familiarity with the cultures of various regions of the world, insights into the workings of international financial institutions, and perhaps a greater wariness of the United States and the "Western" approach to development and diplomacy.

The potential impact of these personnel changes was most vividly demonstrated by the ADB case, when ex-ADB personnel returned to Tokyo to assume positions pivotal for not only ADB policy but for MDB policy in general. It may be only coincidental that Japan embarked on its propounding of the Asian development model and its indirect challenge to the United States in the World Bank during a time period when ex-ADB officials dominated the International Finance Bureau and the vice ministership for international finance. These officials were intimately familiar with the workings of the ADB, the development record of the Asian economies, and the proclivities of the United States on development issues. There is a strong likelihood, therefore, that the knowledge and expertise gained in Manila bore fruit in the assertiveness and self-confidence shown by Japan in the IBRD.

In any case, the prior experiences of MOF officials in one MDB is likely to have an impact on policies toward other MDBs. In the spring of 1993, in the International Finance Bureau, the director-general, the assistant director-general, and seven of the division directors (*kacho*) were veterans of service in an international financial institution. Of these nine officials, four served in the ADB, three in the IBRD, one in the IMF, and one in the AFDB.

There is one personnel problem that the Finance Ministry has not solved—the manpower shortage. Ideas are difficult to propound without individuals to propound them. The paucity of bureaucratic experts on ODA is well documented in Japanese ODA literature, but this is especially striking for MDB policy. In the pivotal Development Institutions Division of the International Finance Bureau, the hub of MDB policy, fewer than 15 career and support staff oversee the IBRD, ADB, EBRD, IADB, and AFDB. Many of Japan's gridlock-like problems may be the result of manpower shortages rather than interministerial battles; MDB policymakers' greatest battle may be with the workload rather than another ministry. This is a vexing problem for the MOF because it would be hard-pressed to justify an increase in its own staff at a time when it forces other ministries to adhere to zero-growth annual budgets.

Third, the ministry created a new Institute of Fiscal and Monetary Policy (IFMP) in 1985 to serve as both a research institute and the MOF's window to the outside world. Originally set up to conduct research and policy studies and to train MOF officials, by the 1990s, IFMP had expanded its activities. It has hosted visiting scholars from abroad, and it has increased the number of foreign trainees, especially government officials from finance ministries of developing nations. Training sessions involve briefings by MOF officials and outside experts on Japan's economy and financial system, and lectures and discussions by visitors on their financial systems. IFMP administered a training program for high-ranking government and central bank officials from ADB member countries until the early 1990s, and delegations of officials from Mongolia and the Central Asian Republics have been especially notable in recent years, in keeping with the ministry's focus on Asia. Therefore, the institute serves a dual role in the internationalization of the MOF: It gathers information on the outside world that can be of use to ministry officials, and, through its briefings to foreign officials, it educates an international audience about Japan's own development experience and political economy.

The fourth development within the MOF was the discovery of something to say within MDBs. The tenets of the Asian development model finally allowed the Japanese to match financial contributions with "ideas." This has been demonstrated especially in the World Bank, but the model has become the foundation for Japanese policy pronouncements in international fora beyond MDBs.

Fifth, the Finance Ministry works more closely with the Foreign Ministry in the area of policy consultation and coordination. The clear demarcation of jurisdictional mandates in MDB policy serves to dampen the usual bureaucratic turf battles and centralizes policymaking more than most public policy arenas in Japan. The standard picture of infighting and backbiting among bureaucratic feudal baronies represented by the four-ministry/agency consultative body is less relevant for multilateral bank policy than for bilateral ODA decisions. The Foreign Ministry has traditionally been one of the MOF's main adversaries, but in recent years, greater cooperation and coordination has occurred between these two institutions. Some of this is attributable to close working relationships among top-level ministry officials on both sides, but the main reason is mutual need. In some ways, the balance of power almost appears to be shifting to MOFA, which has managed to obtain its own "reserved posts" in the ADB legal department, though this may be in jeopardy,[5] and in the EBRD's alternate directorship, traditionally an MOF appointment along with the executive director. But in the end, it is the partnership between these ministries—a division of expertise and labor—that determines policies, and it is the MOF that predominates in the shaping of the technical details of those policies.

The primary reason for MOFA's inroads into MOF territory include the politicization of MDB activities, which requires extensive regional and country expertise and diplomatic acumen. The MOF, with its manpower shortage and lack of this kind of expertise, is hard-pressed to fill these needs, which are the specialty of the MOFA. This cooperation is not always smooth, for MOFA officials still complain about the unwillingness of the MOF to share information, and MOF officials scoff at MOFA's efforts to acquire yet more posts at MDBs. MOF officials also consider MOFA overly acquiescent to external pressures, especially from the United States, while MOF personnel view themselves as exhibiting greater resilience toward *gaiatsu*. But the pattern has taken old of MOF-MOFA consultation and agreement on policy issues before submission to the four-ministry/agency consultative committee.

This cooperative pattern has been visible in specific, high-visibility issues such as the debt plans, aid doubling pledges, Russian aid, and the Central Asian Republics strategy. The MOFA, rather than the MOF, has been the primary initiator of all these policies. But the MOF role is critical, especially because all of these developments involve pledges of financial assistance from national coffers. The MOFA can play an important support role; for example, the International Finance Bureau finds MOFA support helpful in its struggle with the tight-fisted Budget Bureau. It can utilize the ODA Charter as a justification for more funds to fulfill international commitments.

In other words, the MOFA provides the foreign policy context of economic aid, but the MOF pulls rank and takes the lead in fashioning specific policy proposals and in articulating these policies in MDBs. The MOFA can, therefore, establish the diplomatic agenda, but its intrusion into the MDB policy arena can be only at the margins. The unassailable grip of the MOF over international financial institutions mitigates the usual jurisdictional friction that accompanies Japanese bureaucratic policymaking. This arrangement has worked relatively well in our case studies. The marriage of the MOF's technical expertise and knowledge of international financial markets and the workings of MDBs, and the MOFA's expertise and knowledge of recipient nations and regions allows Japan to formulate a more informed policy approach.

This cooperative pattern may necessitate a revision of the commonly accepted view of the ODA policy process. The decentralized *yon-shocho kaigi* system of four-ministry/agency dominance, with its required consensus among all of the participants, is said to reflect and induce policy immobilism. However, the system is undergoing changes in two contradictory directions, with MDB policy clearly reflecting one of these directions.

One the one hand, the decentralization has intensified. Over the past decade, as Japanese ODA emerged as a foreign policy pillar, a further decentralization process has occurred because of the expansion of the ODA budget and activities. At least a dozen ministries and agencies are now involved in the policy process as ODA-related activities proliferated. ODA involves agricultural products, health care and medical equipment, construction projects, and many other technical aspects that fall under several separate ministerial jurisdictions. These ministries were drawn to ODA because it represented new opportunities to increase their own budgets, and they therefore managed to find ODA-related projects to develop. Proliferating actors and increased decentralization makes policy coordination more difficult, but it also does little to weaken the MOF's grip on ministerial budgets. It can, in fact, enhance the MOF's ability to play the divide-and-conquer game among ministries.

On the other hand, a centralization process is also visible, and it is this development that has direct relevance for MDB policy. Some observers have already deemed the system centralized in the sense that their favorite ministries dominate the consultative meetings and determine aid policy. Some argue that the MOF is in control because of its tight hold on the ODA purse strings; others may charge that Ministry of International Trade and Industry's influence is paramount because of the dominance of yen loans and infrastructure projects; others may point to the MOFA as the recipient of the largest portion of the ODA budget, with the largest number of aid personnel and with the ultimate responsibility for diplomatic relations with recipient nations. The Economic Planning Agency is seldom accused of dominating the four-ministry/agency process. Since the mid-1980s, another centralization pattern has emerged. On specific, high-profile diplomatic ODA issues, the Foreign and Finance ministries dominate the process. These two ministries consult and coordinate prior to the four-ministry/agency meetings, which then ratify the policy presented by the two institutions. We have encountered this pattern in our study of MDB policy. Therefore, contrary to expectations of gridlock or immobilism, this policymaking pattern facilitated activism. It led to a rough partnership between two jurisdiction-conscious ministries, and this led to a more active bilateral and regional diplomacy by the MOFA and a more active multilateral diplomacy in MDBs by the MOF. The complementary nature of the roles of these ministries implies greater policy consistency, which in turn implies that bureaucratic politics can produce foreign policy proactivism.

CONCLUSION

The comparative perspective of Japanese policies toward the IBRD, ADB, and EBRD has yielded a revealing picture of Tokyo's policy objectives in all of these MDBs, a clear picture of diplomatic behavior and emerging trends, and a better understanding of an emerging policymaking process that has implications for the nation's overall foreign policy. However, we have extracted our findings from three wide-ranging and quite different international financial institutions and from diplomatic issues that neither originated in nor dominated the agendas of any one institution. We also stated at the outset that an understanding of Japan's MDB policy requires an understanding of the nature and objectives of Japanese diplomacy in general. Our final task, therefore, is to consolidate our findings by applying them to a case study that transcends yet incorporates all of our MDBs. Only then can we begin to see the context and dynamics of Japan's multilateral development bank policy.

Part III

— ◆ —

THE NEW MULTILATERALISM IN A NEW WORLD ORDER

5

— ◆ —

THE MULTILATERALIZATION OF JAPAN'S POLICY TOWARD THE FORMER SOVIET UNION, 1989–1993

Liberality consists less in giving much than in giving at the right moment.

— Jean de la Bruyère

Assistance for Russia and its republics may constitute the greatest challenge to the fashioning of a stable and peaceful new world order. We have touched on the issue throughout our discussion of Japan's multilateral development bank policy. By focusing specifically on this case study, we will get a clearer picture of the interaction and convergence of the themes introduced in previous chapters. Japan's policy provides an interesting case study of post–Cold War multilateral diplomacy and a clue to how Tokyo may approach global responsibilities in a new world order.

The extent of the multilateralization of Japan's Russian aid policy is remarkable. It can be argued that Japan multilateralized its entire diplomacy toward Russia, including negotiations over bilateral political issues and all of its economic assistance, after the collapse of East Europe and the Berlin Wall in 1989. We can therefore observe diversification, politicization, and multilateralization at work in Japan's aid policy toward the former Soviet Union especially from the 1989 Paris Summit to the 1993 Tokyo Summit of the Group of 7.

Specifically, economic aid to the Commonwealth of Independent States is an excellent case study because it is one of the first and most important post–Cold War crises Japan confronted, one with global and historic implications for its international role; it allows us to view the government's interaction with external actors, especially Russia and the G-7, and domestic political forces; and it coincides with the period of Japan's MDB activism, both as a reflection of and catalyst for that activism. It is also a convenient issue in that Russia policy involves all three of our multilateral banks—the World Bank, Asian Development Bank, and European Bank for Reconstruction and Development. This overlap provides a more comprehensive view of the role played by MDBs in Japan's external policy. It will focus our attention where it should be in explaining MDB policy—on the role MDBs play in Japan's total diplomacy, and not on MDBs as policy ends in themselves.

THE MULTILATERALIZATION OF COMMONWEALTH OF INDEPENDENT STATES AID

The Russo-Japanese relationship qualifies as one of the most difficult and intractable of all of Japan's bilateral relationships. The Cold War drove a deep rift between the two nations, but the ambivalence, hostility, and lack of mutual respect is deeply rooted in events that extend back to the nineteenth century. Territorial issues, a war in 1904, Russia's belated entry into World War II two weeks before its end, the treatment of Japanese prisoners of war, tough fisheries negotiations and the seizure of Japanese fishermen, refusal to negotiate or even acknowledge Japanese territorial claims, the downing of Korean Air Lines flight 007 with Japanese passengers on board, persistent violations of Japanese air space, intelligence activities in Japan, the dumping of nuclear wastes in the Sea of Japan—all contributed to an antipathy that translated into inflexible policies.

The Japanese basically view Russia's Japan policy as harsh, hostile, and condescending. As one Japanese Russian expert puts it, "The Russians were seen as being pushy and self-centered, having a crude patriotism lacking in delicacy, having a habit of sticking to rules and depending more on strength than on courtesy, and having a national psyche that is a mix of feelings of superiority and feelings of inferiority."[1]

The advent of Mikhail Gorbachev in 1985 softened Japanese attitudes somewhat.[2] Gorbachev put the Northern Territories issue on the bilateral agenda, a reversal of Leonid Brezhnev's policy, although Russia still rejected Japan's claim to the Kuriles, the four-island chain of Habomai, Shikotan, Kunashiri, and Etorofu.[3] However, Japan clung to its rigid policy of rejecting Soviet requests for large-scale aid until the Northern Territories reverted to it. Japan did respond to Gorbachev with small steps, such as humanitarian aid and removal of the mention of the Soviet threat from defense white papers, but Tokyo was not caught up in the West's Gorbachev fever.[4]

Whatever strides were made by Gorbachev, Boris Yeltsin's reign since 1991 has rekindled strong resentment and challenged Russia's credibility. Japan's Northern Territories policy did exhibit greater flexibility, but without enthusiasm, initiation of large-scale aid, or sacrifice of the core issue of the reversion of the Kuriles. The flexibility was triggered by the fall of Gorbachev, the collapse of the Soviet Union, the West's intense efforts to bolster Yeltsin, and the beginning of Japanese realization that narrow national interests required adjustment to an emerging world order. Given external developments and domestic politics, small-scale economic assistance proved to be the most effective method for, and multilateral fora the most effective channels of, that adjustment. This becomes clear by focusing on the activities surrounding recent G-7 summits.

At the July 1989 Paris Summit, Japan lobbied to soften economic sanctions against China for the massacre of students and workers in Tiananmen Square in June, and announced an additional $35 billion surplus recycling plan intended for developing nation debt relief, bringing total Japanese commitments since 1986 to $65 billion. However, Western partners were turning their attention to East and Central Europe, where the region's political and economic systems collapsed. A multilateral economic assistance framework was forged under G-7 and G-24 auspices, under which the Kaifu cabinet would begin to channel bilateral aid, especially to Poland and Hungary, and multilateral aid, through the new EBRD.

By the 1990 Houston Summit, attention had turned from East Europe toward Gorbachev's Russia. West Germany and France, which had pressed successfully in the spring for Russian membership in the EBRD as a recipient nation, increasingly feared for perestroika's reforms and pushed for massive bilateral and multilateral aid to Moscow. West Germany in particular, which faced the domestic cost of reunifying East and West Germany and feared the flow of refugees from the east, pressed for G-7 endorsement of more Soviet aid.

As in EBRD negotiations, the United States and especially Japan hesitated. Japan in particular opposed large-scale Russian aid and pressed, instead, for resumption of large-scale aid to China. Both the United States and Japan, however, agreed in principle to support Gorbachev, thus granting Germany and France their endorsement. Japan, in turn, received tacit endorsement from the United States and the Europeans for its main agenda item—resumption of economic aid to China. However, for the Japanese government, Houston was the opening round of what would be a long, intense struggle to obtain domestic support for aid to Russia while seeking to moderate G-7 partners' enthusiasm for aid.

By December, both the United States and Japan began to relent on their initial hesitation on food assistance. The United States approved $1 billion in federally guaranteed loans for food purchases and proposed a special association for Russia in the IMF and World Bank. Washington was caught between a desire to strengthen Gorbachev's domestic position and an unwillingness to expend large amounts of aid. The reliance on multilateral methods was visible at the April 1991 G-7 meeting of finance ministers and central bank heads. Secretary of State James Baker emphasized the importance of multilateral aid by reitering U.S. support for Russian special association membership in the IMF and World Bank and urging action by NATO, the CSCE, and the EC.[5]

In November, Japan announced its decision to aid the victims of the Chernobyl nuclear station accident and in December, joined the United States, by pledging $8.3 million in humanitarian aid for food and medicine, but specified that it must be disbursed through a multilateral channel, the Red Cross. In addition, Tokyo promised another $100 million in Export-Import Bank credits. As Kaifu noted, "The United States is taking the same approach as we are."[6] This decision established the shape of Japan's future aid to Russia: Unless the Northern Territories issue is resolved, Japan's aid will remain small scale rather than large scale, humanitarian rather than developmental, semiofficial rather than official, and multilateral rather than purely bilateral. As Chief Cabinet Secretary Sakamoto Misoji pointedly noted, "Economic assistance and humanitarian assistance are two separate matters."[7]

Gorbachev visited Japan in April 1991, leaving empty-handed after virtually pleading for large-scale economic assistance. Japan's policy can be characterized as exactly the opposite of its traditional approach of separating politics from economics (*seikei bunri*). The Japanese refer to their Russian approach as "the inseparability of politics from economics" (*seikei fukabun*). Ironically, Gorbachev complained that Japan "stressed politics" while "we stressed economics."[8]

As the July 1991 London Summit approached, Germany had accepted the U.S. focus on Russian association with the IMF and World Bank as another, though indirect, aid channel.[9] However, the Europeans expressed a wish to invite Gorbachev to London. The United States and Japan opposed the move, with Kaifu strongly opposed. Both countries eventually accepted Gorbachev's presence, but Japan relented only after British Prime Minister John Major proposed that Gorbachev be invited separately from the summit and should not be allowed to request economic aid when addressing the summit.[10]

Gorbachev attended the summit but left without a large G-7 aid commitment. The G-7 agreed on special association for Russia in the IMF and World Bank, but the United States and Japan joined forces to block a request for full IMF membership and more drawing rights at the EBRD, which was limited at the time to Russia's paid-in capital share, as explained in chapter 3. Gorbachev, however, set the stage for future summits as "G-7+1" gatherings.

For the United States and, to some extent, Japan, a turning point came in August. Gorbachev survived an attempted coup d'état, which highlighted his precarious political position. A Foreign Ministry spokesperson stated that "Japan deems it important that there be collaboration within the G-7 framework amid this kind of situation," and Tokyo called for a G-7 meeting.[11] Japanese attitudes changed, accepting the urgency of some kind of substantive support for the Russian government. Japan also began receiving stronger pressures from Germany and from a United States that was galvanized into action.[12]

Japan had pulled together an emergency aid package for the October G-7 ministers' meeting in Bangkok. The package totaled $2.5 billion, divided between $1.8 billion in trade credits, $200 million in export credits, and $500 million in Export-Import Bank loans for food and medicine. Japan noted that this package was in addition to a December 1990 $100 million humanitarian aid pledge, although those funds had not yet been disbursed.[13] It also began to invite Soviets to journey to Japan for training in finance through an EBRD program.[14]

The aid package put Japan on the same level as aid to the Soviet Union by the EC, the United States, and Canada. However, the aid remained small scale, humanitarian, and multilaterally determined. Japan wished to go no further, and said so. It stated that any further steps would be taken in consultation with the United States. Japan's aid, observers noted, contained only $500 million worth of additional aid, and Japan attached conditions. The conditions—Soviet provision of accurate data, economic reform planning in cooperation with the IMF and World Bank, clarification of relations between the central government and the new republics, and determination of who is responsible for paying the national debt to Western institutions— were worked out in consultation between Finance Minister Hashimoto Ryutaro and Secretary of the Treasury Nicholas Brady.[15]

Gorbachev fell from power and the Soviet Union dissolved by the end of 1991. The United States hosted a meeting in Washington in January of 1992, a month after Gorbachev's fall and Yeltsin's election to the presidency. The United States expressed support for full IMF/IBRD membership for Russia, which the G-7 endorsed. Japan pledged a minor increase ($50 million) in its aid, again designated humanitarian and again to be channeled through the Red Cross.[16] And once again, Japan announced conditions, this time political ones, for its aid. Foreign Minister Watanabe Michio cited three conditions: economic reforms that would lead to a market-oriented economy; political reforms that would democratize the nation and halt Russia's military buildup; and a foreign policy based on law and justice.[17] The conditions reflected the new political themes, announced by Kaifu, in Japan's ODA policy, and also its concern about Russia's nuclear and conventional military strength in Asia. "Law and justice" refers to Russia's pledge that the Northern Territories would be settled according to these two principles.

In April, the G-7 announced a $24 billion, one-year aid package for Russia. The package contained $11 billion in bilateral aid, $4.5 billion in IMF/IBRD loans, $2.5 billion in debt payment deferrals, and a $6 billion ruble stabilization fund. Japan openly criticized the circumstances of the package's unveiling, arguing that the specific sums had not been agreed upon and that it had not been consulted about the announcement.[18] On the other hand, Japan could take comfort in the fact that the package did not require new allocations from either it or the other G-7 nations. Much of the $11 billion bilateral portion had been announced previously, and both the United States and Japan could draw their contributions from previously authorized funding sources.[19]

The G-7 urged Russian acceptance of IMF conditions for borrowing from the package. Yeltsin had submitted an economic reform plan to the IMF in March, and the G-7 hoped to hold Russia to its stringent standards.[20] In August 1992, the IMF approved $1 billion for Russia as the first of three scheduled tranches. Subsequent tranches are conditional on implementation of reforms. Japan, strongly skeptical of Russia's ability to manage daily affairs, much less effect reforms, fully supported stringent IMF preconditions.

In June, Russia joined the World Bank. It paid in $26.3 million and 236.5 million rubles, entitling it to 2.99 percent of total shares (or seventh place alongside Canada, India, Italy, and Saudi Arabia). IBRD president Lewis Preston announced that planning was under way that forecasted $20 to 25 billion for Russia and $20 billion for the 14 republics in 1994 and an annual lending program of $4 to 5 billion by 1995.[21] The IBRD's first loan to Russia occurred in August, a "rehabilitation" loan consisting of $250 million for imports by the private sector and $350 million for priority imports in the health, agriculture, transportation, and energy sectors.[22]

The $24 billion aid package represented the July 1992 Munich Summit's commitment to Yeltsin. The largest portion was bilateral, but the IMF and World Bank were assigned a significant role as major conduits for the aid. The IMF, in particular, emerged as the G-7's aid package manager and enforcer by attaching its conditions and policies on the new Russian government's borrowing. By this time, Japan had grown uncomfortable with what it viewed as the G-7's overly Russia-centric emphasis. Within months after the dissolution of the Soviet Union, while still hesitant on aid to Russia, Japan began focusing on the Central Asian Republics as its area of emphasis. Already by March 1992, the government began planning for CAR aid and ended the ban on untied loans by Japanese banks to republics of the former Soviet Union.[23] In April, the government announced an aid package for food, medical supplies, and other basic needs for CAR nations. Foreign Minister Watanabe's visit to Russia included a weeklong swing through Central Asia, the first visit by a Japanese cabinet minister.[24] Also in April, the Finance Ministry's Institute for Fiscal and Monetary Policy inaugurated exchanges with the CARs, hosting visiting scholars, holding seminars, and receiving delegations for briefings on Japanese fiscal and monetary policies.[25]

In October, Japan hosted a G-7 CIS aid conference, at which Japan pledged an additional $100 million. It specified that priority would be given to the Central Asian Republics and the Russian Far East. Japan was bothered that only about 6 percent of its contribution to the previous aid package at the Washington conference was earmarked for CAR; the bulk had been reserved for Russia. This time Japan designated about 15 percent of the new commitment for CAR nations.[26] As a senior Foreign Ministry official explained, "Of course, providing assistance to Russia is regarded as a top priority. But as an Asian nation, we would like to lend greater support to the former Soviet states in the Asian region."[27]

The Tokyo conference accepted the idea of World Bank Consultative Groups to coordinate aid to the republics, and in December, G-7 nations met in Paris to lay the groundwork for IBRD Consultative Groups for Kazakhstan, Kyrgyzstan, Azerbaijan, and Uzbekistan.[28] Watanabe announced plans to invite 300 engineers and experts from the CAR states over the next three years, and Japan announced its intention to open embassies in Ukraine, Kazakhstan, and Uzbekistan from January 1993.[29]

Also in October 1992, the vice minister of finance for international affairs, Chino Tadao, led an MOF fact-finding mission to Uzbekistan, Kyrgyzstan, and Kazakhstan. Chino's delegation talked with Central Asians in great detail about economic reform, the Soviet debt issue, currency problems, and dual EBRD-ADB membership possibilities.[30] Delegation members were struck by the economic inroads already made by South Korea and China and by the political, cultural, and religious involvement of Turkey and Iran in the region. Central Asians expressed a particular interest in receiving training in Japan rather than the United States and Europe. Chino responded by inviting government representatives to Tokyo for three weeks of seminars and briefings at the Finance Ministry's Institute of Fiscal and Monetary Policy in February 1993.[31]

Japan took the initiative in late November to place the CAR nations on the OECD's DAC list of developing nations. It pressed against initial opposition from the United States (concerned about Israel's status) and France (concerned about procedural issues), and against those nations that would be removed from the list. However, Japan felt this step necessary to justify the flow of its official aid to Central Asia. All five CAR states—Kazakhstan, Kyrgyzstan, Tajikistan, Turkmenistan, and Uzbekistan—were placed on the DAC list in early December.[32] By 1993, the doors were open to the one aspect of Russian aid that elicits a positive Japanese response—aid to Russia's Asian republics. In January, Japan announced plans to provide loans of up to $100 million each to Kazakhstan and Kyrgyzstan through the IBRD Consultative Groups.[33]

As 1992 came to a close, Japan became increasingly uncomfortable with its relationship with fellow G-7 members, especially the Europeans, and with its bilateral relationship with Russia and Yeltsin in particular. Germany and France began expressing their disappointment with Japan's cautious and hesitant attitude toward large-scale Russian aid. The year 1993 began with complaints about the failure of an ailing Foreign Minister Watanabe to attend the January Washington conference. The Japanese, in turn, expressed disappointment at the low level of representation at the October Tokyo conference, especially if the G-7 deemed Russian aid so important.[34]

Germany criticized Japan in February, soon after the Washington conference, and took aim at Japan again in May. Chancellor Helmut Kohl noted that Germany pledged about $47 billion to the former Soviet Union and $65 billion to East Europe, with East Germany absorbing the bulk of that aid.[35] Prime Minister Miyazawa Kiichi visited Chancellor Kohl and President François Mitterrand in May, and both leaders pressed Japan for more financial assistance for Yeltsin.

Miyazawa maintained a cautious stance. From the Japanese perspective, Tokyo had already made concessions to Russia when Watanabe raised the possibility in April that Japan might accept Russia retaining administrative control of two of the Northern Territories islands if it accepted Japanese sovereignty over all four. That is, if Russia would return Habomai and Shikotan, Japan would allow Russia to continue to administer Kunashiri and Etorofu.[36] Russia remained unresponsive, however, and both Kohl and Mitterrand offered to mediate the dispute by approaching Yeltsin on Japan's behalf to end the impasse.[37]

Japan followed a multilateral Russian strategy by persuading the G-7 to include a statement supporting Japan's Northern Territories claims in the Houston and Munich Summit communiqués. It hoped that the support from the G-7 would put added pressure on a weakened Russia to relent. As Miyazawa reiterated to Mitterrand, "The territorial dispute should be the common concern of the entire Group of Seven industrialized nations."[38]

However, the Europeans began to attack Japan's stance as inflexible and self-centered and its attitude toward Russia as uncaring and shortsighted. Due to the frequency and the harshness of the criticism, Japanese policymakers became fearful of their isolation from mainstream views on Russian aid. By the end of 1992, Europe had grown increasingly restive with Japan's position, and the United States had shifted toward greater support for Yeltsin. Watanabe was quoted as saying that "Japan will become an orphan if it keeps saying 'no, no' at a time when the whole world is trying to help Russia."[39] The government became caught between opposition at home to unacceptable compromises with Russia on the Northern Territories issue and economic aid friction abroad with G-7 partners at a time when Tokyo was stressing coordinated, cooperative multilateral territorial and aid policies.

G-7 criticism and pressure intensified again in the spring of 1993. By then, Yeltsin was engaged in a bitter struggle with the old guard–dominated Congress of People's Deputies, elected before the breakup of the Soviet Union, and faced an April 25 referendum on his presidency and his reform program. Other G-7 countries sought to demonstrate support for him and his reform platform. In March, Mitterrand called for an early summit.[40] Kohl dispatched a letter to G-7 heads of state expressing concern about Yeltsin's difficulties, and Foreign Minister Klaus Kinkel complained openly that Japan was the main reason why the G-7 could not provide stronger support for Yeltsin.[41] Britain also expressed support for some kind of early summit, but Japan, caught off guard and concerned about detracting from its hosting of the July Summit in Tokyo, responded negatively.

The new American president Bill Clinton met with Yeltsin in Vancouver in April. Clinton pressed for some kind of visible support from G-7 members for Yeltsin before the referendum but took pains to tell Yeltsin that Japan has not been intransigent: "The Japanese have been very forthcoming as the leaders of the G-7. This is their year to lead and they are leading."[42] Clinton suggested a ministerial-level summit instead of a heads-of-state summit prior to the July Tokyo Summit, a position Japan eventually accepted.

The resulting April ministerial meeting in Tokyo drew up a new $43 billion aid package for Russia in time for the referendum. Japan's contribution came to $1.82 billion. Tokyo's package consisted of (1) $320 million in grants, including $100 million for emergency foodstuffs and medical aid, $20 million for human resources development, $30 million for small- and medium-sized enterprises, and $100 million for dismantling nuclear weapons; and (2) $1.5 billion in loans, with $1.1 billion in trade insurance, especially for energy resources, and $400 million in Export-Import Bank loans especially for the energy sector and small to medium size businesses.[43] Japan had originally planned to contribute $1.2 billion, but when the United States announced its $3.6 billion package, Japan raised its contribution to half that amount.[44]

However, in his keynote address, Prime Minister Miyazawa alluded to Japan's lack of confidence in Russia's ability to get its house in order and to the limits of external aid: "In the final analysis, it is the Russians themselves who can make their own reforms work. The task of the international community is to help ease this sometimes painful transition for the Russian people, by providing the necessary 'help for self-help.'"[45]

Miyazawa elaborated on the need for aid to genuinely meet the needs of the Russian people and to build effective institutions that will sustain the transition to a market economy—conditions, in the Japanese view, that should have been met already. Finally, he emphasized two themes of Japan's aid to Russia, G-7 stewardship and multilateralism:

> Our assistance should be closely coordinated through constant consultation among the major donors and international organizations as well as close contact with Russia so that our combined efforts can produce the maximum results. The G-7 countries should play a leading role in this respect, and today's meeting is expected to mark an important step forward in this process.[46]

Some Japanese officials expressed concern about the emphasis on multilateral aid because it did not reduce external criticism of Japan. According to MITI vice minister Tanahashi Yuji, "Japan cannot correct the misperception that we are not giving aid, if we keep channeling the money to international organizations for disbursement."[47] But domestic politics dictated an indirect rather than direct method of aiding Russia.

Japan had formulated another three, albeit informal, conditions for its aid. In the words of a Finance Ministry official, the three expectations were that aid should support the self-help efforts of the Russian people, should be effective and disbursed in accordance with the progress of reforms, and should be pragmatic, visible, and tangible.[48]

By the time of the July Tokyo Summit, Japan's tougher views were in accord with general G-7 opinions. Yeltsin had won his April referendum,[49] which allowed the G-7 to talk tough about needed reforms. But more important, as Russia had not fulfilled its commitment to the IMF, the Fund withheld the first $1.5 billion tranche. In addition, of the $24 billion pledged at Munich, only $16 to $17 billion had been disbursed, and of the $43 billion committed at the April presummit ministerial conference, only $610 million had been utilized (a World Bank loan to the oil sector).[50]

In this atmosphere, even Europeans hesitated to make further commitments of money. At the April conference, Clinton had proposed creating an additional $4 billion privatization support fund and a $3 billion fund for dismantling nuclear weapons.[51] The Europeans as well as Japan balked on both funds. Clinton withdrew his proposal for the nuclear dismantling fund, substituting instead a contribution of $1.6 billion in June; Japan had pledged $100 million in April.[52] The $4 billion fund was scaled down considerably at the Tokyo Summit after strong European resistance to providing more funds.[53] Japan had served as a mediator between the United States and Europe ever since Clinton's proposal in April.

The final result of G-7 negotiations was an aid package that would be disbursed primarily through multilateral institutions:[54]

— IMF Systemic Transformation Facility: $3 billion
— World Bank import rehabilitation loans: $1.1 billion
— IMF standby loans: $4.1 billion
— IMF currency stabilization fund: $6 billion
— World Bank loan commitments: $3.4 billion
— Cofinanced World Bank oil sector loan: $500 million
— EBRD small and medium-size enterprise fund: $300 million
— Export agency credits and guarantees: $10 billion

The Tokyo Summit reflected Japan's stance more closely than did the previous summits. The G-7 emphasis on self-help and effective use of aid echoed Japan's beliefs. The Europeans and Americans were more cautious toward Yeltsin and his government's ability to enact political and economic reforms, and were willing to say so once Yeltsin's power base was steadier than in the prereferendum period. On the other hand, Japan had moved toward a more accommodating stance on both the Northern Territories and the economic aid issues, though grudgingly on the former and unenthusiastically on the latter. It is doubtful that Japan would have moved much on either had it not been Tokyo's turn to lead the G-7 and host the 1993 summit. The government feared possible isolation from other G-7 members, and some officials began to realize the stakes in ignoring Yeltsin's plight for an emerging new world order. Japan's moves responded to both external imperatives and changes in perceptions within the nation. It is clear that Japan responded to external pressure from the G-7. Yeltsin did not trigger its policy change. The Japanese were cool to Yeltsin from the time he assumed power. Tokyo did feel that Gorbachev could not have been saved even if the West had provided the massive aid he had wanted, and they felt it unrealistic to place so much confidence in one person, either Gorbachev or Yeltsin. Russia's problems were beyond the ability of one individual to cure, especially since the country lacked the tradition of democracy and the foundation for a market economy.[55]

Besides, Yeltsin's actions and attitude grated on Japan. Personality had a large impact. The president had been scheduled to visit Tokyo, along with South Korea and China, in early September of 1992.[56] Only four days before his scheduled arrival in Tokyo, he suddenly postponed the visit, citing domestic difficulties in a telephone call to Miyazawa. The canceled visit had caused concern and resentment, but what happened subsequently touched off what can be called a "Yeltsin shock." Yeltsin publicly claimed that Japan's Northern Territories stance was the real reason for the postponement, despite the fact that, in Tokyo's view, Japan had made significant concessions to Moscow. Concessions included the adoption of an "expanded equilibrium" policy that loosened the rigid relationship between the Northern Territories and economic aid; in other words, improved political relations no longer remained an inflexible prerequisite for the extension of aid.[57]

In addition, Yeltsin attacked Japan's economic aid efforts for Russia, asserting that it provided less assistance than any other G-7 nation. This rankled the Japanese since it came on the heels of their first aid package, which elevated Japan to fourth place in total commitments to Russia among G-7 nations. Despite the visit's postponement, Japan went ahead with a $700 million trade insurance commitment for natural gas development and a $100 million loan from the Export-Import Bank.[58]

Finally, Yeltsin made clear that his proposed trips to South Korea and China would continue on schedule. He set no date for the postponed trip to Japan until March of 1993, when he expressed an interest in visiting in May, just before the Tokyo Summit.[59] However, Japan perceived this as a response to Clinton's favorable assessment of Japan's aid efforts. When Yeltsin won his referendum in April, he once again postponed his May visit, leading the Japanese to feel that they were being manipulated and not being rewarded for their policy shift.[60]

Yeltsin's actions confirmed Japan's already ambivalent to hostile perception of the Russian president. The government had to contend with the deep resentment touched off by his actions and attitudes at a time when it had adopted a more positive policy toward the territorial and aid issues. The response within the Liberal Democratic Party was emotional, leading Chief Cabinet Secretary Kato Koichi to urge calm and restraint in the party.[61] Foreign Ministry officials were caught off guard by what they considered a highly unusual diplomatic snub. And Yeltsin's decision reinforced comments heard within the LDP and especially the business community that Russia simply did not appreciate Japan's efforts thus far.[62] As one observer noted,

> The cancellation of Yeltsin's [September] visit to Japan did more than just trample Japan's hopes for a speedy return of the Northern Territories. The Japanese were deeply hurt by the manner in which the trip was called off and by the announcement that Yeltsin would visit South Korea instead. Overbearing Russian diplomacy and contempt for the Japanese, which had lapsed to a large degree during the Gorbachev era, returned at a single stroke.[63]

In short, it is clear that Japan's policy changes and aid packages progressed despite, and not because of, Yeltsin. What Japan found critical was its relationship with the G-7 and not Yeltsin, in whom they had little confidence or trust, and for whom they had minimal personal affinity. Tokyo recognized the strength of Russian national pride, which they saw in EBRD negotiations over Moscow's hesitance in accepting conditions on its borrowing, and thus understood Yeltsin's unwillingness to appear conciliatory on the Northern Territories issue. But the Japanese also recoiled from the perceived slight to their national dignity. The G-7's focus at the Tokyo Summit on Yeltsin's unfulfilled reform commitments and the need for a microeconomic focus on specific projects and sectors reflected Japan's doubts about how effectively Russia would utilize foreign assistance. That perception had not changed.

PATTERNS OF BEHAVIOR

The multilateralization of Japan's Russia policy resulted partly from design and mostly from necessity. The dissolution of the Soviet Union, following the collapse of East and Central Europe, necessitated a multilateral response by the Western nations. The transformation of the international system created problems beyond the ability of individual nations to address and required a coordinated approach. None of the Group of 7 members was willing or able to accept primary responsibility for the task ahead. This was not the Marshall Plan era, when the United States stepped forward with economic aid, leadership, and ideas. Neither could West Europeans step into the breach in their backyard, for their economic aid capability was limited and their leadership focused on getting others to provide aid and ideas. Multilateralism was thus the necessary response to a historic crisis by reactive states.

Like all other nations, Japan did not foresee the transformation of the Second World in Europe and basically reacted to its aftershocks. The past record of Japan's attitudes toward and interaction with Russia also served to constrain domestic policies and narrow diplomatic freedom of action. Japan's multilateral approach thus resulted from both of these facts—that the international environment and general consensus on the multilateral approach were givens and that bilateral diplomacy with Russia was shaped by domestic politics and Russian behavior. Japan's activism was carried out in a reactive context, but this alone did not distinguish the nation from its G-7 partners.

Japanese policy toward the former Soviet Union applies to all three of our MDBs and reflects the patterns of behavior unearthed by our comparative study—a G-7 framework, the primacy of relations with the United States, an Asia-centric foundation, a division of labor among the MDBs, an obsession with national prestige, and a proclivity for a mediatory role.

Japan's multilateral activism was a component of its G-7 diplomacy. Activities centered on G-7-related meetings: annual summits, ministerial conferences, or G-7–initiated working or consultative groups. Tokyo consistently sought coordinated action through G-7 planning and endorsement. The interaction within the G-7, however, was not altogether smooth and unproblematic.

Japan's relationship with its G-7 partners on the Russian aid issue resembled the pattern of interaction witnessed during the formation of the EBRD. Policy initiatives originated in West Europe, especially from Germany and France. The United States and Japan responded halfheartedly in the beginning, moving slowly and reluctantly toward greater attention and aid for Russia. The United States eventually pulled ahead of Japan and, with the Clinton administration, even West Europe to some extent. Europe, which had been critical of Japan, joined with it in moderating Clinton's financial aid proposals leading up to the 1993 Tokyo Summit. Japan, outpaced by the Europeans and then the United States, feared isolation from other G-7 members and gradually moved toward, but not even with, the other six.

From the Washington ministerial conference of 1992 through the April Clinton–Yeltsin and emergency G-7 ministerial conferences, the United States gradually assumed a leadership role for Russian assistance. By the time of the Tokyo Summit, Japan's final aid tally generally matched the level of European commitments.

As in the World Bank (and the IMF), the most notable friction occurred not between the United States and Japan but between the Japanese and the West Europeans. France and Germany, in particular, singled out Japan for criticism for its perceived foot-dragging on aid for both Gorbachev and Yeltsin. Unlike the perceived Japanese challenge to their status within the World Bank through the use of financial contributions, both European nations sought substantial Japanese increases. Vote shares or managerial positions were not involved here. Japan, on the other hand, perceived a threat to its prominent status as chair of the G-7 in 1993 when Europeans suggested a top-level G-7 summit prior to the Tokyo Summit. In this case, the United States mediated Japanese and European differences.

Japan also found the G-7 useful in multilateralizing its bilateral impasse with Russia over the Northern Territories. Annual summit communiqués at Houston and Munich specifically incorporated Japan's position on the Kuriles. Japan obviously found these fora useful for strengthening its bilateral efforts to get the islands returned. It expected the open and explicit backing of the G-7 to bolster its efforts against Moscow, and the multilateralization of the issue played better at home. It did not play well in Moscow, especially after Munich, and may have contributed to renewed intransigence on the issue after Yeltsin's assumption of office. But by making the bilateral issue a G-7 issue, Japan opened a new front and elicited offers by France and Germany to mediate a solution.

Within the trilateral relationship, the centrality of Japan's relationship with the United States is also clearly revealed throughout. Tokyo tries hard to coordinate its policy especially with Washington. Examples include the initial decisions to extend humanitarian aid to Russia in late 1990, the initial hesitation on acceding to German and French insistence on large-scale Soviet aid at Houston, the initial opposition to expanding the G-7 Summit at London to include Gorbachev, the opposition to full IMF/IBRD membership, the veto on increased Russian drawing rights in the EBRD, and the decision to increase its second aid package to half the amount of America's package. There are several instances as well where Japan consulted first with the United States on technical issues, including plans to dismantle Russian nuclear weapons. In these instances, Japan's interests coincided with those of the United States.

Japan, however, was not a camp follower of American policy dictates. As the United States moved toward a more positive attitude toward Russian aid, Japan found itself increasingly out of step with all G-7 members. It remained stubbornly committed to the return of the Northern Territories while making changes in tactics and strategies to effect that return. And it staked out its own areas of emphasis, including assuming the principal role of benefactor for the Central Asian Republics. Initially the United States expressed strong disapproval of the Japanese proposal to seek dual EBRD-ADB membership for the CARs. However, on the Russian aid issue, at no time can Japan's activities be interpreted as a challenge to America's power or status. Like U.S.–Japan relations in MDBs, Japan's role was basically that of a supporter, not a rival. Since Japan opposed large-scale aid to Russia, Tokyo was not even aiming at equality with the United States on this issue. Second-rank status was satisfactory, or even third-rank status, behind West Europe, as long as Japan was not bashed for avoiding its international responsibilities.

At most, Japan could be characterized as a mild challenger of the United States, but, again, this particular issue insured that the "mild" was more appropriate than "challenger." Differences with the United States were occasioned by Japan's own definition of its vital national interests and its sensitivity to domestic political needs and limits. But the essential point is that there were substantial differences between Japan's perceptions, interests, and approaches and those of the Americans and West Europeans. After all, it was the United States that tried to mediate differences between Japanese and West Europeans on the ad hoc pre-Tokyo G-7 Summit; it was Clinton who tried to mediate the rift between Tokyo and Yeltsin in Vancouver; and it was France and Germany that offered to mediate the Northern Territories imbroglio between Japan and Russia.

In other words, Japan was not purely reactive; it did not simply take orders from G-7 partners; it had its own policy agenda that did not completely accord with that of its partners, and thus mediation was required. The multilateral policy framework mitigated these differences in favor of a consensus-oriented united front approach toward Russia. Left alone, Japan probably would have refrained from successive aid commitments, but its desire to contribute to G-7 unity affected the amount and shape of its aid packages.

One of the major differences between Japan and the other Western nations was Tokyo's concern for Asian interests. The issue of reinstituting economic aid to post-Tiananmen China, not Russia, was the overriding priority for Japan at G-7 fora, especially Houston. It is easy to think that

Japan's reluctant endorsement of G-7 aid to Russia was based on a quid pro quo for G-7 endorsement of Japan's wish to resume ODA to China. From Japan's view, the historical importance of China's economic development and integration into the new world order equals that of Russia. In effect, China is Japan's Russia.

Among the G-7 nations, only Japan accorded priority to the Central Asian Republics. The Northern Territories issue did not involve these new states, and Japan's intense interest in them was occasioned in part by a sense of cultural (the Silk Road) and racial affinity. The Japanese felt that if they must participate in Russian aid, the CARs deserve attention because of the West's obsession with Yeltsin and Russia. The needs of the republics were, for all intents and purposes, being ignored, with long-term economic and political consequences given the convergence of Turkish, Iranian, Chinese, Russian, and Western interests.

Japan's interest in Asia was tested during the Tokyo Summit by a demand for an invitation from Indonesian president Suharto, chair of the Non-Aligned Movement. While Japan did not want to snub either Suharto or the movement, it recognized the reluctance of other G-7 nations to allow Suharto to sit at their table. Feelings in Japan ranged from a desire to include Suharto, especially if Yeltsin was to be invited, to a desire to keep the summits a strictly G-7 affair (i.e., without Yeltsin). As a compromise, Miyazawa met with Suharto outside G-7 auspices, as did other G-7 leaders, and dispatched a deputy foreign minister to Jakarta to brief Suharto on the summit upon its completion.

Japan did play its traditional role as spokesperson for Asian interests at G-7 summits. At past summits, Japan made sure that Asian perspectives were not totally overlooked by other participants. At the Tokyo Summit, Japan presented ASEAN views on trade issues, as noted by Philippine President Fidel Ramos: "Japan has been requested by the ASEAN member countries to bat for them in the G-7 meeting in Tokyo" on issues related to protectionism in the West.[64]

Japan's interest in Asia was reflected in its regional division-of-labor approach to world problems. As in bilateral ODA policy, Japan views each region as the primary responsibility of each of the other G-7 nations. Japan's policies toward multilateral banks reveals this regarding multilateral aid. Japan readily accepts responsibility for the Asian region, as reflected in the nation's primacy in the ADB. It assumes Europe and the United States would take primary responsibility in East and Central Europe and in Russia, an assumption visible in Japan's EBRD activities. All G-7 nations would assume joint responsibility for Russia in the global organizations, the World Bank and the IMF, with Japan in a supporting role. Tokyo therefore pledged aid early through World Bank consultative groups for Central Asia and supports CAR membership in the ADB partly out of fear that the EBRD will ignore the region. Throughout this time period, Japan utilized MDBs in a way we now expect. Economic aid through MDBs served as its international contribution, and these institutions certainly compensated for Japan's lack of knowledge about these countries and regions, whether East Europe or Central Asia. Japan did not even have embassies in these countries. Also, the funneling of aid through multilateral institutions softened domestic criticism of aid to Russia and legitimized a controversial policy in political circles. In the early stages, the government made sure its people understood that aid is humanitarian, small scale, and designated for the Red Cross. These MDBs allowed Japan to transcend the bilateral impasse on the Northern Territories issue by providing multilateral aid without the precondition of the islands' return.

Japan certainly found MDBs useful for enhancing national resources. The Russian aid issue exploded on the international scene just as the bubble economy of the 1980s burst. Japan was heading into a persistent recession, which made it difficult to commit large amounts of financial aid to a country disliked by the overwhelming majority of the Japanese people. The nation's multilateral aid could thus be presented as supplemental to G-7 and MDB resources.

In the Russian aid case, however, there is a twist: MDBs allowed Japan to avoid substantial aid-giving. The government consistently stressed the small-scale nature of this assistance; successive aid packages utilized very little new money; and the government constantly sought the participation of the private sector and its large surplus. While Japan haggled over aid increases to Russia of hundreds of millions of dollars, it announced a $120 billion aid package for traditional developing nations, including $70 to $75 billion in official aid, prior to the Tokyo Summit. MDBs therefore played a dual positive and negative role: enhancing Japan's resources, while at the same time providing a rationale for limiting commitments of its resources.

There is no question that Japan worried about its international status throughout this period. Japanese policymakers did not worry much about Yeltsin's criticisms, although his snub made it more difficult for the government to rally support for Russian aid. But ruling party politicians in particular voiced concern that Japan's perceived stubbornness was resulting in isolation from other G-7 nations. When the United States moved toward a more positive attitude on Russian aid, Japan was exposed to harsh criticism from Europeans and from the United States. In view of its antipathy toward Russia and its strong opposition to the pro-Russian policies of its developed-nation partners, prestige motives must have motivated and been the basis of Tokyo's aid. In large part, Japan's aid activism had been a defensive strategy to avoid tarnishing its post–Cold War stature as a global actor.

Japan's penchant for mediatory activities was also on view within the G-7. At Houston, Japan assumed a self-appointed role as intermediary between China and the G-7, and at Tokyo, Japan juggled many diplomatic balls. It mediated the gap between Europe and the United States over Clinton's proposal for a $4 billion privatization fund. The figure was substantially reduced, and Japan supported a new transformation facility within the IMF. Japan also represented Asian interests to the G-7 on trade issues, as mentioned previously, and it worked on Central Asian membership in the ADB. These were successful examples of Japan's mediatory efforts.

On the other hand, Japan seemed awkward in its dealings with Suharto and the Non-Aligned Movement, and fairly unsuccessful in its attempt to refocus G-7 attention to the needs of traditional developing nations. In February, Japan expressed its intention to stress LDCs at the July Tokyo Summit: Tokyo stated that it would propose a comprehensive aid package to promote democracy and free market systems, citing the Asian success story in the process.[65] The cabinet approved the $120 billion LDC aid package in June to succeed the previous $50 billion Medium-Term Program in time for formal unveiling at the summit.

Japan used the aid pledge as an attempt to counteract what it perceived as the G-7's preoccupation with Russia. It suggested a division of labor to deal with traditional Third World needs, including the United States taking responsibility for Russia, East Europe, and regional conflicts, German responsibility for East Europe, and British and French oversight of commonwealth or former colonial possessions.[66] However, Japan encountered interest but not strong commitment. As stated by a Foreign Ministry official: "The G-7 members, especially the United States, are more concerned about aiding Russia and have lost interest in the developing nations. We want to correct that."[67] Japan's activities in the World Bank reflect this new concern for traditional recipients in the post–Cold War world.

Significantly, the fact that Japan also was on the other side of mediatory efforts confirms its new status as a major player on the international scene. Japan's participation was essential to Western efforts. Its wishes could not be ignored, and contrary to previous periods, the nation now seemed to have strong wishes. Japan emerged in the 1990s as an integral and relatively equal player in the G-7 forum.

In sum, Japan's Russian aid policy puts MDB policy into its international and diplomatic context. MDB policy reflects Japan's overall diplomatic emphasis on a trilateral/G-7 framework, U.S.-Japan relations, concern for Asia, defense of national prestige, and preference for a mediatory role, both among G-7 countries and between the G-7 and outside countries. This context provides a more complete picture of Japan's policy not possible by focusing only on individual multilateral institutions or by relying only on the U.S.-Japan nexus.

THE POLICYMAKING PROCESS

Japan's Russian aid policymaking process, though hardly smooth, cannot be described as immobile. Japan hewed closely to its core policy position on the Northern Territories and decided on policy changes or flexibility as the occasion warranted. In a sense, given its commitment to the return of the Kuriles, hesitation on aid to Russia, preference for Central Asia, commitment to the G-7 consultation process, and sensitivity to domestic attitudes toward Russia, the government managed to achieve its minimal objectives. It was not a great lesson in Japanese global leadership but constituted an example of forced leadership (as the chair of the 1993 G-7 Summit) and the diplomacy of mitigation.

The central policy actor remains the bureaucracy, and among the ministries, the Foreign Ministry constituted the core of Japan's Russia policy: "While the decision-making process governing Japan's relations with other major powers includes input from other governmental agencies, various pressure groups, and a number of businesses, the MFA has virtually monopolized Japan's Soviet policy."[68]

The MOFA has consistently taken tough positions against the Soviet Union throughout the postwar period:

> They are earnest supporters of the "Yoshida Doctrine" and consider the maintenance of friendly relations with the United States to be essential for the national interests of Japan. They are basically hard-liners toward Moscow, and hold a deep rooted mistrust against the Russians for declaring war against Japan in violation of the Neutrality Pact and for occupying the northern territories.[69]

The greater flexibility of MOFA attitudes toward Russia is attributed to the rise of a new, more moderate generation within the ministry and the loosening of the grip of the hard-line Soviet Desk on Russia policy.[70] The moderates were aided by the fear of isolation from the thinking and policies of fellow G-7 members, which implies that the policy change "was not necessarily prompted by a fundamental re-examination of Japan's policy toward the Soviet Union."[71] These individuals and this fear operated on MOFA policymaking during the 1990s, with initiatives originating in the offices of the vice minister and deputy foreign ministers for political and economic affairs.

The Ministry of Finance remained on the sidelines of Russia policy until the collapse of East Europe in 1989. The multilateralization of Second World aid, especially the portion channeled through international financial institutions, elevated the aid issue beyond a budgetary matter. The politicization of ODA policy through Kaifu's 1991 four principles and the Cabinet's adoption of the 1992 ODA charter coincided with the MOF's adjustment to Kaifu's political initiatives in East European aid and the political mandate of the EBRD.

The MOF remained strongly skeptical of Moscow's ability to absorb and utilize financial aid effectively, and it focused much attention on the problems of ruble stabilization and convertibility and on responsibility for debt repayment. As EBRD negotiations showed, the MOF strongly opposed, first, membership for Russia and then large-scale borrowings by supporting the "voluntary" limit to paid-in capital.

The Finance and Foreign ministries began closer coordination of policy after the collapse of the Soviet Union into a confederation of republics. The Foreign Ministry's enthusiasm for aid to the Central Asian Republics became infectious. The MOFA began raising the issue with the MOF in the spring of 1992. The MOF's initial response was negative, but the top leadership turned favorable by the summer. Mid-level officials remained skeptical until the fall. The turning point came with a G-7 ministerial conference with the heads of all republics in Moscow. At that time, the Central Asian finance ministers approached the vice minister for international finance and established a sense of camaraderie that resulted in the vice minister's delegation to three of the republics in October 1992.

By late November, the MFA and the MOF were in accord on the importance of Central Asian aid, with both coordinating Japanese strategy to get the CAR nations onto the DAC list and to obtain CAR membership in the ADB as well as the EBRD. This policy shift in the MOF can be attributed to the personal initiatives taken by Finance Vice Minister Chino and supported by what some perceived as a slant toward Asia by "Asianists" in the ministry's International Finance Bureau in 1992-93.

Japan's 1993 aid package reflects the dominance of the MOF and MOFA as channels for the official portion of Russian aid: The $320 million in grants would be administered by MOFA; IMF, World Bank, and EBRD contributions would be overseen by the MOF. The Export-Import Bank would disburse the $400 in loans, and MITI would decide on the $1.1 billion in trade insurance. Neither MITI nor the Export-Import Bank, however, played a major role in the decision-making process. The Export-Import Bank is under MOF auspices, and the low level of economic ties with Russia weakened MITI's interest. Besides, government officials privately acknowledge the strong possibility that these loans and credits eventually will be unused because of absorptive problems on the Russian side. The Japan Defense Agency, with a policy view in accord with that of the MOFA's hard-liners, is often credited with some impact on policy, but its involvement in political matters remains restricted by the Constitution and by public opinion.[72]

In short, by the Tokyo Summit, the MOFA and the MOF served as the spark plugs and overseers of aid to the former Soviet Union because of changes in personnel and perceptions. The EBRD negotiations provide one reflection of this partnership: During the founding process, the MOFA delegate on the Japanese negotiating team, Russian specialist Tamba Minoru, raised the Northern Territories issue, while the technical financial aspects were discussed by Finance Vice Minister Utsumi Makoto. And once the EBRD had been established, the Japanese executive director came from the MOF and the alternate director from the MOFA, a configuration not duplicated in any other MDB.

In general, the softening of MOFA and MOF attitudes toward Russia was greatly aided by the fact that Japan became the chair of the G-7 after the 1992 Munich Summit. Tokyo assumed a leadership role for Russian aid by default, and the MOFA consistently argued that Japan must not lose face as the chair by providing inadequate aid compared with other G-7 nations. This tactic applied to the cabinet-level G-7 meetings in October 1992 and April 1993 as well as the Tokyo Summit itself. The MOF response was measured, relying on a minimum of new money commitments, but favorable. It too recognized the need to contribute to the international effort and to provide support especially for the United States. At Tokyo, the MOF took the lead in mediating the rift between the U.S. desire to create a $4 billion privatization fund and West Europe's refusal to contribute the requested amount. One official contends that the United States could not have prevailed against Europe and that only Japan's mediation saved this fund.

Among other political actors, the involvement of the prime ministers, cabinet ministers, and LDP leaders is notable. Prime ministers intervened sporadically in Russian policy. Nakasone is notable for his activism during and after his tenure to effect a breakthrough of some kind in bilateral relations. Takeshita is credited with adopting the "expanded equilibrium" policy and internationalizing the Northern Territories issue by persuading the United States to put the subject on the agenda for U.S.-Soviet summits and by raising the issue at the 1988 Toronto Summit.[73] Kaifu is credited with placing Japan's Northern Territories issue into the Houston Summit joint communiqué and with instructing the Defense Agency to drop references to the "Soviet threat" from defense white papers. Miyazawa strongly pushed the aid packages for Yeltsin while holding the line on American and European demands for what was viewed as extravagant demands for more aid.

In general, the prime ministers' involvement in Russia policy was sporadic, selective, and often at the behest of the Foreign Ministry. No prime minister wanted to be credited with forging close relations with Russia and forcing the nation to provide massive aid to Yeltsin unless it entailed the reversion of the Northern Territories. In the absence of a breakthrough on the territorial issue, Russian relations were a liability for prime ministers at the polls and within the ruling party.

LDP faction leaders were notably active on Russia policy, especially Abe Shintaro and Watanabe Michio. Both served as foreign minister while leading major factions within the party. Abe served as Nakasone's Foreign Minister until 1985 and maintained his activism on Russia policy into the 1990s. Watanabe was the prime spokesperson for the Miyazawa cabinet during the dissolution of the Soviet Union and into the spring of 1993. For both, their activism can be explained by the usefulness of a breakthrough on the Northern Territories for their ambitions to succeed their respective prime ministers. However, both succumbed to serious illnesses that forced their withdrawal from the political scene; Abe died of cancer, and Watanabe, while remaining politically active, never reentered the foreign policy arena. The LDP secretary general, Ozawa Ichiro, a contender for the leadership of the Takeshita faction and as Kaifu's successor before bolting from the LDP in 1993, was also a major player on Soviet policy; however, he retreated behind the scenes because of the LDP's loss of a local election in 1988, for which he took responsibility, and because of allegations of involvement in a scandal.[74]

In some ways, politicians took the lead in attempting to effect a breakthrough in the impasse in bilateral relations. One commentator felt that "It is clear that the Liberal Democratic Party is one step ahead of the Ministry of Foreign Affairs on policy toward the Soviet Union. This is a completely new departure from the past, and must be putting additional pressure on the MFA."[75]

On the other hand, some feel that prime ministers became more "muffled" after 1988 and into the 1990s, and that the LDP leaders' attempt at personal diplomacy never seriously succeeded in challenging the MOFA's authority over Russia policy: "Never having been seriously threatened, the autonomy of the Gaimusho [MOFA] had apparently been fully restored despite backstage jostling by LDP potentates aimed at personal diplomacy."[76]

Through the early 1990s, LDP leaders, though active, did not remain consistently involved in Russian policy, and they basically accepted the thrust of ministerial positions on Russian aid. As one observer notes, "Although Japan's *attitude* has become more flexible, neither the Japanese government nor the LDP has abandoned the *substance* of their basic demand, which remains the return of the four islands."[77]

The difference from the past was the focus not on the Northern Territories alone but on the issue of economic aid. The financial dimension, and especially its multilateralization, served as the catalyst for the prominence of the Finance Ministry in the policymaking process.

One must also remember that the Russian aid issue hit Japan during the last gasp of LDP rule in Japan. Successive major scandals involving payoffs, bribery, women, and gangsters rocked the ruling party in a way that forced it from office after almost four decades of monopolizing power. The major actors on Russia policy were touched by scandal (Nakasone, Takeshita, Abe, Watanabe, Ozawa, Miyazawa, and many more), and the LDP experienced a Soviet-type phenomenon—dissolution, as two groups bolted the ruling party to form new parties, the Shinseito and Shinto Sakigake. The politicians had to deal with the Russian aid issue amid the historic changes occurring in domestic politics. The Tokyo Summit was held in the midst of the national election that ousted the Miyazawa cabinet and the LDP and ushered in a coalition government comprised of seven opposition parties headed by the minor Japan New Party. Few politicians found the time to focus attention on Russia, which left the field to the bureaucrats.

As for other domestic forces, the business community was peripheral to Russia policy, including aid. Simply put, Japanese enterprises have little interest in the Russian market or in the economies of the new republics. The business community was wrestling with a recession, and to the extent it was interested in new economic frontiers abroad, its focus rested on the potential of the fast-rising Chinese market. Russia appeared a backwater, especially with the absence of management know-how, low technical levels, inadequate infrastructure, currency convertibility problems, and failure to create an investment environment more friendly to foreign corporations.

Public opinion does play an important role in Russia policy by establishing the limits of the possible for the government. Opinion polls consistently give Russia the dubious distinction of being the country most disliked by the Japanese, and over 90 percent of the people favor the return of all four islands. No government dared to step over the line by abandoning claims to the islands. The government feared that even the compromises—offering to accept Russian administrative rights in return for a recognition of sovereignty, or a staged return of two and then four islands—would provoke a national outcry. This accounts for a view within some political circles that if aid must be given, it should be used as a carrot to induce the return of the islands. Only then might the Japanese people support large-scale aid to Moscow.

In sum, five general lessons can be drawn from the case of aid to Russia.

First, the bureaucracy is central. Specifically, we witnessed the gradual convergence of Foreign and Finance Ministry interests. There emerged a mutual reliance on each other's areas of knowledge and expertise. The Finance Ministry required the MOFA's ability to deal with political and diplomatic aspects and implications of policy in far corners of the world in order to fashion appropriate financial aid projects. The Foreign Ministry therefore pressed its advantage in areas where the political intruded on the financial and technical. On the other hand, the Foreign Ministry lacked the technical expertise in international financial issues, the know-how needed to gain leverage over the MOF Budget Bureau, and detailed knowledge of the workings of international financial institutions. The convergence of needs led to a cooperative partnership that still showed signs of jurisdictional tension and strain and also to greater coordination of policy.

Second, politicians can play a significant role, but not consistently or independently. They remain locked into party and factional politics and to public opinion, reliant on the bureaucracy for information and policy guidance. They remain prisoners of their own political ambitions, becoming involved when Russia looks like a plus for their careers and avoiding it when it looks like a liability. However, the prime minister and cabinet ministers can play a formative and timely role in initiating or legitimizing changes in long-standing policies, something that bureaucrats find difficult to accomplish on their own. At crucial junctions, using their role as national spokespersons, political leaders can take the nation in new directions, but they cannot sustain or implement these moves on their own.

Third, other political forces play a peripheral role. The business community, the opposition parties, and nongovernmental citizens groups did not significantly influence policy. To the contrary, it was the government that sought to mobilize one interest group, the business community, to enter Second World markets through the use of trade insurance and credits and cofinancing arrangements in official economic aid packages. In this area, the government can claim only minimal success, as businesses remain hesitant to leap into CIS economies, but it cannot be argued that the government responded to business pressure or lobbying. On the other hand, most of these interest groups basically agreed with the government's stance and attitude toward the Russians and the Northern Territories, and thus provided the justification for pursuing policies tougher than other G-7 nations.

Fourth, public opinion, often reflected through the mass media, plays an important role in establishing the parameters of policy. Policymakers are well aware of the limits of their freedom of action. Public opinion can thus serve two functions, as a legitimizer of national policy or as an obstacle to overcome if change is desired. However, the government does have room to maneuver, for the shifts on the territorial issue and on the aid issue itself occurred without the explicit endorsement of the people. The LDP's political problems and eventual fall had little to do with public sentiment on Russia policy.

Finally, the external environment plays a significant role in shaping Japanese behavior, but not because Japan lacks a policy or is particularly vulnerable to external pressure. The international environment offered Japan opportunities to pursue national interests as well as acting as a constraint on its freedom of action. It served a dual role, as did the domestic environment. As in the case of all G-7 states, Japan's Russian aid policy was made in the context of both internal and external pressures and imperatives.

A focus on only one dimension will not explain Japan's behavior. If Japan was simply responding to external pressure from the G-7 and Russia, it would have been much more forthcoming toward Gorbachev and Yeltsin, and its aid commitments would be much larger and would have come much sooner. If Japan was simply responding to domestic pressure, it would not have readied aid packages until Russia agreed to return the Northern Territories. It is the interaction of these complementary and conflictual external and domestic factors, and the government's role in mediating, adjusting to, or overcoming these forces, that explains the particular shape of Japan's Russia policy and its economic aid packages.

6

— ◆ —

REQUIEM FOR THE REACTIVE STATE?

Success or failure lies in conformity to the times.
                                    —Niccolo Machiavelli

No wind favors him who has no destined port.
                                    —Michel de Montaigne

If judged by its economic and financial performance and resources, Japan entered the 1990s as a great power; if judged by its global prominence and political performance, it was a middle power; if judged by its international agenda-setting and rule-making leadership record, it was a small power. The pressing question is how Japan will enter the next century. What goals will Japan pursue, and what form will that diplomacy take? How should we analyze this foreign policy?

Japan's performance toward multilateral development banks provides clues. It illustrates the gradual, but incomplete, emergence of a small power to middle or great power status in one type of fora. It introduces themes and behavioral patterns that may prove instructive in understanding Japan's overall foreign policy in the future. MDBs also raise the question: what kind of power, reactive or pro-active?

DIPLOMATIC THEMES AND PATTERNS

Japan's ODA policy reflects the emerging themes in its search for a role in the post–Cold War world—diversification, politicization, multilateraliza-tion, and a search for "ideas." From the 1980s, multilateral bank policy has served as one of the testing grounds for these themes. Therefore, the evolving configuration of Japan's behavioral patterns in multilateral banks may provide one vision of the shape of things to come. To consolidate and recapitulate our findings, the following four features of Japan's behavior seem most salient.

First, Japanese diplomacy is increasingly conducted within a trilateral configuration both globally and within multilateral banks. The U.S.-Japan nexus remains undisputedly the most important pillar of Japan's foreign policy, but increasingly, Tokyo has sought to strengthen its ties with the European leg of the triangular partnership. We know that Japan is increasing its contacts with the CSCE, NATO, and the EC, but it is in the G-7 that the nation appears especially active of late. Japan has placed special emphasis on the G-7 at a time when critics downgrade the importance or effectiveness of G-7 summits and cooperative efforts. Relations with Europe may encounter strains over specific issues, but on the whole, Japan's efforts have been aimed in particular at persuading or placating France and Germany. Japan views England as the origin of half the problems caused by those "Anglo-Saxons" and associates London's positions with those of the United States.

Japan's activities within MDBs reflect this broader configuration. The U.S.-West Europe-Japan nexus is critical in understanding Japanese activities in the World Bank, IMF, and EBRD. Issues such as aid for East Europe and Russia demand close coordination among the world's principal donor nations. The controversial tenure of Jacques Attali pitted the EBRD management against a united G-7 concern with mismanagement. This does not necessarily mean that Japan and Europe avoid all confrontation in favor of cooperation, for differences of opinions have emerged, ranging from vote shares, to development philosophy, to Japanese reticence on Russian aid. But Japan's overall approach reflects its concern with maintaining trilateral consensus on specific issues.

In the ADB, Japan's relationship with European members is weaker than at the IBRD. Tokyo has focused more on the U.S. role since the bank's founding, and it recently has perceived a weakening of European commitment to the Bank. However, the triangular configuration still applies, with either the Asian developing member states or the bank management substituting for Europe as the third leg. We have seen that the dynamics of Japanese activities often involve the United States and a particular DMC, such as China or Vietnam, or the president, such as Fujioka or Tarumizu. In the IBRD, the U.S.-IBRD management-Japan nexus constituted the context of Japan's call for a study of the Asian economic miracles by the bank. Therefore, Japan often considered the MDB management as either one of the trilateral legs or the target of a trilateral coalition.

Second, the role Japan seeks to play within this trilateral context is that of an intermediary. In numerous instances, Japan has mediated difficulties between two other participants on a particular issue. It has mitigated tension between the United States and Europe, notably in the EBRD on issues such as exclusive emphasis on the private sector, and at the Tokyo G-7 Summit over Clinton's $4 billion plan for Russian privatization; between the United States and Asian countries, especially in the ADB; and between the EBRD and ADB on Central Asian Republic dual membership. Japan also has served as intermediary between MDB recipient nations and the United States and European donors, and the promotion of the Asian development model stems in large part from Japan's effort to play an educative role for Western nations on behalf of Asians.

We have observed a Japan that defines activism and leadership as the ability to effect tension-reduction within a collective and cooperative framework. Leadership does not connote striking out on one's own in pursuit of narrow self-interest. A leader promotes, effects, and maintains harmony and cooperation, while at the same time pursuing its own interests.

On the other hand, in a tribute to Japan's new status, its strong policy positions also occasion other trilateral partners to attempt mediation between it and third parties. We have seen this process when Germany, France, and the United States all attempted to mediate differences between Tokyo and Yeltsin prior to the Tokyo Summit. The Japanese occasionally require the services of a mediator as well.

Third, Japan's activism is based on an assumption of a global division of labor, or burden-sharing, among G-7 countries. Japan defines division of labor functionally and regionally.

Functionally, in the security arena, the United States would take charge of maintaining global peace and stability, with West Europe and Japan playing support roles in their regions and globally. For Japan this means primarily nonmilitary assistance, as with the $13 billion in the Gulf War and with military contributions severely restricted to UN-type peacekeeping operations (and these on a very selective and conditional basis). In the international economic arena, the United States would continue to play a leading role in maintaining the world economy, but here West Europe and Japan would play more of an equal role, occasionally taking initiatives to bolster U.S. difficulties and weaknesses. Japan views this to be its prime role given its national strengths: economic, financial, technological, human resources, and knowhow. An active, expanded ODA and MDB policy is one means of fulfilling this role.

The Russian aid issue is significant in that it spans both the security and economic dimensions. Japan considered economic assistance both bilaterally (together with the United States) and multilaterally (through the EBRD) for dismantling Moscow's military-industrial complex and its transition to civilian production. And if we consider the supplementary role of Japanese humanitarian, development, and refugee assistance for UN-related peacekeeping activities and the Gulf War, we now see that in the 1990s, Japan's foreign aid has come to undergird multilateral military exercises.[1] For a pacifist nation, searching for nonmilitary contributions to the world community, the gap between economic and military aid will close no further. Yet this gap has closed more than ever since Japanese provided aid to its colonies in the pre–World War II era.

Regional division of labor means, for Japan, the assumption of a leadership role in Asia. Japan would funnel the majority of its bilateral ODA to the region, based on feelings of kinship and wartime guilt, and on the recognition of the limits of its global reach, interests, and knowledge. The United States would focus on global issues and assume special responsibility for Latin America, while France looks after Africa and Britain its Commonwealth members. The United States and West Europe, especially Germany, could assume of responsibility for the democratization and liberalization of East and Central Europe and Russia. Japan can provide limited financial support in Europe's backyard while focusing on the Central Asian and the Russian Far Eastern theaters.

Simply put, Japan does not intend to abandon Asia to enter the West. Rather, regional division of labor entails serving as the intermediary between Asia and the West, a pattern seen consistently at G-7 summits. And Japan is seeking to expand its definition of Asia, to include former Soviet republics. Asia serves as the base for the globalization of Japan's diplomacy. Tokyo believes that its activities in Asia, whether economic or strategically related, impact favorably on the international economy and on world stability. Japan considers Asia policy as its contribution to international responsibilities. This traditional view of Japan's role in Asia has been adapted to a post–Cold War world.

Multilateral development banks fit into this larger foreign policy configuration. From the Japanese perspective, MDBs are useful and effective tools in its multilateral diplomacy. They address and reflect policy needs in all three dimensions—trilateralism, functionalism, and regionalism. We have seen how these banks contribute to Japanese efforts to attain institutional, diplomatic, and development objectives, but a comparative analysis enabled us further to piece together the broader implications and significance of policy toward individual institutions. We have thus been able to determine the big picture, the diplomatic context, of Japan's MDB activities.

Fourth, the Japanese government was not paralyzed by policy immobilism. The MDB policymaking process worked relatively well under bureaucratic auspices given Japan's limited objectives and conceptualization of its role in multilateral fora. The cooperative relationship between two rival ministries, Finance and Foreign, actually served the nation well in view of the sporadic involvement of politicians, the lack of a long-term vision, and the chaos reigning in party politics. The bureaucracy fashioned and implemented policy and even forged the "ideas" that distinguish Japan's development strategy today.

The bureaucrats maintained their advantage by default. The Diet maintained the power to approve or reject the economic assistance budget, and it did push the Finance Ministry to secure a larger vote share and seek more staff and management posts in MDBs. But the Diet never rejected, or held hostage for political purposes, the increases in annual ODA outlays, and it left the task of obtaining vote shares and positions to the ministry—which, for the most part, succeeded in its efforts. Prime ministers urged ministries to fashion economic and ODA packages and policy rationales before the convening of international summits, and the ministries did put together debt plans, aid packages, ODA principles and philosophies, and development models.

On the other hand, however effective the bureaucrats' stewardship of an activist policy, the MDB case does expose the weaknesses of the policy process. The process works well when ministry interests and objectives coincide and do not diverge, and when personnel between ministries get along. This favorable environment characterized the atmosphere of the late 1980s and 1990s in multilateral aid policy. The consensus on Russian aid and the six-month consensus building process on Central Asian aid symbolized the mood of the times. Yet in the trade arena, divisiveness, jurisdictional battles, transnational alliances, and foreign pressure have been hallmarks of the policy process.

Also, bureaucrats have more technical expertise and information than politicians, which gives them a decided advantage in policy determination, but that knowledge and expertise still cannot match the expertise of MDBs and other governments. The generalist nature of bureaucratic career patterns and the shortage of manpower severely hinder the long-term acquisition of expertise and experience. A major attraction of MDBs is that they compensate for Japan's policymaking shortcomings, and if knowledge is power, then the advantage is often in the hands of MDB managements, staffs, and other members of the board of directors.

The bureaucracy has been a linchpin of an evolving but stable MDB policy. Bureaucratic politics need not degenerate into immobile politics. But bureaucrats also may be the Achilles' heel of Japan's activism. MDB policy requires further integration into Japanese foreign policy overall; it cannot always be treated as narrow, technical, or philosophical problems. Individual ministries and their differing jurisdictions, interests, and perspectives are ill-equipped for that task. Activism requires the stewardship of Japan's political leadership, but that appears a distant prospect in the 1990s. In the meantime, the bureaucracy will remain the headquarters for MDB policy, and as a result, Japan's activism will continue to be characterized by caution, incrementalism, and a preference for a mediatory, middle-of-the-road role.

This diplomatic pattern presents an evolutionary picture of Japanese foreign policy since the 1970s. Diplomacy does not appear static, mired in a passive and reactive syndrome, and it offers hope for significant and substantive contributions to the world community. However, if Japan can be viewed as an activist state, we still need to answer one final question: What kind of activist state?

REQUIEM FOR THE REACTIVE STATE?

All states are basically reactive, adapting to the external environment while reflecting domestic interests. The issue posed by the reactive state approach is whether Japan is somehow an extreme case of reactivity, different from other nations. Japan's reactiveness is portrayed as a congenital defect of the body politic, deeply embedded in the postwar national psyche and the policy process. It constitutes the identity of the Japanese state and nation. This picture argues or implies that reactiveness applies to Japan's entire diplomacy, not just to the political dimension, that it subordinates indigenous motives or interests, deemphasizes will or choice, and makes few efforts to shape, rather than take the shape of, the environment. This is not the profile of a great power; it is the profile of a dysfunctional state and a passive, stagnant diplomacy.

The study of Japan's multilateral development bank policy both confirms and contradicts this depiction. On the one hand, the reactive state approach retains strong explanatory power. The international system is a given and its developments are often beyond Japan's control, which forces Tokyo to respond out of self-interest and necessity. MDB policy often reflects the temper of the times and takes the shape of its environment. However, we also have seen that Japan exhibits purposive, strategic behavior. External stimuli often serve as a catalyst for policy, but domestic factors provide policy parameters, and it is the government that mediates and molds these external imperatives and domestic demands into policies that often have an impact on other nations and international institutions. Japan's diplomacy is not passive or stagnant. Japan manages to capture the temper of the times and manages to do some shaping. There are many indications of Japanese proactive as well as reactive behavior.

If all states are reactive to some extent, and if proactivism occurs within a reactive context, we need to clarify the definition of reactive and proactive and to focus on the relationship between the two. In other words, the challenge is to delineate the border between reactivity and proactivity, if this is possible in the real world. Were France and Germany proactive, seizing the moment, in their mobilization of the G-7 on East European and Russian aid, pressing their own national interests amid German unification, French leadership aspirations, and American decline? Or were they simply reacting to the collapse of the Second World in Europe, fearful of the impact on their own economies, realizing their lack of adequate financial resources to aid these nations, worried about of a flood of refugees from the East into their societies? Or were they both reactive and proactive, depending on the circumstances? Or must we choose? Are these not two sides of the same coin as forms of normal, typical nation-state behavior?

Our earlier discussion of four ideal types of activism—proactivist, acquiescent, defensive, and anticipatory—may assist us here. All of these types can accommodate both proactive and reactive behavior, though in varying degrees and under certain conditions.

Acquiescent and defensive activism come closest to activism purely within a reactive context. They provide two types of responses to the outside world—subservient or defiant. Both assume that the domestic dimension is overshadowed by external imperatives and that the government's role is to adapt to the international environment either through placation or resistance.

Acquiescent activism is a somewhat extreme depiction of the reactive state: Japan is like a billiard ball, bouncing off the movement of others. Japan's objectives are externally determined, and they are concerned primarily with survival through adaptation to the environment. Policy immobilism robs Japan of a vision and is the reason for reactiveness. The nation merely reacts. In many ways, this definition comes closest to the reactive state conception of Japanese foreign policy. However, this depiction applies poorly to our MDB and Russian aid cases. Japan's behavior in the ADB, IBRD, EBRD, and G-7 summits reveals a Japanese agenda, often pursued against the wishes of others. Japan eventually produced an aid package for Russia that, arguably, suited G-7 and Russian interests more than its own wishes, but neither Americans nor Europeans—nor Moscow—would depict the

Japanese as pushovers. Japan brought quid pro quos to the negotiating tables and extracted concessions. While Japan may not have held the cue stick, neither did it crash uncontrollably into other balls or fall into the pockets.

Neither is defensive activism completely appropriate for our cases. Japan is too fearful of isolation from the G-7 and other countries to be defiantly and uncompromisingly intransigent toward external demands. The extreme "no retreat, no surrender" behavior does not apply to our cases, although Japan's attitude (but not policy) toward Russia comes close. Much of Japan's foreign policy is defensive, but its activism was not designed to avoid compliance but to accommodate and mediate. MDBs, by definition, are fora that require cooperative and flexible behavior, not intransigence and naysaying. In our cases, we found neither a frightened nor fully self-confident "Japan that can say no" to outside threats or entreaties. Japanese responses ranged from "yes, but . . ." to "no, but . . . ." Japan's behavior in our case studies rests somewhere between the extremes of surrender and defiance.

The other two ideal types of activism allow for greater attention to proactivism. The proactive approach, which differentiates between promotive and induced proactivism, and anticipatory activism both focus on purposive and strategic behavior. Both allow for some reactivity, but this is not the dominant feature of Japanese policy or policymaking.

Promotive activism comes closest to a purely proactive approach devoid of reactivity. In this view Japan's behavior is purposive, dynamic, and strategic. Tokyo does not seek merely to adapt, to take the shape of the environment, but rather to influence or mold that environment in a manner favorable to itself. External influences have little to do with Japan's domestically determined national interests, and pursued policies cannot be linked easily to specific external stimuli. The government is not wracked by immobilism and knows where to go.

Our cases uncover some instances of this type of behavior. Japan would assign priority to the Asia Pacific region with or without external pressure; this desire to identify with and lead Asia comes from within. In this context, Japan's intense effort to restore aid to China after Tiananmen Square reflects a self-appointed mission. Japan's tendency toward independence on China policy has a long history in the postwar period; its diplomacy fits into the context of overall Sino-Japanese relations since normalization of relations in 1972. Thus, the Tiananmen incident may be seen as the immediate catalyst for policy but not the formative influence in that the overall policy context already existed. The incident itself did not dictate the specific response taken by Japan; the direction had already been set in 1972. In this context, Japan struggled to obtain the approval of G-7 members for its policies, and MDBs clearly served as diplomatic tools utilized by Japan to pursue a course determined in Tokyo.

Nor is it clear what external pressure led Japan to engage in a long, persistent campaign to achieve the number-two position in the World Bank/IMF against opposition from West Europeans or the number-one position within the ADB against American opposition. Numerous general answers are possible—everything from a response to the decline of American hegemony to the world's expectation that Japan do more—but the most convincing ones are internal, especially the leadership's recognition of a window of opportunity, given the nation's newfound financial power as largest creditor and aid great power, to contribute to the international community in some way and to enhance its national prestige. The view that interprets Japan's initiative-taking in these banks as a U.S.-Japan power struggle fits here: Japan, recognizing a golden opportunity, seizes the moment and challenges a vulnerable United States.

However, most instances of proactivism do seem to come within a reactive context, thus limiting proactivism to a certain stage or certain aspects of a more general policy. Proactivism does not seem to apply to the whole life of the policy. Cases of pure promotive activism are therefore difficult to find—especially if states, by definition, are reactive to begin with. Therefore, definitions of reactivism and activism, and the question of where to draw the line between them, become of paramount importance. Induced proactivism and anticipatory activism thus become extremely useful, and perhaps more relevant, general frameworks.

Induced proactivism is similar to promotive activism but allows for some external causation. However, unlike acquiescent and defensive activism, it puts greater distance between an external stimulus and national policy and is thus useful in cases where the international environment induces action but does not shape the specific policy response. Japan's policy is still defined as a response, but there is greater free will in attempting to overcome obstacles and mold the environment to its liking. In other words, at some point Japan's policy takes off, and whatever the initial cause of that policy, it gains a life of its own where domestic interests—aspirations, pressure group interests, public opinion, bureaucratic jurisdictional conflicts, politicians' electoral needs, and the like—begin to shape it more than external influences.

This approach is useful in cases where we are convinced that activism is, at least initially, a response to external stimuli but where we cannot determine exactly which outside stimulus triggered which Japanese actions. For example, it is difficult to determine what specific external stimulus led Japan to question the Anglo-American development orthodoxy and to call for a major IBRD study of the East Asian economic miracles. Neither Americans nor Europeans wanted Japan to call them naive on development issues or to have their deeply held beliefs challenged. We can assume that the main impetus came from within Japan, linked directly to its financial ascendance internationally and the search for "ideas," but we also know that debates within the international development community, the economic rise of Asia, and shifts in American and European standing within the IBRD provided Tokyo with the window of opportunity.

This phenomenon is visible even in policy toward Russia. We know that Japan's policy was heavily influenced by the collapse of East Europe and the Soviet Union and the end of the Cold War. Japan could not, for example, ignore Russia, as it preferred to do given its dislike of Moscow and the intractable territorial issue. Yet historic developments did not, in themselves, dictate a particular Japanese response. Japan chose to take the issue to the G-7 forum, including the Northern Territories in summit communiqués, while floating trial balloons on the Kuriles and compromising on Russian aid. It also put emphasis on the Central Asian Republics, though nothing dictated that it should focus so intently on these new nations and carve out its own role in the region. Tokyo maintained its basic position against pressure to sacrifice a national interest for the greater good of the new world order. The Japanese government, responding to its own needs and to domestic political demands, formulated and followed its own course within the context of an international environment in considerable flux.

Both promotive and induced proactivism, with or without the presence of external stimuli, concentrates on Japan's indigenously defined national interests and strategic behavior. They relegate external pressures to the realm of the policy environment, allowing a catalytic but not necessarily formative role.

Anticipatory activism restores a tighter link between specific policies and the environment by emphasizing the latter's influence more than induced activism. Environmental stimuli are formative, not solely catalytic. Policies can take on lives of their own and policymakers can mobilize and strategize (thus assuming characteristics of promotive or induced proactivism at some point), but policies clearly remain responses to and linked with identifiable external stimuli. But unlike acquiescent or defensive activism, Japan's response is not necessarily either submissive or defiant. It is an exercise in preventive diplomacy.

So much of Japan's diplomacy is based on concerns about what others think and expect; so many of its policies are results of anticipated criticisms and requests from abroad. It is no coincidence that each of Japan's aid doubling plans and debt plans were formulated just prior to international gatherings, especially G-7 summits and ministerial conferences. Japan expected criticism at these public fora and prepared specific responses accordingly, hoping not only to forestall attacks but also to garner kudos. Japan expected rewards for formulating surplus recycling programs, filling the West's aid fatigue gap, championing the needs of Third World nations amid emphasis on the former Second World, and promoting the principles of democratization, privatization, human rights, and free and open markets through a formal ODA Charter. It clearly expected the appreciation not only of the United States but also Europe, Asia, the developing world, and international organizations.

One of the strongest motive forces that propelled Japan into the area of Russian aid was the fear that the nation would be isolated in the G-7, charged with being concerned only with its own narrow, selfish territorial interests while ignoring a historic global transformation. Japan's final Russian aid package was readied, along with the $120 billion economic aid package for developing nations, in time for the 1993 Tokyo Summit. Japan carefully calibrated the amount of its package to American and European shares. Obviously Tokyo devised these packages in the full knowledge that much more was expected of it as the host of the summit. Japan formulated its polices amid expectations of criticism for doing nothing or doing little if it did not make that extra effort at the summit. But again, Japan maintained its basic policy line toward Russia, maintaining cool but proper relations without sacrificing its national objectives on the Northern Territories.

It seems clear that none of these four approaches alone is adequate to the task of explaining the totality of MDB policy. Complex real-world policies do not conform easily to neat, academic analytical categories. Policies need to be broken down into their components and stages or time spans. The flexible use of appropriate ideal types in a sequential pattern seems most appropriate for the analysis of Japanese foreign policy, provided we can delineate and clarify the borders between reactive and active behavior. That task is a little easier now.

We can define reactive policies narrowly as those policies that are direct responses to specific demands emanating from specific, identifiable external sources. These demands and Japanese policy are causally linked. External pressure has two intentions or effects: to attain a desired response, or to prevent or forestall an undesired action. In either case, whether Japan's response is positive or negative, the environment determines its policy. This definition omits the more general and amorphous mood-of-the-times types of international stimuli that are harder to link to specific policies. It resembles features of crisis decision making—with its reactive nature, shortened decision-making time span, restricted number of key policymakers—and is basically the classic definition of *gaiatsu* (external pressure), which usually refers to a particular Japanese reaction to a specific policy stimulus.

We can define as proactive those policies that are purposive and strategic, aimed at influencing the outside environment, and that reflect ideas, interests, and objectives determined domestically and not so much by outside forces. These are cases where Japan is acting and not just reacting, shaping and not just being shaped by the environment. The external environment is one-step removed from specific Japanese policies, and those policies may be formulated within either a restricted or protracted time period. The key to identifying the border is to determine the importance and extent of state and domestic determinants in policymaking and the promotive intent and objectives (but not necessarily the success or failure) of policy.

Induced and anticipatory proactivism are especially appropriate in explaining Japan's policies toward multilateral development banks. The reason lies in the inescapable conclusion that so much of Japan's foreign policy is tailored to responding, either in anticipation or after-the-fact, to the expectations, hopes, and fears of foreign actors, both nation-state and non–nation-state. So much of Tokyo's perceptions and actions are tied to the vicissitudes of a changing international system. This is the overriding framework for and motive force behind Japan's search for status, respectability, and acceptance as well as for its promotion of concrete national interests.

Promotive activism is of limited utility because MDB policies are often derivative of broader diplomatic interests and objectives, both regional and functional. MDBs constitute policy tools more than policy ends. And yet, this approach is helpful under certain conditions and at certain stages of policy designing in explaining behavior that does not neatly conform to a specific external stimuli. The main restriction on the unlimited use of promotive activism is our initial definition of states as basically reactive entities.

Within this framework, we find in our case study a sequential pattern where external stimuli—both the specific and "mood" types—provide the initial push, but Japan then incorporates the stimuli into its own policy objectives and fashions a policy that may or may not respond directly to the intent or wishes of that stimuli. On Russian aid policy, for example, the immediate catalysts were developments outside Japan, both indirect (e.g., the collapse of the Soviet Union) and direct (e.g., specific demands for Japanese aid from France and Germany). The policy then took on a life of its own when Japanese policymakers juxtaposed the Northern Territories issue, domestic sentiments, relations with Western allies, fears of aid loss by Asian and Third World recipients, and the newly discovered interest in the CARs. This case was induced activism in that historic events beyond Japan's control confronted Tokyo with the need to respond. It was anticipatory activism in that Japan feared isolation and estrangement from G-7 nations eager to assist Russia if it failed to act. It was promotive activism in that Japan's actual response was based mostly on its own definition of national interest, whereby Tokyo sought to manipulate the G-7 to induce favorable Russian policy changes on the Northern Territories, using aid as one carrot, and to utilize Russian aid as leverage to resume Chinese aid. Its aid package did not fully meet the expectations of the G-7 but represented what Japan was willing to give at the time—small scale, humanitarian aid—and hoping to avoid—isolation.

What we see is a multidimensional foreign policy rather than a one-dimensional economic or reactive diplomacy. We see the nuances and subtleties of a diversified, politicized, multilateralized diplomacy. We see activity rather than passivity and decisiveness rather than immobilism.

The advantage of proactive perspectives is that the environment is not portrayed only in negative terms, as presenting obstacles and imposing limits to national behavior. Proactive perspectives recognize the positive, empowering function of the external environment as encouraging and providing opportunities for activism. Nation-states can shape, revise, and generally influence that environment. In our cases, Japan realized that its policies can have a significant effect on MDBs; Tokyo can make things happen. Therefore, the environment can be both a hindrance and an opportunity, and activism can be formative as well as defensive.

In conclusion, there is no need to jettison the reactive state approach. We must acknowledge and use its explanatory strengths. There will be no requiem for the reactive state. However, if we treat proactivism as simply an anomaly or an exception to the rule, the analysis of Japan's twenty-first century international role may become just as reactive as the foreign policy that reactive statists seem to explain. Perhaps the greatest virtue in applying proactive approaches is the granting of some benefit of the doubt to the Japanese. Reactivism basically views Japanese policies and policymaking negatively, assuming that the Japanese do not have the will or the ability to determine their own interests and direction without the help of more dynamic and prescient actors abroad. A reactive state will never fully fulfill its international responsibilities. But according to our cases, Japanese behavior appears rather normal, neither mired in immobilism and excessive reactivism nor consumed with the quest for power regardless of international opinion. Japan, like all nations in the post–Cold War world, is finding its way through the uncertainties of an international system in flux by balancing the need to act and react.

Throughout the postwar era, the Japanese ship of state had concentrated on filling its cargo bay and sailing along the coast, trying to avoid rough waters and dangerous shoals. As familiar landmarks crumble and Japan heads into the open sea, however, it is imperative for the navigators to focus not only on the currents and tides but also on the yet unspecified destined port. The elevation of multilateralism in the post–Cold War era reflects the growing perception that neither Japan nor any nation can afford to sail alone. For Japan, that journey requires seaworthy vessels such as multilateral development banks. The task at hand is not so much to get access to the bridge, for that has been accomplished. The real challenge is to take the helm, find that favorable wind, and pilot the ship to its destination. Throughout the postwar era, Japan has skillfully found and ridden the winds; in the post–Cold War era, it must find its port.

NOTES

CHAPTER 1

1. See Atsushi Kusano, "Kokusai Seiji Keizai to Nihon," in Akio Watanabe (ed.), *Sengo Nihon no Taigai Seisaku* (Tokyo: Yuhikaku, 1985), 264.

2. For background, see Michael Yoshitsu, *Caught in the Middle East: Japan's Diplomacy in Transition* (Lexington, MA: Lexington Books, 1984); Marvin Ott, "Japan's Growing Involvement in the Middle East," *SAIS Review* (Summer-Fall 1985), 221-32; Robert M. Orr, Jr., "Japanese Foreign Aid: Over a Barrel in the Middle East," in Bruce M. Koppel and Robert M. Orr, Jr. (eds.), *Japan's Foreign Aid: Power and Policy in a New Era*, 289-304 (Boulder, CO: Westview Press, 1993); and Ronald A. Morse (ed.), *Japan and the Middle East in Alliance Politics* (Washington, D.C.: The Wilson Center, 1986).

3. Observers at the time all noted that the 1977 pledge constituted the first time Japan pledged to double its ODA. However, technically speaking, this was the second time. Japan pledged to double its ODA in 1969. That pledge was also announced by Fukuda, then minister of finance, at the annual board of governors Meeting of the Asian Development Bank in Sydney. Fukuda pledged a doubling in five years, "our economic resources permitting." See Asian Development Bank, *Summary of Proceedings: Second Annual Meeting of the Board of Governors, 1969* (Manila: ADB Printing Office, 1969), 41-42; See also *Nihon Keizai Shimbun*, April 10, 1969, for background.

4. See Terutomo Ozawa, *Recycling Japan's Surpluses for Developing Countries* (Paris: Development Centre of the Organization For Economic Co-Operation and Development, 1989); Hiroshi Okuma, "Japan in the World: The Capital Recycling Programme," *Trocaire Development Review* (1988), 69-88; Toshihiko Kinoshita, "Developments in the International Debt Strategy and Japan's Response," *EXIM Review* (January 1991), 62-80; Kinoshita, "Ruiseki Saimu Mondai to Shikin Kanryu," in Takatoshi Ito (ed.), *Kokusai Kinyu no Genjo* (Tokyo: Yuhikaku, 1992), chap. 7; and Kinoshita, "Ruiseki Saimu Mondai no Sui-i to Sekai-teki Shikin Kyokyu Shisutemu no Sai-Kochiku no Hoko to Tenbo," *Finashiaru Rebyuu* (March 1993), 42-76.

5. See Dennis T. Yasutomo, *The Manner of Giving: Strategic Aid and Japanese Foreign Policy* (Lexington, MA: Lexington Books, 1986), chap. 3; on Korea, see also Hong N. Kim, "Politics of Japan's Economic Aid to South Korea," *Asia Pacific Community* (Spring 1984), 80-102.

6. See Alan Rix, *Japan's Aid Program: Quantity Versus Quality* (Canberra: Australian Government Publishing Service, 1987), 31-34.

7. "Takeshita Announces 'International Cooperation Initiative,'" *Japan Report* (May 1988), 1-2.

8. For the Japanese response to the Gulf War, see Courtney Purrington, "Tokyo's Policy Responses During the Gulf War and the Impact of the 'Iraqi Shock' on Japan," *Pacific Affairs* (Summer 1992), 161-81; Takashi Inoguchi, "Japan's Response to the Gulf Crisis: An Analytical Overview," *Journal of Japanese Studies* (Summer 1991), 257-73; Kenichi Ito, "The Japanese State of Mind: Deliberations on the Gulf Crisis," *Journal of Japanese Studies* (Summer 1991), 275-90; and Ito, "Force Versus Sanctions in the Middle East," *Japan Echo* (Spring 1991), 16-31.

9. As stated in an ODA White Paper, "In the wake of the Gulf Crisis, we also need to consider the lessons that should be learnt from the circumstances that allowed Iraq to become a militarily strong power." See Ministry of Foreign Affairs, *Japan's ODA 1991* (Tokyo: Association for Promotion of International Cooperation, 1992), 4.

10. See Dennis T. Yasutomo, "Foreign Aid and Japan's Economic Diplomacy," in Nihon Kokusai Mondai Kenkyujo (ed.), *Nihon no Keizai Gaiko no Arikata ni Kansuru Sogoteki Kenkyu*, 35-63 (Tokyo: Kokusai Mondai Kenkyujo, 1994).

11. See K. V. Kesavan, "Japan and the Tiananmen Square Incident," *Asian Survey* (July 1990), 671-77; and Zhao Quansheng, "Japan's Aid Diplomacy in China," in Koppel and Orr (eds.), *Japan's Foreign Aid*, 163-202.

12. Gaimusho Keizai Kyoryoku Kyoku and Keizai Kyoryoku Kenkyukai, *Keizai Kyoryoku no Rinen: Seifu Kaihatsu Enjo wa Naze Okonau no ka* (Tokyo: Kokusai Kyoryoku Suishin Kyokai, 1981).

13. On comprehensive national security, see Anzen Hosho Kenkyu Guruppu, *Sogo Anzen Hosho Senryaku* (Tokyo: Okurasho Insatsu Kyoku, 1980); Heiwa Mondai Kenkyukai, *Kokusai Kokka Nihon no Sogo Anzen Hosho Seisaku* (Tokyo: Okurasho Insatsu Kyoku, 1985); Anzen Hosho Kenkyukai, *Ekonomisuto ga Kaita Sogo Anzen Hosho no Kozu* (Tokyo: Nihon Seisansei Honbu, 1981); Robert W. Barnett, *Beyond War: Japan's Concept of Comprehensive National Security* (Washington, D.C.: Pergamon Brassey's International Defense Publishers, 1984); J. W. M. Chapman, R. Drifte, and I. T. M. Gow, *Japan's Quest for Comprehensive Security: Defence, Diplomacy and Dependence* (New York: St. Martin's Press, 1982); and Yasutomo, *Manner of Giving*, especially chap. 2.

14. Ministry of Foreign Affairs, *Japan's ODA 1991*, 22.

15. Tom Minehart, "Japan Will Be Strong Actor on New World Stage," Associated Press, February 6, 1990. Emphasis added. See also Dennis T. Yasutomo, "The Politicization of Japan's 'Post-Cold War' Multilateral Diplomacy," in Gerald L. Curtis (ed.), *Japan's Foreign Policy After the Cold War: Coping with Change*, 323-46 (New York: M. E. Sharpe, 1993).

16. A copy of the ODA Charter can be found in *Gaiko Foramu* (March 1993), 8.

17. See Tamio Amau, *Ta-Kokkan Gaiko Ron; Kokuren Gaiko no Jisso* (Tokyo: PMC Shuppan, 1990), and Yasuhiro Ueki, "Japan's UN Diplomacy: Sources of Passivism and Activism," in Curtis, ed., *Japan's Foreign Policy*, 347-70.

18. For examples of ODA literature during this period, see Toshio Shishido, *Tonan Ajia Enjo o Kangaeru* (Tokyo: Toyo Keizai Shimposha, 1973); Jiro Kawakita, *Kaigai Kyoryoku no Tetsugaku: Himaraya de no Jissen kara* (Tokyo: Jissen Chuo Sinsho, 1974); Keisuke Suzuki, *Ni-So Keizai Kyoryoku: Shiberia Kaihatsu Kyoryoku to Nihon* (Tokyo: Kokusai Mondai Kenkyujo, 1974); Tsuneo Iida, *Enjo Suru Kuni, Sareru Kuni* (Tokyo: Nikkei Shinsho, 1974); Kunihiko Ogawa, *Kuroi Keizai Kyoryoku: Kono Ajia no Genjitsu o Miyo* (Tokyo: Shimpo Shinsho, 1974); Toshio Watanabe and Kakuten Hara (eds.), *Tei-Kaihatsu Koku Keizai Enjo-ron* (Tokyo: Ajia Keizai Shuppan-kai, 1970); Masao Sakurai, *Waga Kuni no Keizai Kyoryoku* (Tokyo: Ajia Keizai Kenkyujo, 1972); Akira Onishi, *Tei-Kaihatsu Koku to Nihon* (Tokyo: Besuto Bookusu, 1969); Sangyo Kozo Shingikai Kokusai Keizai Bukai (ed.), *Nihon no Taigai Keizai Seisaku: Shinrai Sareru Nihon e no Michi* (Tokyo: Diamondo-sha, 1972); and the ten volume series edited by Kajima Heiwa Kenkyujo, *Taigai Keizai Kyoryoku Taikei* (Tokyo: Kajima Kenkyujo Shuppan-kai, 1973-74).

19. It could be noted that the first English-language studies of Japanese aid also appeared at this time and reflected the contents of the Japanese language materials. See J. Alexander Caldwell, "The Evolution of Japanese Economic Cooperation (1950-1970)," in Harald B. Malmgren (ed.), *Pacific Basin Development: The American Interests*, 66-80 (Lexington, MA: Lexington Books, 1972); Martha Loutfi, *The Net Cost of Japanese Foreign Aid* (New York: Praeger, 1973); John White, *Japanese Aid* (London: Overseas Development Institute, 1974); and Sukehiro Hasegawa, *Japanese Foreign Aid: Policy and Practice* (New York: Praeger, 1975).

20. The major recent books are: Alan Rix, *Japan's Foreign Aid Challenge: Policy Reform and Aid Leadership* (London: Routledge, 1993); Robert M. Orr, Jr., *The Emergence of Japan's Foreign Aid Power* (New York: Columbia University Press, 1990); Koppel and Orr, Jr. (eds.), *Japan's Foreign Aid*; Yasutomo, *The Manner of Giving*; Margee M. Ensign, *Doing Good or Doing Well: Japan's Foreign Aid Program* (New York: Columbia University Press, 1992); Shafiqul Islam (ed.),

Yen for Development: Japanese Foreign Aid and the Politics of Burden-Sharing (New York: Council on Foreign Relations Press, 1991).

21. For example, see U.S. Department of State, *Japan's Foreign Aid: Program Trends and U.S. Business Opportunities* (February 18, 1993); U.S. Agency for International Development, *Japan's Development Financing: Opportunities for U.S. Business* (May 1989); U.S. General Accounting Office, *Economic Assistance: Integration of Japanese Aid and Trade Policies* (May 1990).

22. To date, Yasutomo, *Strategic Aid,* and Orr, *Foreign Aid Power,* have been translated into Japanese, and Islam, *Yen for Development,* is cited frequently by aid analysts. See also a special issue devoted to Japanese ODA with a roundtable discussion moderated by Isami Takeda with Orr, Rix, and Yasutomo in "Sho-Gaikoku wa Doo Miteriru ka: Hihan to Hyoka," *Gaiko Foramu,* no. 54 (March 1993), 16-27.

23. For example, three conferences were held in Tokyo in October and November of 1992, cohosted by Japanese and American sponsors. American sponsors included the Overseas Development Council, the Department of Commerce, and the Citizens Network for Foreign Affairs. The ODC and Citizens Network conferences held follow-up conferences in Washington, D.C., the following spring.

24. Kazuo Sumi, *ODA Enjo no Genjitsu* (Tokyo: Iwanami Shinsho, 1990); Sumi, *Kirawareru Enjo: Segin-Nihon no Enjo to Narumada Damu* (Tokyo: Tsukiji Shokan, 1990); and Sumi, *No Moa ODA; Baramaki Enjo* (Tokyo: JICC Shuppan Kyoku, 1992); Yoshinori Murai, *Nippon no ODA* (Tokyo: Gakuyo Shobo, 1992); and Murai, *Musekinin Enjo Taikoku Nippon* (Tokyo: JICC Shuppan Kyoku, 1989).

25. In addition to periodic articles or series critical of aid projects, both the Asahi and Mainichi have published volumes on ODA. See Asahi Shimbun "Enjo" Shuzaihan, *Enjo Tojokoku Nippon* (Tokyo: Tosho Insatsu Kabushiki-Gaisha, 1985), and Mainichi Shimbun Shakaibu Shuzaihan, *Kokusai Enjo Bijinesu; ODA wa Doo Kawarete iru ka* (Tokyo: Aki Shobo, 1990).

26. The standard annual white papers are the Ministry of International Trade and Industry's *Keizai Kyoryoku no Genjo to Mondaiten* (Tokyo: Tsusho Sangyo Chosakai), the Ministry of Foreign Affairs' *Waga Kuni no Seifu Kaihatsu Enjo,* 2 volumes (Tokyo: Kokusai Kyoryoku Suishin Kyokai), and, in English, *Japan's Official Development Assistance Annual Report* (Tokyo: Association for Promotion of International Cooperation).

27. See, in particular, Koichiro Matsuura, *Enjo Gaiko no Saizensen de Kangaeta Koto* (Tokyo: Dai-Nihon Insatsu Kabushikigaisha, 1990); Isao Kubota, *Q and A: Wakariyasui ODA; Sono Shikumi to Yakuwari* (Tokyo: Gyosei, 1992); Michihiro Sasanuma, *ODA Hihan o Kangaeru* (Tokyo: Kogyo Jiji Tsushinsha,

1991); Sadao Higuchi, *Seifu Kaihatsu Enjo* (Tokyo: Keiso Shobo, 1986); Kazumi Goto, "OECF Through the Looking-Glass and What Alice Found There: Japan Loan Aid in Perspective," manuscript (March 5, 1993); and Takao Kawakami, "21 Seiki ni Muketa Nihon no Enjo Seisaku," *Gaiko Foramu,* no. 54 (March 1993), 4-15.

28. For example, see Ichiro Ozawa, *Blueprint for a New Japan; The Rethinking of a Nation,* chap. 6 (Tokyo: Kodansha International, 1994). See also Takujiro Hamada, "Taikenteki Enjo-ron," in Takeshi Igarashi (ed.), *Nihon no Oda to Kokusai Chitsujo* (Tokyo: Nihon Kokusai Mondai Kenkyujo, 1990), 153-70. Many LDP Diet members who are considered interested or knowledgeable about ODA left the party in June 1993 and joined the new conservative parties, either the Shinseito or the Sakigake. Hamada, an LDP Diet member, lost his seat in the general election of July 1993.

29. For example, Keidanren follows ODA developments through its economic cooperation bureau and publishes periodic reports and policy proposals, and the private sector recently created the Japan International Development Organization (JAIDO).

30. See Toshio Watanabe and Atsushi Kusano, *Nihon no ODA o Doo Suru ka* (Tokyo: Nihon Hoso Kyokai Shuppan Kyokai, 1991); Hirohisa Kohama, *ODA no Keizaigaku* (Tokyo: Nihon Hyoronsha, 1992); Ken Matsui, *Kokusai Kyoryokuron Enshu* (Tokyo: Koyo Shobo, 1988); Tsuneo Iida, *Nihon Keizai no Mokuhyo* (Tokyo: PHP Kenkyujo, 1993); and Iida, "Rinen ni Tsuite no Ikkosatsu," *Tsusan Januaru* (July 1990), 22-23.

31. ODA studies that directly address the arguments of the aid critics, especially Sumi and Murai, are Sasanuma and Watanabe and Kusano. The works of Sumi and Sasanuma provide the most comprehensive and detailed explications of their respective views and, therefore, serve as an excellent introduction to the debate.

32. The term is used loosely to refer to the general thrust of positive views of Japan's ODA that the author consolidated by drawing from a variety of sources.

33. For a taste of this aspect of the aid debate, see the give and take in the works of Murai, Sumi, and Watanabe and Kusano.

34. The official annual aid evaluation report is Gaimusho Keizai Kyoryoku Kyoku, *Keizai Kyoryoku Hyoka Hokokusho,* usually released every summer.

35. For example, see Ensign, *Doing Well or Doing Good.*

36. For example, see the works of Rix and Orr.

37. See, for example, the edited volume by Islam, *Yen for Development.*

38. I hope, therefore, that readers will excuse the incorporation of some non-Japanese works in this section. In addition, this section incorporates views

distilled from interviews in Japan that stretch back at least ten years. I am attempting to draw a composite picture and not worry about footnoting each and every point or idea.

39. This is a central tenet of the thinking of Robert M. Orr, Jr.; for example, see *Foreign Aid Power*. See also Rix, *Challenge*.

40. See the works of Sumi and Murai for articulation of this view.

41. I associate these ideas with development experts such as Ryokichi Hirono, a former official in United Nations Development Program (UNDP) from Seikei University, along with Ministry of Finance officials and aid technicians and policy implementers in OECF and Japan International Cooperation Agency (JICA).

42. See especially the works of Robert M. Orr, Jr.

43. See Dennis T. Yasutomo, "Why Aid? Japan as an Aid Great Power," *Pacific Affairs* (Winter 1989-90), 490-503.

44. This view has taken hold throughout the various ministries, agencies, media, political parties, and academia. See, for example, Goto, "Alice."

45. The works of Juichi Inada emphasize the existence of a political-strategic agenda for aid from the 1960s. For example, refer to "Japan's Aid Diplomacy: Increasing Role for Global Security," *Japan Review of International Affairs* (Spring/Summer 1988), 91-112; "Stick or Carrot? Japanese Aid Policy and Vietnam," in Koppel and Orr (eds.), *Power and Policy*, 111-34; "ODA to Nihon Gaiko: Tai-Filipin Enjo ni Tsuite no Jirei Kenkyu," in Igarashi (ed.), *Kokusai Chitsujo*, 52-81; and "Hatten Tojo Koku to Nihon: Taigai Enjo Seisaku no Henyo Katei," in Akio Watanabe (ed.), *Sengo Nihon no Taigai Seisaku*, 285-314. Critics, of course, argue that Japan had a political agenda provided by the United States.

46. I associate this view with development experts such as Ryokichi Hirono. See also Kohama, *Keizaigaku*, and Tsuneo Iida, *Nihon Keizai no Mokuhyo* (Tokyo: PHP Kenkyujo, 1993), chaps. 5 and 6, and "Rinen."

47. This view is prevalent within the Ministry of Foreign Affairs, especially the Economic Cooperation Bureau, which produced the ODA Charter (and the prior conceptualizations found in the 1981 principles). The MFA's ODA white papers, as well as Miti's, explain the official philosophy.

48. The author's previous work reflects this view; see especially *Manner of Giving*.

49. Scattered writings touch upon the development side of Japan's philosophy. Start with Kohama, *Keizaigaku*, and Matsui, *Enshu*.

50. Perhaps the most popular and influential of the recent works in this genre is Graham Hancock, *Lords of Poverty: The Power, Prestige, and Corruption of the International Aid Business* (New York: Atlantic Monthly Press, 1989).

51. See Sumi, *Kirawareru Enjo*.

CHAPTER 2

1. *Japan Times,* June 17, 1990.
2. *Japan Times Weekly International,* July 8-14, 1991.
3. Seizaburo Sato, "The Foundations of Modern Japanese Foreign Policy," in Robert A. Scalapino (ed.), *The Foreign Policy of Modern Japan,* 389 (Berkeley: University of California Press, 1977).
4. For a discussion of the foreign policy debate within Japan, see Kenneth B. Pyle, "Japan, The World, and the Twenty-First Century," in Takashi Inoguchi and Daniel I. Okimoto (eds.), *The Political Economy of Japan: Volume 2: The Changing International Context* 446-86 (Stanford, CA: Stanford University Press, 1988).
5. For representative views, see the following works by

   Donald Hellmann: *Japanese Domestic Politics and Foreign Policy; The Peace Agreement with the Soviet Union* (Berkeley: University of California Press, 1969); "The Confrontation with Realpolitik," in James William Morley (ed.), *Forecast for Japan: Security in the 1970s,* 135-69 (Princeton, NJ: Princeton University Press, 1972); "Japanese Security and Postwar Japanese Foreign Policy," in Scalapino (ed.), *Foreign Policy,* 321-40; "Japanese Politics and Foreign Policy: Elitist Democracy Within An American Greenhouse," in Inoguchi and Okimoto (eds.), *Political Economy,* 345-80.

   By Kent Calder: especially "Japanese Foreign Economic Policy Formation: Explaining the Reactive State," *World Politics,* 40 (July 1988), 517-41; "Halfway to Hegemony?: Japan in a Changing Global Economic Order," *Harvard International Review* (April/May 1988), 12-16.

   By Robert M. Orr, Jr.: especially *The Emergence of Japan's Foreign Aid Power* (New York: Columbia University Press, 1990).

   By Yoichi Funabashi: "Japan and the New World Order," *Foreign Affairs* (Winter 1991-92), 58-74.

   By Yashichi Ohata and Sadao Tamura: *Nihon no Kokusai Tekio-ryoku* (Tokyo: Yuhikaku, 1989).

   By Michael Blaker: "Probe, Push, and Panic: The Japanese Tactical Style in International Negotiations," in Scalapino (ed.), *Foreign Policy,* 55-101; "Evaluating Japan's Diplomatic Performance," in Gerald L. Curtis (ed.), *Japan's Foreign Policy After the Cold War: Coping with Change* (Armonk, NY: M.E. Sharpe, 1993), 1-42.
6. Hellmann, "Confrontation," 135.
7. Hellmann, "Japanese Politics," 351.

8. Calder, "Reactive State," 518.
9. Blaker, "Diplomatic Peformance," 3.
10. Funabashi, "New World Order," p. 60.
11. Tetsuya Kataoka, *Waiting for a 'Pearl Harbor'; Japan Debates Defense* (Stanford, CA: Hoover Institute Press, 1980), 7.
12. Ikutaro Shimizu, "The Nuclear Option: Japan, Be a State!" *Japan Echo,* 8, no. 3 (1980), 33-45.
13. Hellmann, "Japanese Politics," 358.
14. Orr, *Emergence,* 20-21.
15. Ohata and Tamura, *Tekio-ryoku,* p. ii.
16. Calder, "Reactive State," 520.
17. Ibid., 519.
18. Hellmann, "Confrontation," 138.
19. Ibid., 135 and 137.
20. Calder, "Reactive State," 520.
21. Funabashi, "New World Order," p. 62.
22. Orr, *Emergence,* 108.
23. Ibid., especially 121.
24. Ibid., 125.
25. Ibid., 113.
26. Hellmann, "Japanese Politics," 346.
27. Ibid., 358-68.
28. Hellmann, *Japanese Domestic Politics,* 18.
29. Hellmann, "Confrontation," 135-36.
30. Funabashi, "New World Order," 72.
31. Hellmann, *Japanese Domestic Politics,* 154.
32. Calder, "Reactive State," 528-29.
33. Ibid., 529.
34. Ibid., 530.
35. Ibid., 530.
36. Leonard Schoppa, "Zoku Power and LDP Power: A Case Study of the Zoku Role in Education Policy," *Journal of Japanese Studies* (Winter 1991), 79-106.
37. Calder, "Reactive State," 532.
38. Orr, *Emergence,* 19.
39. Ibid., 12.
40. Ibid., 21.
41. He states that "parochial" interest groups "have virtually no international interests other than to resist foreign encroachments into Japanese domestic markets" and that "in the absence of outside pressures for action, the media

structure in Japan creates strong incentives toward hesitant initial behavior." See Calder, "Reactive State," 529 and 530.

42. Funabashi, "New World Order," 72 and 73.
43. See Orr, *Emergence*, 107-31. ✓
44. Hellmann, "Japanese Security," 330.
45. Hellmann, "Japanese Politics," 369.
46. Calder, "Reactive State," 541.
47. Blaker, "Diplomatic Performance," 37-38.
48. Hellmann, "Japanese Security," 332.
49. Calder, "Reactive State," 519.
50. Martin E. Weinstein, *Japan's Postwar Defense Policy, 1947-1968* (New York: Columbia University Press, 1971); Weinstein, "Strategic Thought and the U.S.-Japan Alliance," in Morley (ed.), *Forecast*, 135-69.
51. See Chae-Jin Lee, *Japan Faces China* (Baltimore: Johns Hopkins Press, 1976); Michael M. Yoshitsu, *Japan and the San Francisco Peace Settlement* (New York: Columbia University Press, 1983); and Alexander Ching-an, "The Policy Making Process in Japan's Policy Toward The People's Republic of China" (Ph.D. diss., Columbia University, 1969).
52. See Dennis T. Yasutomo, "The Politicization of Japan's 'Post-Cold War' Multilateral Diplomacy," in Curtis (ed.), *Japan's Foreign Policy*, 338.
53. Michael Yoshitsu, *Caught in the Middle East: Japan's Diplomacy in Transition* (Lexington, MA: Lexington Books, 1984); Marvin Ott, "Japan's Growing Involvement in the Middle East," *SAIS Review* (Summer-Fall 1985), 221-32; and Yasumasa Kuroda, "Japan and the Arabs: The Economic Dimension," *Journal of Arab Affairs* (Spring 1984).
54. Mike M. Mochizuki, "Japan's Search For Strategy," *International Security* 8 (Winter 1983-84), 52-79.
55. J.W.M. Chapman, R. Drifte, and I.T.M. Gow, *Japan's Quest for Comprehensive Security: Defence, Diplomacy, and Dependence* (New York: St. Martin's Press, 1982); Robert W. Barnett, *Beyond War: Japan's Concept of Comprehensive National Security* (Washington, D.C.: Pergamon-Brassey's International Defense Publishers, 1984; Dennis T. Yasutomo, *The Manner of Giving: Strategic Aid and Japanese Foreign Policy* (Lexington, MA: Lexington Books, 1986).
56. Calder, "Reactive State," 518.
57. J.A.A. Stockwin, "Dynamic and Immobilist Aspects of Japanese Politics," in J.A.A. Stockwin et al., *Dynamic and Immobilist Politics in Japan*, 1 (Honolulu: University of Hawaii Press, 1988).
58. Stockwin, "Dynamic," 19.

59. Alan Rix, "Dynamism, Foreign Policy and Trade Policy," in Stockwin (ed.), *Dynamic*, 314.
60. Alan Rix, "Bureaucracy and Political Change in Japan," in Stockwin (ed.), *Dynamic*, 54.
61. Rix, "Dynamism", in Stockwin et al., *Dynamic*, 297.
62. Aurelia George, "Japanese Interest Group Behaviour: An Institutional Approach," in Stockwin et al., *Dynamic*, 120.
63. Ibid., 122.
64. Stockwin, "Dynamic," in Stockwin et al., *Dynamic*, 19-20.
65. Rix, "Dynamism," 320.
66. Ibid., 318.
67. To cite one example involving Japan, see Holsti's study of Japan's China policy. He argues that economic interests did predominate for a while but that Japan returned to power considerations in the end. K.J. Holsti, "Politics in Command: Foreign Trade as National Security Policy," *International Organization* (Summer 1986), 643-72.
68. Robert Keohane, cited in John G. Ikenberry, David A. Lake, and Michael Mastanduno, "Introduction: Approaches to Explaining American Foreign Economic Policy," *International Organization*, 42 (Winter 1988), 4.
69. Kenneth Waltz, *Theory of International Politics* (Reading, MA: Addison-Wesley, 1979), 65.
70. Ibid., 60.
71. Ibid., 96-97.
72. Stephen D. Krasner, *Structural Conflict: The Third World Against Global Liberalism* (Berkeley: University of California Press, 1985), 28.
73. Bruce E. Moon, "Consensus or Compliance? Foreign Policy Change and External Dependence," *International Organization*, 39 (Spring 1985), 297.
74. Stephen Krasner, "Regimes and the Limits of Realism: Regimes as Autonomous Variables," in Stephen D. Krasner (ed.), *International Regimes* (Ithaca, NY: Cornell University Press, 1983), 356.
75. Waltz, *Theory*, 94.
76. Ikenberry, Lake, and Mastanduno, "Introduction," 1-2.
77. Peter J. Katzenstein, "Introduction: Domestic and International Forces and Strategies of Foreign Economic Policy," in Peter J. Katzenstein, *Between Power and Plenty: Foreign Economic Policies of Advanced Industrialized States,* 11 (Madison: University of Wisconsin Press, 1978).
78. Jeff Frieden, "Sectoral Conflict and Foreign Economic Policy," *International Organization*, 42 (Winter 1988), 88.
79. Lynn H. Miller, *Global Order: Values and Power in International Politics* (Boulder, CO: Westview Press, 1990), 144.

80. Ikenberry, Lake, and Mastanduno, "Introduction," 1-2.

81. David A. Lake, "The State and American Trade Strategy in the Pre-Hegemonic Era," *International Organization*, 42 (Winter 1988), 35-36.

82. Ibid., 57.

83. Katzenstein, "Introduction," in Katzenstein, *Foreign Economic Policies*, 18.

84. Lake, "The State," 37.

85. Katzenstein, "Introduction," in Katzenstein, *Foreign Economic Policies*, 18.

86. Ibid.

87. Ikenberry, Lake, and Mastanduno, "Introduction," 10.

88. Judith Goldstein, "Ideas, Institutions, and American Trade Policy," *International Organization*, 42 (Winter 1988), 182.

89. Ibid., 179-217.

90. Ibid.

91. Ibid., 36.

92. Stephen D. Krasner, *Defending the National Interest: Raw Materials Investments and U.S. Foreign Policy* (Princeton, NJ: Princeton University Press, 1978).

93. Peter J. Katzenstein, "Conclusion: Domestic Structures and Strategies of Foreign Economic Policy," in Katzenstein, *Foreign Economic Policies*, 306-8.

94. Steven M. Smith, *Foreign Policy Adaptation* (New York: Nichols Publishing Company, 1981), 40.

95. Katzenstein, "Introduction," in Katzenstein, *Foreign Economic Policies*, 18.

96. John G. Ikenberry, "The State and Strategies of International Adjustment," *World Politics*, 39 (October 1986), 54.

97. Ikenberry, Lake, and Mastanduno, "Introduction," 12-13.

98. Ikenberry, "Strategies," 59.

99. See Robert C. Angel, "Prime Ministerial Leadership in Japan: Recent Changes in Personal Style and Administrative Organization," *Pacific Affairs* (Winter 1988-1989), 583-602; and Kenji Hayao, *The Japanese Prime Minister and Public Policy* (Pittsburgh, PA: University of Pittsburgh, 1993).

100. Harold K. Jacobson, *Networks of Interdependence: International Organizations and the Global Political System* (New York: Alfred A. Knopf, 1979), 121.

101. Ibid., 120-22.

102. Ibid., 122.

103. Ibid., 120.

104. Ibid.

105. Ernst B. Haas, *When Knowledge Is Power: Three Models of Change in International Organizations* (Berkeley: University of California Press, 1990), 30.

106. Quoted in Jayed A. Ansari, *The Political Economy of International Economic Organization* (Boulder, CO: Lynn Rienner Publishers, 1986).

107. Charles Pentland, "International Organizations and Their Roles," in Paul F. Diehl (ed.), *The Politics of International Organizations: Patterns and Insights,* 6 (Pacific Grove, CA: Books/Cole Publishing Company, 1989).
108. Haas, *Knowledge,* 15.
109. Jahangir Amuzegar, "The IMF Under Fire," in Diehl (ed.), *International Organizations,* 303-4.
110. Gayl D. Ness and Steven R. Brechin, "Bridging the Gap: International Organizations as Organizations," *International Organization* (Spring 1988), 252.
111. Ibid., 270.
112. Robert O. Keohane, *International Institutions and State Power: Essays in International Relations Theory* (Boulder, CO: Westview Press, 1989), 6; and Keohane, *After Hegemony: Cooperation and Discord in the World Political Economy* (Princeton, NJ: Princeton University Press, 1984), 13.
113. Keohane, *International Institutions,* 5.
114. Keohane, *Hegemony,* 13.

CHAPTER 3

1. Toru Yanagihara, "Japan's Foreign Aid to Bangladesh: Challenging the Dependency Syndrome," in Bruce M. Koppel and Robert M. Orr, Jr. (eds.), *Japan's Foreign Aid; Power and Policy in a New Era,* 198 (Boulder, CO: Westview Press, 1993).
2. See Masaki Shiratori, *Sekai Ginko Guruppu; Tojokoku Enjo to Nihon no Yakuwari* (Tokyo: Kenkyusha Insatsu Kabushikigaisha, 1993), chap. 6.
3. Ibid., 225. See also Nobuaki Kemmochi, *Sekai Ginko to Nihon* (Tokyo: Sekai Ginko Tokyo Jimusho, 1990).
4. See *Japan Times Weekly,* August 6-12, 1990.
5. Information found in Shiratori, *Sekai Ginko,* chap. 6, and Kemmochi, *Sekai Ginko,* 22-30.
6. Kemmochi, *Sekai Ginko,* 1.
7. See Shiratori, *Sekai Ginko,* 230-31.
8. Interview with a former Ministry of Finance official, October 20, 1992.
9. Shiratori, *Sekai Ginko,* 232-4.
10. The Japanese consider the regional offices the core of bank activities. Interview with a member of the Japanese delegation to the bank, May 26, 1992.
11. Shiratori, *Sekai Ginko,* 239-40.
12. Ibid.
13. Personnel issues are discussed at length in Shiratori, *Sekai Ginko,* chap. 6, and an insider's perspective can be found in a book written by two Japanese staff

members of the World Bank and IMF: Kenichi Ono and Izumi Ono, *IMF to Sekai Ginko; Uchigawa Kara Mita Kaihatsu Kinyu Kikan* (Tokyo: Nihon Hyoronsha, 1993).

14. Sadako Ogata, "Shifting Power Relations in Multilateral Development Banks," *The Journal of International Studies* (January 1989), 10-15.
15. Interview with Finance Ministry official, November 11, 1992.
16. Interview, May 26, 1992.
17. Interview, November 12, 1992.
18. For details, see Toshihiko Kinoshita, "Developments in the International Debt Strategy and Japan's Response," *Exim Review* (January 1991), 62-80, and "Ruiseki Saimu Mondai no Sui-i to Sekai-teki Shinkin Kyokyu Shisutemu no Sai-Kochiku no Hoko to Tenbo," *Fainanshiaru Rebyu* (March 1993), 42-76.
19. "Exim Japan's Commitments Under $65 billion Recycling Plan," mimeo.
20. "Shikin Kanryu Jisshi Jokyo (Chiiki-betsu)," mimeo.
21. For recent studies of post–Tiananmen Square Sino-Japanese relations, see Zhao Quansheng, "Japan's Aid Diplomacy With China," in Koppel and Orr, Jr. (eds.), *Japan's Foreign Aid,* 163-87; and K. V. Kesavan, "Japan and the Tiananmen Square Incident," *Asian Survey* (July 1990), 671-77.
22. MOF officials, April 21 and 22, 1993.
23. MOF official, March 4, 1993.
24. For Japan's activities on China at the Houston Summit, see Dennis T. Yasutomo, "The Politicization of Japan's 'Post–Cold War' Multilateral Diplomacy," in Gerald L. Curtis (ed.), *Japan's Foreign Policy After the Cold War: Coping with Change* (Armonk, NY: M.E. Sharpe, 1993), 323-46.
25. MOF official, November 20, 1992.
26. MOF official, February 2, 1993.
27. Interview, November 10, 1990.
28. Interview, October 2, 1992.
29. See "Issues Related to the World Bank's Approach to Structural Adjustment— Proposal from a Major Partner," OECF Occasional Paper No. 1 (October 1991), in *The OECF Research Quarterly,* no. 73 (February 1992), 11-18.
30. Ibid., 16.
31. Ibid., 17.
32. Interview, October 2, 1992.
33. Interview with MOF official, November 20, 1992.
34. Interview, April 21, 1993.
35. Former MOF official, April 21, 1993.
36. Interview, April 21, 1993.
37. Interview, April 21, 1993.

38. *World Development Report 1991: The Challenge of Development* (Oxford: Oxford University Press, 1991).

39. Ibid., 3 and 4.

40. World Bank, *The East Asian Miracle: Economic Growth and Public Policy* (Oxford: Oxford University Press, 1993).

41. Interview with a former MOF official, April 21, 1993.

42. Isao Kubota, "Higashi Ajia no Kiseki—Saikin no Kaihatsu Enjo Seisaku no Ronten (1)," *Fainansu* (December 1993), 40.

43. Ibid., 41.

44. Isao Kubota, "Higashi Ajia no Kiseki—Saikin no Kaihatsu Enjo Seisaku no Ronten (2)," *Fainansu* (January 1994), 28.

45. Interview, February 2, 1993.

46. Kubota, "Higashi Ajia (2)," 28.

47. Shiratori, *Sekai Ginko*, p. 243.

48. Interview with MOF official, October 20, 1992.

49. Information on Japan's involvement in the ADB from the initial conceptualization of a regional bank idea through 1982 comes from the author's previous study, *Japan and the Asian Development Bank* (New York: Praeger Special Studies, 1983). The analysis of Japan-ADB relations during the 1980s—President Fujioka's reign from 1981 to 1989—owes much to my recent article, "Japan and The Asian Development Bank: Multilateral Aid Policy in Transition," in Koppel and Orr, Jr. (eds.), *Japan's Foreign Aid,* 305-40. Information on the President Tarumizu years (1989-1993) was gathered during the author's nine-month stay at the Ministry of Finance in 1992-93.

50. The story of Japan's involvement in the founding of the ADB can be found in my earlier study, *Japan and the Asian Development Bank*. See also Takeshi Watanabe, *Ajia Kaigin Sosai Nikki* (Tokyo: Nihon Keizai Shimbunsha, 1973); Po-Wen Huang, Jr., *The Asian Development Bank: Diplomacy and Development in Asia* (New York: Vantage Press, 1975); R. Krishnamurti, *ADB—The Seeding Days* (Manila: ADB Printing Section, 1977).

51. According to a former Japanese executive director, "It's funny to have a policy implementer's salary go higher than a policymaker's salary. If a policymaker's salary is lower, integrity is threatened. The World Bank uncapped its salary, but why follow a bad example?" Interview, July 17, 1990.

52. Interview, July 17, 1990.

53. Based on discussions with ADB staff members and former staff members over the past few years.

54. See "Dai-Niju-go Kai Ajia Kaihatsu Ginko Nenji Sokai Somu Enzetsu," *Fainansu* (July 1992), 46-47.

55. Interview with an MOF official, May 27, 1993.

56. Interview, June 19, 1990.
57. Interview, August 11, 1989.
58. Interview, May 6, 1993.
59. Interview, October 16, 1992.
60. A former ADB staff member, June 14, 1990.
61. Interview, August 1, 1989.
62. Interview, August 21, 1989.
63. Interview, August 11, 1989.
64. For a critical view that Japan pushed its own development agenda in agriculture in the ADB, see Robert Wihtol, *Asian Development Bank and Rural Development* (New York: St. Martin's Press, 1988).
65. See the addresses of Japanese finance ministers at the ADB annual meetings in Vancouver and, especially, Hong Kong: "Dai Niju-yon Kai Ajia Kaihatsu Ginko Nenji Sokai Somu Enzetsu," in *Fainansu* (June 1991), 34-36, and "Dai-Niju-go Kai Ajia Kaihatsu Ginko Nenji Sokai Somu Enzetsu," *Fainansu* (July 1992), 46-48. For background on both meetings, consult Hiroshi Toyoda, "Dai-Niju-go Ajia Kaihatsu Ginko Hon Kon Sokai ni Tsuite," *Fainansu* (July 1992), 40-45, and Satoru Miyamura, "Dai-Niju-yon Ajia Kaihatsu Ginko Bankoobaa Sokai ni Tsuite," *Fainansu* (June 1991), 28-33.
66. Interview, October 6, 1992.
67. Masao Fujioka, *Ajia Kaigin Sosai Nikki: Manira e no Sato-Gaeri* (Tokyo: Toyo Keizai Shimposha, 1986), 152-68.
68. Interview, August 1, 1989.
69. Interview, May 17, 1993.
70. Kevin Rafferty, "Asian Development Bank: The Manila Agenda," *Institutional Investor* (April 1983), 168.
71. An observation by a non-Japanese former bank associate. Interview, July 18, 1990.
72. Interview, June 19, 1990.
73. Interview, June 19, 1990.
74. Interview, June 14, 1990.
75. Interview with a former non-Japanese ADB official, July 18, 1990.
76. Interview at the Finance Ministry, June 19, 1990.
77. Interview, July 18, 1990.
78. Interview, May 17, 1993.
79. A former ADB staff member, June 21, 1990.
80. Interview with a former Japanese executive director, May 17, 1993.
81. Interview, May 27, 1993.
82. *Mainichi Shimbun,* July 6, 1993.
83. Interview, May 17, 1992.

84. Philip Bowring, "Asia Outgrowing Its Bank," *Daily Yomiuri*, May 19, 1993.

85. Karen Donfried, *CRS Report for Congress: The European Bank for Reconstruction and Development: An Institution of and for the New Europe* (Washington, D.C.: Congressional Research Service, August 15, 1991), CRS-3.

86. Interview with a member of Japan's negotiating team, March 12, 1993.

87. Interview, July 8, 1993.

88. European Bank for Reconstruction and Development, *Summary Proceedings of the Inaugural Meeting of the Board of Governors, London, 15-17 April 1991,* 97.

89. Interview, May 26, 1992.

90. Samantha Sparks, *Policy Focus: The European Bank for Reconstruction and Development* (Washington, D.C.: Overseas Development Council, 1990), 2.

91. An MOF observer remarked that "the whole process was funny. France made its own Finance Ministry the headquarters [of the EBRD establishment process], not the EC. Mitterrand took all the initiatives, and the EC approved. Ireland was the chair, but it was bypassed by France, which had stepped down the previous year as chair." Interview, July 19, 1990.

92. Interviews at MOF, March 12 and May 20, 1993.

93. For a detailed, article-by-article comparison of the EBRD's Articles of Agreement with those of other MDBs, see Ibrahim F. I. Shihata, *The European Bank for Reconstruction and Development: A Comparative Analysis of the Constituent Agreement* (London: Graham and Trotman/Martinus Nijhoff, 1990). Similarities between the EBRD and ADB include operational principles, powers and procedures of the boards of directors, special fund provisions, private sector development operations, and underwriting securities issues.

94. Interview with an MOF delegate, March 12, 1993.

95. Tetsuma Fujikawa, "Roshia-To-O ga Kawaru, Sekai ga Kawaru (Saishukai): Oshu Fukko Kaihatsu Ginko no Riji San Kagyo," *Finansu* (December 1993), 86-87.

96. Fujikawa, "Roshia-To-O," 86.

97. Interview, July 12, 1993.

98. Fujikawa, "Roshia," 94.

99. "In early November 1989, he told Treasury Director Jean-Claude Trichet to flesh out the structure for an organization that would rebuild the economies of Eastern Europe. A month later, Mitterrand submitted his Treasury's quickly drawn plan to the 11 other members of the European Community, and they gave France the authority to convene a conference to negotiate the details." See Anthony J. Blinken, "Jacques of All Trades," *New York Times Magazine,* October 31, 1991, 46.

100. According to one observation, "He had immense self-confidence, was frankly immodest about his own abilities, but had no practical banking experience. . . .

Many of the shareholders, such as the US, had never really wanted him, and the sniping began almost immediately. He was notorious for being late for meetings, for agreeing to initiatives and then doing little about them; few dispute the fact that he lacked the ability to put his vision into effect and provided ineffectual leadership at the bank. And he had a remarkable ability for rubbing people up the wrong way." See *Daily Yomiuri*, July 2, 1993.

101. See *Daily Yomiuri*, April 15 and May 9, 1992.

102. "Oshu Fukko Kaihatsu Ginko Dai-Ikkai Nenji Sokai: Chino Zaimukan Enzetsu," *Fainansu* (June 1992), 57-58.

103. Hiroshi Toyoda, "Dai-Ikkai Oshu Fukko Kaihatsu Ginko Nenji Sokai ni Tsuite," *Fainansu* (June 1992), 53-54.

104. For details on the charges against Attali, see *Japan Times*, June 15, June 27, and July 18, 1993; Knight Ridder, July 14, 1993; and *Daily Yomiuri*, July 2, 1993.

105. Jacques Attali, *Millennium: Winners and Losers in the Coming World Order* (New York: Times Books, 1991), 55.

106. Attali writes, "The United States can (with great difficulty) resist Japan's advance by taking an alternate route. . . . The United States may attempt to become a part of the European sphere. And this attempt will be welcomed because it is in Europe's interest to see that America no longer declines. This will strengthen Europe in its competition with Japan." Ibid., 54.

107. Ibid., 58.

108. Ibid., 63.

109. European Bank for Reconstruction and Development, *Summary Proceedings of the Inaugural Meeting of the Board of Governors, London, 15-17 April 1991*, 15.

110. *Japan Times*, June 27, 1993. Actually, Gyohten's name surfaces whenever any international financial organization position opens up, illustrating the small pool of internationalists in Japan qualified to serve in such positions. His name has been raised in connection with a World Bank vice presidency, the IMF's managing directorship, and the ADB presidency (twice).

111. Eugene Moosa, "Japan Takes Timid First Step in Global Role," Reuters, January 17, 1990.

112. Eugene Moosa, "Kaifu Says Japan Should Play Political Role," Reuters, January 9, 1990.

113. See Barbara Wanner, "Japan's Relations with the 'Soviet Bloc,'" *JEI Report*, January 19, 1990.

114. Interview, July 19, 1990.

115. *Japan Times*, July 21, 1990.

116. Shigemitsu Sugisaki, "Kyu-Soren/To-O no Doko to Oshu Fukko Kaihatsu Ginko (EBRD) ni Tsuite," *Shihon Shijo* (July 1992), 19.

117. Interview, March 12, 1993.
118. The letter can be found in Shihata, *European Bank,* 164-65.
119. The story of the compromise on Soviet membership and borrowing is well known. See, for example, Donfried, *CRS Report,* and Shihata, *European Bank,* 70-71, and for the text of Gerashchenko's letter, see 164-65.
120. Sparks, *Policy Focus,* 3.
121. Interview with a Department of the Treasury official, May 26, 1992.
122. See Sparks, *Policy Focus,* 3.
123. Sparks, *Policy Focus,* 3.
124. "Delegates were anxious to show that the focus of the Bank's functions was the private sector but, given that the private sector in the potential recipient countries was at present either small or nonexistent, that the Bank would also support the public sector in its transition from purely centralised control to demonopolisation, decentralisation or privatisation and to a competitive business environment. . . ." See Shihata, *European Bank,* 167.
125. Interview, March 12, 1993.
126. Interview with an MOF official, May 20, 1993.
127. EBRD, *Inaugural Meeting,* 24.
128. "Oshu Fukko Kaihatsu Ginko," 57. See also Toyoda, "Dai-Ikkai," 54.
129. European Bank for Reconstruction and Development, *Proceedings of the First Annual Meeting of the Board of Governors, Budapest, 13-14 April 1992,* 74-75.
130. Ibid., 172-3.
131. Ferdinand Protzman, "$1 Billion Plan for Poland and Hungary," *New York Times,* January 10, 1990.
132. "Prime Minister Kaifu Leaves on European Tour," Associated Press, August 1, 1990.

CHAPTER 4

1. Figures come from a Finance Ministry document, dated July 1990.
2. Finance Ministry document, July 1990.
3. Ministry of Foreign Affairs, *Seifu Kaihatsu Enjo Taiko/Japan's Official Development Assistance Charter* (June 30, 1992), 2 (A dual-language edition released by the Foreign Ministry).
4. Ibid., 2.
5. Two MOFA officials have been seconded to the ADB since the late 1980s. However, the ministry failed to replace its second official in 1992, citing the need for personnel at home to prepare for Tokyo's hosting of the 1993 G-7 Summit.

CHAPTER 5

1. Hiroshi Kimura, "Coming Apart," *Look Japan* (December 1992), 7.
2. For a detailed history of Russo-Japanese relations during the Gorbachev era, see Gilbert Rozman, *Japan's Response to the Gorbachev Era, 1985-1991: A Rising Superpower Views a Declining One* (Princeton, NJ: Princeton University Press, 1992).
3. Tsuyoshi Hasegawa, "Soviet-Japanese Relations in the 1990s," in Mike Mochizuki et al., *Japan and the United States: Troubled Partners in a Changing World*, 63 (Washington, D.C.: Brassey's (US), 1991).
4. See Motohide Saito, "Gorubachofu Tai-Nichi 'Shin-Shiko' Gaiko no Kiseki to Hyoka," *Hogaku Kenkyu* (February 1992), 207-27.
5. *New York Times,* June 19, 1991.
6. See *Japan Times Weekly,* December 24 and 30, 1990; *New York Times,* December 5, 11, 13 and 14, 1993; and Yoji Takagi, "Getting on Track," *Look Japan* (December 1992), 8-11.
7. *Japan Times Weekly,* December 24-30, 1990.
8. *New York Times,* April 22, 1991. See also *New York Times,* April 18 and 22, 1991, and *Japan Times Weekly,* April 29-May 5, 1991.
9. *New York Times,* July 9, 1991.
10. *Japan Times Weekly,* June, 17-23, 1991.
11. Kyodo News Service, August 21, 1991.
12. *Daily Yomiuri,* October 9 and 14, 1991.
13. The Japanese maintain that the problem rested on the Soviet side since there was a problem of who should receive this aid, the central government or the republics. See *Daily Yomiuri,* October 9, 1991.
14. Takagi, "Getting on Track," 10.
15. *Daily Yomiuri,* October 11 and 22, 1991.
16. *New York Times,* January 20-24, 1992.
17. *Daily Yomiuri,* January 24, 1992.
18. *New York Times,* April 5, 1992, and Margo Grimm, "International Aid Package for Russia Announced But Far From Wrapped Up," *JEI Report* (April 10, 1992), 6-8.
19. *Daily Yomiuri,* April 17, 1992, and *New York Times,* April 5, 1992.
20. *New York Times,* April 28, 1992. The IMF conditions included reduction of the budget deficit, bringing inflation under control, establishing a legal framework, reforming farming and the energy sector, developing a fiscal system that raises enough hard currency to meet international obligations, and establishing a single exchange rate for the ruble.

21. *World Bank News,* June 19, 1992.
22. *World Bank News,* August 7, 1992.
23. *Daily Yomiuri,* March 8, 1992.
24. *Daily Yomiuri,* April 15, 1992.
25. Interview with an institute official, April 21, 1993.
26. *Asahi Shimbun,* October 28, 1992.
27. *Japan Times,* October 29, 1992.
28. *World Bank News,* December 23, 1992.
29. *Japan Times,* October 30, 1992.
30. For a details of this trip, and the impressions of one of the delegation members, see Hiroshi Toyoda, "Chikakute Toi Kuni—Chuo Ajia no San-Kyowakoku o Homon Shite," *Fainansu* (December 1992), 84-94.
31. The delegation included eight Russian officials and two each from Uzbekistan, Kazakhstan, Kyrgyzstan, and Turkmenistan. For details of this training session, see Zaisei Kinyu Kenkyujo Kokusai Koryu Shitsu, "Keizai Kaikaku no Hikari to Kage: Roshia Rempo to Kyowa Koku to Okurasho to no Taiwa o Tsujite," *Fainansu* (March 1993), 51-60.
32. Reuter-Kyodo, December 3, 1992. Among the nations removed from the list over a three year period are the Bahamas, Kuwait, Qatar, Singapore, United Arab Republic.
33. *Japan Times,* January 5, 1993.
34. Only four nations were represented by minister-level delegates, including Japan and the United States. The European Community delegate canceled at the last minute. See *Asahi Shimbun,* October 30, 1992.
35. *New York Times,* May 6, 1992.
36. *Daily Yomiuri,* April 19, 1992.
37. *Daily Yomiuri,* May 1, 1992.
38. Ibid., May 1, 1992.
39. *Asahi Shimbun,* September 11, 1993.
40. *Japan Times,* March 11, 17 and 18, 1993.
41. *Daily Yomiuri,* March 19, 1993, and *Japan Times,* March 23, 1993.
42. *Japan Times,* April 5, 1993.
43. See *Japan Times,* April 15, 1993. For extensive coverage of the ministerial conference, see Motomichi Ikawa, "Tai-Ro Shien G7 Kakuryo Godo Kaigo ni Tsuite," *Fainansu* (May 1993), 50-60.
44. *Japan Times,* April 14, 1993.
45. *Japan Times,* April 15, 1993.
46. Ibid.
47. *Japan Times,* April 11, 1993.
48. Isao Kubota, "Aid for Japan and Russia," *Japan Times,* April 19, 1993.

49. The results show that 58.7 percent of the Russian people supported Yeltsin and 52.7 percent supported his reform policies. *Japan Times*, April 27, 1993.
50. *Japan Times*, April 14 and June 3, 1993.
51. *Japan Times*, April 15, 1993.
52. *Japan Times*, June 3, 1993.
53. *Japan Times*, July 1, 1993, and *Daily Yomiuri*, June 17, 1993.
54. From *Japan Times*, April 16, 1993.
55. For a reflection of this view, Hiroshi Kimura, "Doubts About Aid to Russia," *Japan Times*, March 30, 1993.
56. See *Asahi Shimbun*, September 10 and 11, 1993.
57. Saito explains "expanded equilibrium" as follows: "The core of 'expanded equilibrium' was that Japan would give humanitarian, technological, intellectual, and financial aid . . . in proportion to the degree of settlement reached on the northern territories issue." But he adds that "this implied that Tokyo would not provide massive financial aid to Moscow unless some sort of agreement on the territorial issue was reached." See Motohide Saito, "Japan's 'Northward' Foreign Policy," in Gerald L. Curtis (ed.), *Japan's Foreign Policy After the Cold War: Coping with Change*, 285 (Armonk, NY: M. E. Sharpe, 1993).
58. Takagi, "Getting on Track," 10.
59. *Japan Times*, April 15, 1993.
60. *Japan Times*, May 7, 1993.
61. *Asahi Shimbun*, September 10 and 11, 1993.
62. See *Asahi Shimbun*, October 30, 1992.
63. Kimura, "Coming Apart," 7.
64. *Japan Times*, July 18, 1993.
65. *Japan Times*, February 7, 1993.
66. *Japan Times*, July 18, 1993.
67. *Japan Times*, July 10, 1993.
68. Hasegawa, "Soviet-Japanese Relations," 72.
69. Saito, "Northward," in Curtis (ed.), *Japan's Foreign Policy*, 290.
70. Rozman, *Japan's Response*, 29-31.
71. Hasegawa, "Soviet-Japanese Relations," 81.
72. Saito, "Northward," in Curtis (ed.), *Japan's Foreign Policy*, 290.
73. Ibid., 285.
74. See Rozman, *Japan's Response*; Saito, "Northward," in Curtis (ed.), *Japan's Foreign Policy*; and Hasegawa, "Soviet-Japanese Relations" for the involvement of LDP players.
75. Hasegawa, "Soviet-Japanese Relations," 73.
76. Rozman, *Japan's Response*, 22.

77. Hasegawa, "Soviet-Japanese Relations," 75.

CHAPTER 6

1. See Dennis T. Yasutomo, "Foreign Aid and Japan's Economic Diplomacy," in Nihon Kokusai Mondai Kenkyujo (ed.), *Nihon No Keizai Gaiko No Arikata Ni Kansuru Sogo-Teki Kenkyu* (Tokyo: Nihon Kokusai Mondai Kenkyujo, 1994), 35-62.

BIBLIOGRAPHY

SELECTED BOOKS

Amau, Tamio. *Ta-Kokkan Gaiko Ron; Kokuren Gaiko no Jisso.* Tokyo: PMC Shuppan, 1990.

Ansari, Jayed A. *The Political Economy of International Economic Organization.* Boulder, CO: Lynn Rienner Publishers, 1986.

Anzen Hosho Kenkyukai. *Ekonomisuto ga Kaita Sogo Anzen Hosho no Kozu.* Tokyo: Nihon Seisansei Honbu, 1981.

Anzen Hosho Kenkyu Gurupu. *Sogo Anzen Hosho Senryaku.* Tokyo: Okurasho Insatsu Kyoku, 1980.

Asahi Shimbun "Enjo" Shuzaihan. *Enjo Tojokoku Nippon.* Tokyo: Tosho Insatsu Kabushiki-Gaisha, 1985.

Asian Development Bank. *Summary of Proceedings,* Annual Meetings of the Board of Governors. Manila: ADB Printing Office, 1968–present.

Association for Promotion of International Cooperation. *Japan's Official Development Assistance Annual Report.* Tokyo: Association for Promotion of International Cooperation, annual.

Attali, Jacques. *Millennium: Winners and Losers in the Coming World Order.* New York: Times Books, 1991.

Barnett, Robert W. *Beyond War: Japan's Concept of Comprehensive National Security.* Washington, D.C.: Pergamon Brassey's International Defense Publishers, 1984.

Chapman, J. W. M., Drifte, R., and Gow, I. T. M. *Japan's Quest for Comprehensive Security: Defence, Diplomacy and Dependence.* New York: St. Martin's Press, 1982.

Curtis, Gerald L., ed. *Japan's Foreign Policy After the Cold War: Coping with Change.* New York: M. E. Sharpe, 1993.

Donfried, Karen. *CRS Report for Congress: The European Bank for Reconstruction and Development: An Institution of and for the New Europe.* Washington, D.C.: Congressional Research Service, August 15, 1991.

Ensign, Margee M. *Doing Good or Doing Well: Japan's Foreign Aid Program.* New York: Columbia University Press, 1992.

European Bank for Reconstruction and Development. *Proceedings of the First Annual Meeting of the Board of Governors, Budapest, 13-14 April 1992.*

———. *Summary Proceedings of the Inaugural Meeting of the Board of Governors,* London, 15-17 April 1991.

Fujioka, Masao. *Ajia Kaigin Sosai Nikki: Manira e no Sato-gaeri.* Tokyo: Toyo Keizai Shimposha, 1986.

Gaimusho. *Seifu Kaihatsu Enjo Taiko/Japan's Official Development Assistance Charter* (June 30, 1992).

———. *Waga Kuni no Seifu Kaihatsu Enjo* (2 volumes). Tokyo: Kokusai Kyoryoku Suishin Kyokai, annual).

———. Keizai Kyoryoku Kyoku. *Keizai Kyoryoku Hyoka Hokokusho* (annual).

———. Keizai Kyoryoku Kyoku and Keizai Kyoryoku Kenkyukai. *Keizai Kyoryoku no Rinen: Seifu Kaihatsu Enjo wa Naze Okonau no ka.* Tokyo: Kokusai Kyoryoku Suishin Kyokai, 1981.

Haas, Ernst B. *When Knowledge Is Power: Three Models of Change in International Organizations.* Berkeley: University of California Press, 1990.

Hancock, Graham. *Lords of Poverty: The Power, Prestige, and Corruption of the International Aid Business.* New York: Atlantic Monthly Press, 1989.

Hasegawa, Sukehiro. *Japanese Foreign Aid: Policy and Practice.* New York: Praeger, 1975.

Hayao, Kenji. *The Japanese Prime Minister and Public Policy.* Pittsburg: University of Pittsburg, 1993.

Heiwa Mondai Kenkyukai. *Kokusai Kokka Nihon no Sogo Anzen Hosho Seisaku.* Tokyo: Okurasho Insatsu Kyoku, 1985.

Hellmann, Donald. *Japanese Domestic Politics and Foreign Policy: The Peace Agreement with the Soviet Union.* Berkeley: University of California Press, 1969.

Higuchi, Sadao. *Seifu Kaihatsu Enjo.* Tokyo: Keiso Shobo, 1986.

Huang, Po-Wen. *The Asian Development Bank: Diplomacy and Development in Asia.* New York: Vantage Press, 1975.

Iida, Tsuneo. *Enjo Suru Kuni, Sareru Kuni.* Tokyo: Nikkei Shinsho, 1974.

———. *Nihon Keizai no Mokuhyo.* Tokyo: PHP Kenkyujo, 1993.

International Bank for Reconstruction and Development. *The East Asian Miracle: Economic Growth and Public Policy.* Oxford: Oxford University Press, 1993.

———. *World Development Report 1991: The Challenge of Development.* Oxford: Oxford University Press, 1991.

Islam, Shafiqul, ed. *Yen for Development: Japanese Foreign Aid and the Politics of Burden-Sharing.* New York: Council on Foreign Relations Press, 1991.

Jacobson, Harold K. *Networks of Interdependence: International Organizations and the Global Political System.* New York: Alfred A. Knopf, 1979.

Kajima Heiwa Kenkyujo, ed. *Taigai Keizai Kyoryoku Taikei* (10-volume series). Tokyo: Kajima Kenkyujo Shuppan-kai, 1973-74.

Kataoka, Tetsuya. *Waiting for a "Pearl Harbor": Japan Debates Defense.* Stanford, CA: Hoover Institution Press, 1980.

Katzenstein, Peter J., ed. *Between Power and Plenty: Foreign Economic Policies of Advanced Industrialized States.* Madison: University of Wisconsin Press, 1978.

Kawakita, Jiro. *Kaigai Kyoryoku no Tetsugaku: Himaraya de no Jissen kara.* Tokyo: Jissen Chuo Sinso, 1974.

Kenmochi, Nobuaki. *Sekai Ginko to Nihon.* Tokyo: Sekai Ginko Tokyo Jimusho, 1990.

Keohane, Robert O. *After Hegemony: Cooperation and Discord in the World Political Economy.* Princeton, NJ: Princeton University Press, 1984.

————. *International Institutions and State Power: Essays in International Relations Theory.* Boulder, CO: Westview Press, 1989.

Kohama, Hirohisa. *ODA no Keizai Gaku.* Tokyo: Nihon Hyoronsha, 1992.

Koppel, Bruce M. and Robert M. Orr, Jr., eds. *Japan's Foreign Aid: Power and Policy in a New Era.* Boulder, CO: Westview Press, 1993.

Krasner, Stephen. *Defending the National Interest: Raw Materials Investments and U.S. Foreign Policy.* Princeton, NJ: Princeton University Press, 1978.

————. *Structural Conflict: The Third World Against Global Liberalism.* Berkeley: University of California Press, 1985.

Krishnamurti, R. *ADB—The Seeding Days.* Manila: ADB Printing Section, 1977.

Kubota, Isao. *Q and A: Wakariyasui ODA; Sono Shikumi to Yakuwari.* Tokyo: Gyosei, 1992.

Lee, Chae-Jin. *Japan Faces China.* Baltimore, MD: Johns Hopkins Press, 1976, 1976.

Loutfi, Martha. *The Net Cost of Japanese Foreign Aid.* New York: Praeger, 1973.

Mainichi Shimbun Shakaibu Shuzaihan. *Kokusai Enjo Bijinesu: ODA wa Doo Kawarete iru ka.* Tokyo: Aki Shobo, 1990.

Mason, Edward S., and Asher, Robert E. *The World Bank Since Bretton Woods: The Origins, Policies, Operations, and Impact of the International Bank for Reconstruction and Development and Other Members of the World Bank Group.* Washington, D.C.: Brookings Institution, 1973.

Matsui, Ken. *Kokusai Kyoryokuron Enshu.* Tokyo: Koyo Shobo, 1988.

Matsuura, Koichiro. *Enjo Gaiko no Saizensen de Kangaeta Koto.* Tokyo: Dai-Nihon Insatsu Kabushikigaisha, 1990.

Miller, Lynn H. *Global Order: Values and Power in International Politics.* Boulder, CO: Westview Press, 1990.

Ministry of Foreign Affairs. *Japan's ODA* (annual). Tokyo: Association for Promotion of International Cooperation.

Morse, Ronald A., ed. *Japan and the Middle East in Alliance Politics.* Washington, D.C.: The Wilson Center, 1986.

Murai, Yoshinori. *Musekinin Enjo Taikoku Nippon.* Tokyo: JICC Shuppan Kyoku, 1989.

————. *Nippon no ODA*. Tokyo: Gakuyo Shobo, 1992.

Ogawa, Kunihiko. *Kuroi Keizai Kyoryoku: Kono Ajia no Genjitsu o Miyo*. Tokyo: Shimpo Shinsho, 1974.

Ohata, Yashichi, and Tamura, Sadao. *Nihon no Kokusai Tekio-ryoku*. Tokyo: Yuhikaku, 1989.

Onishi, Akira. *Tei-Kaihatsu Koku to Nihon*. Tokyo: Besuto Bookusu, 1969.

Ono, Kenichi, and Ono, Izumi. *IMF to Sekai Ginko: Uchigawa Kara Mita Kaihatsu Kinyu Kikan*. Tokyo: Nihon Hyoronsha, 1993.

Orr, Robert M., Jr. *The Emergence of Japan's Foreign Aid Power*. New York: Columbia University Press, 1990.

Ozawa, Ichiro. *Blueprint for a New Japan: The Rethinking of a Nation*. Tokyo: Kodansha International, 1994.

Ozawa, Terutomo. *Recycling Japan's Surpluses for Developing Countries*. Paris: Development Centre of the Organization for Economic Co-Operation and Development, 1989.

Putnam, Robert D., and Bayne, Nicholas. *Hanging Together: Cooperation in the Seven-Power Summits*. Cambridge, MA: Harvard University Press, 1987.

Rix, Alan. *Japan's Aid Program: Quantity Versus Quality*. Canberra: Australian Government Publishing Service, 1987.

————. *Japan's Foreign Aid Challenge: Policy Reform and Aid Leadership*. London: Routledge, 1993.

Rozman, Gilbert. *Japan's Response to the Gorbachev Era, 1985-1991: A Rising Superpower Views a Declining One*. Princeton, NJ: Princeton University Press, 1992.

Sangyo Kozo Shingikai Kokusai Keizai Bukai, ed. *Nihon no Taigai Keizai Seisaku: Shinrai Sareru Nihon e no Michi*. Tokyo: Diamondo-sha, 1972.

Sasanuma, Michihiro. *ODA Hihan o Kangaeru*. Tokyo: Kogyo Jiji Tsushinsha, 1991.

Shihata, Ibrahim F. I. *The European Bank for Reconstruction and Development: A Comparative Analysis of the Constituent Agreement*. London: Graham and Trotman/Martinus Nijhoff, 1990.

Shiratori, Masaki. *Sekai Ginko Guruppu: Tojokoku Enjo to Nihon no Yakuwari*. Tokyo: Kenkyusha Insatsu Kabushikigaisha, 1993.

Shishido, Toshio. *Tonan Ajia Enjo o Kangaeru*. Tokyo: Toyo Keizai Shimposha, 1973.

Smith, Steven M. *Foreign Policy Adaptation*. New York: Nichols Publishing Company, 1981.

Sparks, Samantha. *Policy Focus: The European Bank for Reconstruction and Development*. Washington, D.C.: Overseas Development Council, 1990.

Stockwin, J. A. A., et. al. *Dynamic and Immobilist Politics in Japan*. Honolulu: University of Hawaii Press, 1988.

Sumi, Kazuo. *Kirawareru Enjo: Segin-Nihon no Enjo to Narumada Damu*. Tokyo: Tsukiji Shokan, 1990.

————. *No Moa ODA: Baramaki Enjo.* Tokyo: JICC Shuppan Kyoku, 1992.

————. *ODA Enjo no Genjitsu.* Tokyo: Iwanami Shinso, 1990.

Suzuki, Keisuke. *Ni-So Keizai Kyoryoku: Shiberia Kaihatsu Kyoryoku to Nihon.* Tokyo: Kokusai Mondai Kenkyujo, 1974.

Tsusho Sangyo Sho. *Keizai Kyoryoku no Genjo to Mondaiten.* Tokyo: Tsusho Sangyo Chosakai, annual.

United States. Agency for International Development. *Japan's Development Financing: Opportunities for U.S. Business* (May 1989).

————. Department of State. *Japan's Foreign Aid: Program Trends and U.S. Business Opportunities* (February 18, 1993).

————. General Accounting Office. *Economic Assistance: Integration of Japanese Aid and Trade Policies* (May 1990).

Waltz, Kenneth. *Theory of International Politics.* Reading, MA: Addison-Wesley, 1979.

Watanabe, Takeshi. *Ajia Kaigin Sosai Nikki.* Tokyo: Nihon Keizai Shimbunsha, 1973.

Watanabe, Toshio, and Kusano, Atsushi. *Nihon no ODA o Doo Suru ka.* Tokyo: Nihon Hoso Kyokai Shuppan Kyokai, 1991.

Watanabe, Toshio, and Hara, Kakuten, eds. *Tei-Kaihatsu Koku Keizai Enjo-ron.* Tokyo: Ajia Keizai Kenkyujo, 1972.

Weinstein, Martin E. *Japan's Postwar Defense Policy, 1947-1968.* New York: Columbia University Press, 1983.

White, John. *Japanese Aid.* London: Overseas Development Institute, 1974.

Wihtol, Robert. *Asian Development Bank and Rural Development.* New York: St. Martin's Press, 1988.

Yasutomo, Dennis T. *Japan and the Asian Development Bank.* New York: Praeger Special Studies, 1983.

————. *The Manner of Giving: Strategic Aid and Japanese Foreign Policy.* Lexington, MA: Lexington Books, 1986.

Yoshitsu, Michael. *Caught in the Middle East: Japan's Diplomacy in Transition.* Lexington, MA: Lexington Books, 1984.

————. *Japan and the San Francisco Peace Settlement.* New York: Columbia University Press, 1983.

SELECTED ARTICLES

Amuzegar, Jahangir. "The IMF Under Fire." In Paul Diehl, ed., *The Politics of International Organizations: Patterns and Insights,* 242-57. Pacific Grove, CA: Books/Cole Publishing Company, 1989.

Angel, Robert C. "Prime Ministerial Leadership in Japan: Recent Changes in Personal Style and Administrative Organization." *Pacific Affairs* (Winter 1988-89), 583-602.

Blaker, Michael. "Evaluating Japan's Diplomatic Performance." In Gerald L. Curtis, ed., *Japan's Foreign Policy After the Cold War: Coping with Change*, 1-42. Armonk, NY: M.E. Sharpe, 1993.

————. "Probe, Push, and Panic: The Japanese Tactical Style in International Negotiations." In Robert Scalapino, ed., *The Foreign Policy of Modern Japan*, 55-101. Berkeley: University of California Press, 1977.

Blinken, Anthony J. "Jacques of All Trades." *New York Times Magazine*, October 31, 1991, 37 & 44-48.

Bowring, Philip. "Asia Outgrowing Its Bank." *Daily Yomiuri*, May 19, 1993.

Caldwell, J. Alexander. "The Evolution of Japanese Economic Cooperation (1950-1970)." In Harald B. Malgren, ed., *Pacific Basin Development: The American Interests*, 61-80. Lexington, MA: Lexington Books, 1972.

Calder, Kent. "Halfway to Hegemony? Japan in a Changing Global Economic Order." *Harvard International Review* (April/May 1988), 12-16.

————. "Japanese Foreign Economic Policy Formation: Explaining the Reactive State." *World Politics* (July 1988), 517-41.

Chino, Tadao. "Oshu Fukko Kaihatsu Ginko Dai-Ikkai Nenji Sokai: Chino Zaimukan Enzetsu." *Fainansu* (June 1992), 57-58.

"Dai-Niju-yon Kai Ajia Kaihatsu Ginko Nenji Sokai Somu Enzetsu." *Fainansu* (June 1991), 34-36.

"Dai-Niju-go Kai Ajia Kaihatsu Ginko Nenji Sokai Somu Enzetsu." *Fainansu* (July 1992), 46-48.

Frieden, Jeff. "Sectoral Conflict and Foreign Economic Policy." *International Organization* (Winter 1988), 59-90.

Fujikawa, Tetsuma. "Roshia-To-O ga Kawaru, Sekai ga Kawaru (Saishukai): Oshu Fukko Kaihatsu Ginko no Riji San Kagyo." *Fainansu* (December 1993), 82-95.

Funabashi, Yoichi. "Japan and the New World Order." *Foreign Affairs* (Winter 1991-92), 58-74.

Goldstein, Judith. "Ideas, Institutions, and American Trade Policy." *International Organization* (Winter 1988), 179-218.

Goto, Kazumi. "OECF Through the Looking-Glass and What Alice Found There: Japan Loan Aid in Perspective," manuscript (March 5, 1993).

Grimm, Margo. "International Aid Package for Russia Announced But Far From Wrapped Up." *JEI Report* (April 10, 1992).

Hamada, Takujiro. "Taikenteki Enjo-ron." In Takeshi Igarashi, ed., *Nihon no ODA to Kokusai Chitsujo*, 153-70. Tokyo: Nihon Kokusai Mondai Kenkyujo, 1990.

Hasegawa, Tsuyoshi. "Soviet-Japanese Relations in the 1990s." In Mike Mochizuki, et al., *Japan and the United States: Troubled Partners in a Changing World*, 57-89. Washington: Brassey's (US), 1991.

Hellmann, Donald. "The Confrontation with Realpolitik." In James William Morley, ed., *Forecast for Japan: Security in the 1970s*. Princeton, NJ: Princeton University Press, 1972.

————. "Japanese Politics and Foreign Policy: Elitist Democracy Within An American Greenhouse." In Takashi Inoguchi and Daniel I. Okimoto, eds., *The Political Economy of Japan: Volume 2: The Changing International Context*, 345-80. Stanford, CA: Stanford University Press, 1988.

————. "Japanese Security and Postwar Japanese Foreign Policy." In Robert A. Scalapino, ed., *The Foreign Policy of Modern Japan*, 321-40. Berkeley: University of California Press, 1977.

Hirono, Ryokichi. "Japan's Leadership Role in the Multilateral Development Institutions." In Shafiqul Islam, ed., *Yen for Development: Japanese Foreign Aid and the Politics of Burden-Sharing*, 171-81. New York: Council on Foreign Relations, 1991.

Holsti, K. J. "Politics in Command: Foreign Trade as National Security Policy." *International Organization* (Summer 1986), 643-72.

Iida, Tsuneo. "Rinen ni Tsuite no Ikkosatsu." *Tsusan Janaru* (July 1990), 22-23.

Ikawa, Motomichi. "Tai-Ro Shien G7 Kakuryo Godo Kaigo ni Tsuite." *Fainansu* (May 1993), 50-60.

Ikenberry, John G. "The State and Strategies of International Adjustment." *World Politics* (October 1986), 53-77.

Ikenberry, John G., Lake, David A., and Mastanduno, Michael. "Introduction: Approaches to Explaining American Foreign Economic Policy," *International Organization* (Winter 1988), 1-14.

Inada, Juichi. "Hatten Tojo Koku to Nihon: Taigai Enjo Seisaku no Henyo Katei." In Akio Watanabe, ed., *Sengo Nihon no Taigai Seisaku*, 285-314. Tokyo: Yuhikaku, 1985.

————. "Japan's Aid Diplomacy: Increasing Role for Global Security." *Japan Review of International Affairs* (Spring-Summer 1988), 91-112.

————. "ODA to Nihon Gaiko: Tai-Filipin Enjo ni Tsuite no Jirei Kenkyu." In Takeshi Igarashi, ed., *Nihon no ODA to Kokusai Chitsujo*, 52-81. Tokyo: Nihon Kokusai Mondai Kenkyujo, 1990.

————. "Stick or Carrot? Japanese Aid Policy and Vietnam." In Bruce M. Koppel and Robert M. Orr, Jr., eds., *Japan's Foreign Aid: Power and Policy in a New Era*, 111-34. Boulder, CO: Westview Press, 1993.

Inoguchi, Takashi. "Japan's Response to the Gulf Crisis: An Analytical Overview." *Journal of Japanese Studies* (Summer 1991), 257-73.

"Issues Related to the World Bank's Approach to Structural Adjustment—Proposal from a Major Partner; OECF Occasional Paper No. 1 (October 1991)." *The OECF Research Quarterly* (February 1992), 11-18.

Ito, Kenichi. "Force Versus Sanctions in the Middle East." *Japan Echo* (Spring 1991), 16-31.

———. "The Japanese State of Mind: Deliberations on the Gulf Crisis." *Journal of Japanese Studies* (Summer 1991), 275-90.

Kawakami, Takao. "21 Seiki ni Muketa Nihon no Enjo Seisaku." *Gaiko Foramu* (March 1993), 4-15.

Keohane, Robert O. "Multilateralism: An Agenda for Research." *International Journal* (Autumn 1990), 731-64.

Kesavan, K. V. "Japan and the Tiananmen Square Incident." *Asian Survey* (July 1990), 671-77.

Kim, Hong. "Politics of Japan's Economic Aid to South Korea." *Asia Pacific Community* (Spring 1984), 80-102.

Kimura, Hiroshi. "Coming Apart." *Look Japan* (December 1992), 4-7.

———. "Doubts About Aid to Russia." *Japan Times* (March 30, 1993).

Kinoshita, Toshihiko. "Developments in the International Debt Strategy and Japan's Response." *EXIM Review* (January 1991), 62-80.

———. "Ruiseki Saimu Mondai no Sui-i to Sekai-teki Shikin Kyokyu Shisutemu no Sai-Kochiku no Hoko to Tenbo." *Fainanshiaru Rebyuu* (March 1993), 42-76.

———. "Ruiseki Saimu Mondai to Shikin Kanryu." In Takatoshi Ito, ed., *Kokusai Kinyu no Genjo,* chap. 7. Tokyo: Yuhikaku, 1992.

Krasner, Stephen. "Regimes and the Limits of Realism: Regimes as Autonomous Variables." In Stephen D. Krasner, ed., *International Regimes,* 355-68. Ithaca, NY: Cornell University Press, 1983.

Kubota, Isao. "Aid for Japan and Russia." *Japan Times* (April 19, 1993).

———. "Higashi Ajia no Kiseki—Saikin no Kaihatsu Enjo Seisaku no Ronten (1)." *Fainansu* (December 1993), 38-41.

———. "Higashi Ajia no Kiseki — Saikin no Kaihatsu Enjo Seisaku no Ronten (2)." *Fainansu* (January 1994), 27-30.

Kuroda, Yasumasa. "Japan and the Arabs: The Economic Dimension." *Journal of Arab Affairs* (Spring 1984).

Kusano, Atsushi. "Kokusai Seiji Keizai to Nihon." In Akio Watanabe, ed., *Sengo Nihon no Taigai Seisaku,* 254-84. Tokyo: Yuhikaku, 1985.

Lake, David A. "The State and American Trade Strategy in the Pre-Hegemonic Era." *International Organization* (Winter 1988), 33-58.

Miyamura, Satoru. "Dai-Niju-yon Ajia Kaihatsu Ginko Bankoobaa Sokai ni Tsuite." *Fainansu* (June 1991), 28-33.

———. "Oshu Fukko Kaihatsu Ginko Soritsu Sokai ni Tsuite." *Fainansu* (June 1991), 22-26.

Mochizuki, Mike M. "Japan's Search for Strategy." *International Security* (Winter 1983-84), 52-79.

Moon, Bruce E. "Consensus or Compliance? Foreign Policy Change and External Dependence." *International Organization* (Spring 1985), 297-330.

Ness, Gayl D., and Brechin, Steven R. "Bridging the Gap: International Organizations as Organizations." *International Organization* (Spring 1988), 245-74.

Ogata, Sadako. "Shifting Power Relations in Multilateral Development Banks." *Journal of International Studies* (January 1989), 1-25.

Okuma, Hiroshi. "Japan in the World: The Capital Recycling Programme." *Trocaire Development Review* (1988), 69-88.

Orr, Robert M., Jr. "Japanese Foreign Aid: Over a Barrel in the Middle East." In Bruce M. Koppel and Robert M. Orr, Jr., eds., *Japan's Foreign Aid: Power and Policy in a New Era,* 289-304. Boulder, CO: Westview Press, 1993.

Oshiba, Ryo. "Tai-So-To-O Kinyu Shien Mondai Kara Mita Reisengo no Sekai Chitsujo." *Hitotsubashi Ronso* (January 1991), 18-30.

Ott, Marvin. "Japan's Growing Involvement in the Middle East." *SAIS Review* (Summer-Fall 1985), 221-32.

Pentland, Charles. "International Organizations and Their Roles." In Paul F. Diehl, ed. *The Politics of International Organizations: Patterns and Insights.* Pacific Grove, CA: Brooks/Cole Publishing Company, 1989, 5-14.

Purrington, Courtney. "Tokyo's Policy Responses During the Gulf War and the Impact of the 'Iraqi Shock' on Japan." *Pacific Affairs* (Summer 1992), 161-81.

Pyle, Kenneth B. "Japan, The World, and The Twenty-First Century." In Takashi Inoguchi and Daniel I. Okimoto, eds., *The Political Economy of Japan: Volume 2: The Changing International Context,* 446-86. Stanford, CA: Stanford University Press, 1988.

Rafferty, Kevin. "Asian Development Bank: The Manila Agenda." *Institutional Investor* (April 1983).

Saito, Motohide. "Gorubachofu Tai-Nichi 'Shin-Shiko' Gaiko no Kiseki to Hyoka." *Hogaku Kenkyu* (February 1992), 207-27.

Saito, Tadashi. "Japan's 'Northward' Foreign Policy." In Gerald L. Curtis, ed., *Japan's Foreign Policy After the Cold War: Coping with Change,* 274-302. Armonk, NY: M. E. Sharpe, 1993.

———. "Japan's Role in Multilateral Financial Organizations." *JEI Report* (February 22, 1991).

Sato, Seizaburo. "The Foundations of Modern Japanese Foreign Policy." In Robert A. Scalapino, ed., *The Foreign Policy of Modern Japan,* 367-90. Berkeley: University of California Press, 1997.

Schoppa, Leonard. "Zoku Power and LDP Power: A Case Study of the Zoku Role in Education Policy." *Journal of Japanese Studies* (Winter 1991), 79-106.

Sherk, Donald R. "U.S. Policy Toward the Multilateral Development Banks." *Washington Quarterly* (Summer 1993), 77-86.

Shimizu, Ikutaro. "The Nuclear Option: Japan, Be A State!" *Japan Echo* 8, no. 3 (1980), 33-45.

"Sho-Gaikoku wa Doo Miteiru ka: Hihan to Hyoka." *Gaiko Foramu* (March 1993), 16-27.

Sugisaki, Shigemitsu. "Kyu-Soren/To-O no Doko to Oshu Fukko Kaihatsu Ginko (EBRD) ni Tsuite." *Shihon Shijo* (July 1992), 18-28.

Takagi, Yoji. "Getting on Track." *Look Japan* (December 1992), 8-11.

"Takeshita Announces 'International Cooperation Initiative.'" *Japan Report* (May 1988), 1-2.

Toyoda, Hiroshi. "Chikakute Toi Kuni—Chuo Ajia no San-Kyowakoku o Homon Shite." *Fainansu* (December 1992), 84-94.

———. "Dai-Ikkai Oshu Fukko Kaihatsu Ginko Nenji Sokai ni Tsuite." *Fainansu* (June 1992), 53-55.

———. "Dai-Niju-go Ajia Kaihatsu Ginko Hon Kon Sokai ni Tsuite." *Fainansu* (June 1991), 28-33.

Ueki, Yasuhiro. "Japan's UN Diplomacy: Sources of Passivism and Activism." In Gerald L. Curtis, ed., *Japan's Foreign Policy After the Cold War: Coping With Change*, 347-70. Armonk, NY: M. E. Sharpe, 1993.

Wanner, Barbara. "Japan's Relations with the 'Soviet Bloc.'" *JEI Report*, January 19, 1990.

Yanagihara, Toru. "Japan's Foreign Aid to Bangladesh: Challenging the Dependency Syndrome." In Bruce M. Koppel and Robert M. Orr, Jr., eds., *Japan's Foreign Aid: Power and Policy in a New Era*, 188-202. Boulder, CO: Westview Press, 1993.

Yasutomo, Dennis T. "Foreign Aid and Japan's Economic Diplomacy." In Nihon Kokusai Mondai Kenkyujo, ed., *Nihon no Keizai Gaiko no Arikata ni Kansuru Sogoteki Kenkyu*, 35-63. Tokyo: Kokusai Mondai Kenkyujo, 1994.

———. "Japan and the Asian Development Bank: Multilateral Aid Policy in Transition." In Bruce M. Koppel and Robert M. Orr, Jr., eds., *Japan's Foreign Aid: Power and Policy in a New Era*, 305-40. Boulder, CO: Westview Press, 1993.

———. "Why Aid? Japan as an Aid Great Power." *Pacific Affairs* (Winter 1989-90), 490-503.

———. "The Politicization of Japan's 'Post-Cold War' Multilateral Diplomacy." In Gerald L. Curtis, ed., *Japan's Foreign Policy After the Cold War: Coping with Change*, 323-46. Armonk, NY: M. E. Sharpe, 1993.

Zaisei Kinyu Kenkyujo Kokusai Koryu Shitsu. "Keizai Kaikaku no Hikari to Kage: Roshia Rempo to Kyowa Koku to Okurasho to no Taiwa o Tsujite." *Fainansu* (March 1993), 51-60.

Zhao, Quangsheng. "Japan's Aid Diplomacy in China." In Bruce M. Koppel and Robert M. Orr, Jr., eds., *Japan's Foreign Aid: Power and Policy in a New Era*, 163-87. Boulder, CO: Westview Press, 1993.

INTERVIEWS AND ASSISTANCE

Interviews were conducted and assistance was rendered between 1987 and 1993. Institutional affiliations reflect positions held at the time of the interview (or the last interview in the case of multiple meetings).

Aichi, Kazuo: Liberal Democratic Party
Akao, Nobutoshi: Ministry of Foreign Affairs
Anami, Koreshige: Ministry of Foreign Affairs
Asahi, Hideaki: Ministry of Foreign Affairs
Asakawa, Masatsugu: Ministry of Finance
Atoji, Hiroshi: Liberal Democratic Party
Bresnick, Ronda: United States Department of the Treasury
Brooks, William: United States Department of State
Carnes, Carol: United States Department of the Treasury
Chino, Tadao: Ministry of Finance
Cohen, Josh: Agency for International Development
Crowe, Brian: United States Department of the Treasury
Dehmlow, Jay: United States Department of State
Engel, Tom: United States Department of State
Feltman, Jeffrey: United States Department of State
Fujikawa, Tetsuma: Ministry of Finance
Goto, Kazumi: Overseas Economic Cooperation Fund
Gyohten, Toyoo: Bank of Tokyo
Hasumi, Yoshihiro: Japanese Consulate, Shanghai
Hasegawa, Koichi: Ministry of Finance
Hayashi, Akira: Ministry of Foreign Affairs
Hosono, Katsuya: Ministry of Finance
Ijima, Toshiro: Ministry of Foreign Affairs
Ikawa, Motomichi: Ministry of Fianance
Imai, Kazuo: Export-Import Bank of Japan
Inada, Juichi: Yamanashi University
Isaka, Yoshihiro: Ministry of Finance
Iwasaki, Fumio: Ministry of Finance
Iwasaki, Mika: World Bank Tokyo Office
Kaizuka, Masaaki: World Bank/Ministry of Finance
Kajiyama, Naoki: Ministry of Finance
Kato, Takatoshi: Ministry of Finance
Kawamata, Shinichiro: World Bank Tokyo Office
Kinoshita, Toshihiko: Export-Import Bank of Japan

Kitamura, Takanori: Ministry of Foreign Affairs
Kiyoi, Mikie: Ministry of Foreign Affairs
Klemm, Hans: United States Embassy, Tokyo
Kobayashi, Eiji: Asian Development Bank
Kojima, Seiji: Ministry of Foreign Affairs
Kubota, Isao: Ministry of Finance
Laudato, George: Agency for International Development
MacDonald, Larry: United States Department of the Treasury
Matsunaga, Daisuke: Ministry of Foreign Affairs
Matsuura, Koichiro: Ministry of Foreign Affairs
Mattsson, Jan: United Nations Development Programme, Beijing
Miyamura, Satoru: Ministry of Finance
Miyazaki, Yukiji: Wako Securities
Mizoguchi, Zembei: Ministry of Finance
Monma, Daikichi: Ministry of Finance
Mori, Shoji: Ministry of Finance
Moriarity, Lauren: United States Department of State
Morris, Elizabeth: United States Department of the Treasury
Naito, Junichi: Ministry of Finance
Nakahira, Kosuke: Ministry of Finance
Nakamura, Morio: Ministry of Foreign Affairs
Nicholson, Norm: Agency for International Development
Nishizawa, Toshiro: Ministry of Foreign Affairs
Nogami, Yoshiji: Ministry of Foreign Affairs
Noma, Osamu: Ministry of Foreign Affairs
Obe, Kazuaki: Ministry of Foreign Affairs
Ohsawa, Fumiaki: Ministry of Finance
Oku, Katsuhiko: Ministry of Foreign Affairs
Okuma, Hiroshi: Seijo University
Ono, Hisashi: Ministry of Finance
Orr, Robert M.: Nippon Motorola and Temple University Japan
Osono, Haruo: Ministry of Finance
Paulson, Sara: United States Department of the Treasury
Reis, Robert: United States Embassy, Tokyo
Rouge, Michel: Embassy of France
Saito, Norio: Japanese Embassy, Beijing
Sakumoto, Naoyuki: Institute of Developing Economies
Sakurai, Toshihiro: Overseas Economic Cooperation Fund
Sanada, Akira: Japanese Consulate, Shanghai
Sewell, John: Overseas Development Council

Sherk, Donald: Development Alternatives, Incorporated
Shiratori, Masaki: Overseas Economic Cooperation Fund
Stillman, Grant: Aoyama Gakuin University
Sugimoto, Nobuo: Ministry of Foreign Affairs
Sugisaki, Shigemitsu: Ministry of Finance
Takagi, Shinji: Ministry of Finance and Osaka University
Takase, Kunio: International Development Center
Tanaka, Hitoshi: Ministry of Foreign Affairs
Taniuchi, Tetsuro: Ministry of Foreign Affairs
Totsune, Haruhito: Ministry of Finance
Toyoda, Hiroshi: Ministry of Finance
Tsukagoshi, Yasusuke: Ministry of Finance
Tsuneishi, Takao: Institute of Developing Economies
Upton, Barbara: Agency for International Development
Utsumi, Makoto: Ministry of Finance and Keio University
van der Lugt, Robert: World Bank Resident Mission, Beijing
Watanabe, Akio: Aoyama Gakuin University
Watanabe, Tatsuo: Ministry of Finance
Wethington, Olin: United States Department of the Treasury
White, Paul: United States Embassy, Tokyo
Wright, Maurice: University of Manchester
Yagi, Ken: Ministry of Finance
Yamazaki, Setsuko: United Nations Development Programme, Beijing
Yang, Linda Tsao: Asian Development Bank
Yen, Michael: United States Embassy, Tokyo
Yonezawa, Junichi: Ministry of Finance
Yoshimura, Yukio: Ministry of Finance

INDEX